Trade Facilitation and the Global Economy

OECD
BETTER POLICIES FOR BETTER LIVES

Please cite this publication as:
OECD (2018), *Trade Facilitation and the Global Economy*, OECD Publishing, Paris.
http://dx.doi.org/10.1787/9789264277571-en

ISBN 978-92-64-27756-4 (print)
ISBN 978-92-64-27757-1 (PDF)
ISBN 978-92-64-300316 (ePub)

Photo credits : Cover © Jeffrey Fisher.

Corrigenda to OECD publications may be found on line at: *www.oecd.org/publishing/corrigenda*.

Foreword

Trade facilitation – transparent, predictable and straightforward border procedures that expedite the movement of goods – promises large gains domestically and globally. In a globalised world, where production is spread across countries and goods cross borders many times before reaching consumers, trade facilitation is essential to lowering trade costs and increasing economic welfare. Efficient border procedures allow firms to reduce losses of perishables, cut inventory costs, be more responsive to changing consumer preferences, and participate in time-sensitive global value chains. The OECD Trade Facilitation Indicators (TFIs) provide a powerful tool to assess these gains and to monitor worldwide efforts to improve border procedures, reduce trade costs, boost trade flows, and contribute to inclusive growth. They are the most precisely targeted instrument for monitoring and benchmarking country performance on trade facilitation across more than 160 countries.

The TFIs show that implementation of the WTO Trade Facilitation Agreement (TFA) is well underway, but progress is uneven and some significant challenges remain, in particular regarding domestic and cross-border agency co-operation. Technical and financial assistance is playing an important role in enabling implementation. The TFA is expected to reduce trade costs between 12% and 18%, and to increase world trade. Developing and emerging economies are likely to benefit the most from reduced import and export costs and faster delivery times, leading to efficient participation in time-sensitive global value chains.

Beyond the obvious effects on trade and production, trade facilitation is critical for inclusiveness. Lowering trade costs is disproportionately more significant for small firms, increasing opportunities for start-ups generally and for female entrepreneurs in particular to move from the informal to formal economy, and to grow their businesses. Implementing the TFA also contributes to reducing opportunities for illicit trade, bribery, and corruption that stifle entrepreneurship. The importance of trade facilitation in removing layers of additional costs becomes even more important in the digital era, with growing numbers of parcels crossing international borders, both raising demand and creating new challenges for government controls and facilitation.

The TFA, and its early success, represent a promising approach for future multilateral trade reform, providing flexibilities for adjusting implementation in line with country capacities, underpinned by technical and, where necessary, financial support. In brief, the TFA is a compelling example of effective international co-operation.

Ken Ash, Director

OECD Trade and Agriculture Directorate

Acknowledgements

The work that this book draws on was prepared under the aegis of the OECD Trade Committee and its Working Party. Countries covered in the Trade Facilitation Indicators (TFI) database contributed significantly through their verification of the data and by discussions of the underlying work synthesised in this book. The assistance of the express and logistics industries in providing factual information on implementation of trade facilitation on the ground is gratefully acknowledged. The assistance of the Costa Rican and Swiss authorities in exploring success factors and challenges of border agency co-operation is gratefully acknowleged. The assistance of the Inter-American Development Bank, the Inter-American Network of International Trade Single Windows, the Asia-Pacific Economic Cooperation Forum and the US-ASEAN Connectivity through Trade and Investment in exploring success factors and challenges of Single Windows is gratefully acknowleged.

The book was prepared by Evdokia Moise, Silvia Sorescu, Dorothee Flaig, Emanuele Mazzini, Tom Butterly, Florian Le Bris and Clarisse Legendre, under the supervision of Julia Nielson. Jackie Maher provided assistance in formatting the book and Michèle Patterson supervised the publication process. The authors would like to thank Ken Ash, Carmel Cahill, Steve Pope and Cezary Sowinski for useful comments and suggestions.

Table of contents

Executive summary 9

Chapter 1. Overview 13
Why trade facilitation? 14
The WTO Trade Facilitation Agreement 15
Introducing the OECD Trade Facilitation Indicators 16
Overview of this publication 19
Notes 20
Bibliography 21

PART 1

Trade facilitation, a growing global footprint

Chapter 2. Trade facilitation around the world: The state of play 25
The entry into force of the TFA brought new momentum to trade facilitation efforts 26
The big picture: Current state of play on trade facilitation globally 27
A closer look: Key challenges in relation to the TFA 31
Way forward: Paving the way for full implementation of the TFA 46
Notes 47
Bibliography 47

Chapter 3. Border agency co-operation 49
Co-operation among agencies, including across borders, matters 50
Measuring effective domestic border agency co-operation 50
Measuring effective cross-border agency co-operation 55
Notes 59
Bibliography 60

Chapter 4. Single Window systems 61
Single Windows bring benefits, but are challenging to design and implement 62
Indicators on Single Windows in the TFIs 62
Creating a regional Single Window: The experience of ASEAN 73
Notes 76
Bibliography 77

Chapter 5. Costs and challenges 79
The costs of TFA implementation are manageable compared to the expected benefits 80

Assessing the costs of implementing trade facilitation measures 80
Identifying the main cost components of trade facilitation reforms 81
What does country experience tell us? 85
Notes 87
Bibliography 88

PART 2

The economic case for trade facilitation

Chapter 6. Trade facilitation, trade and global value chains 91
The impact of the Trade Facilitation Agreement on trade costs 93
The potential impact of trade facilitation on the operation of supply chains 96
Notes 98
Bibliography 98

Chapter 7. Economy-wide impacts of trade facilitation 101
Capturing the economy-wide impacts of trade facilitation 102
A new approach to assessing the economy-wide impacts of trade facilitation reforms 104
Notes 113
Bibliography 113

Annex A. The Trade Facilitation Indicators: Methodology 117

Annex B. Trade Facilitation Indicators: Country lists 121

Annex C. Trade Facilitation Indicators questionnaire 123

Tables

1.1. Overall structure of the OECD Trade Facilitation Indicators................ 17
4.1. Economy groupings.. 63
7.1. Trade facilitation raises welfare over the longer term..................... 111
A.2.1. Country groupings.. 121

Figures

1.1. TFIs data collection process 18
1.2. TFIs as an evaluation tool 19
2.1. Implementation of areas covered by the TFA is underway worldwide 29
2.2. In general, more advanced economies perform better 30
2.3. But there is positive momentum on implementation for all countries 30
2.4. TFIs 2017: Full sample snapshot, regional groupings 31
2.5. Availability of information provisions are already widely implemented 32
2.6. Dialogue with the private sector is progressing but modalities remain challenging 33
2.7. Binding advance rulings are generally available, but other aspects remain a work in progress 34
2.8. The right to appeal is widely available but timeliness and communication of processes varies 35

2.9. Implementation of disciplines on fees and charges is modest and varies by income 36
2.10. Implementation of disciplines on penalties is relatively homogenous among MICs, but remains problematic for LICs 37
2.11. Progress has been generally good on trade formalities 37
2.12. Automating border procedures remains a challenge 39
2.13. Implementation of risk management has significantly improved, but mostly in higher income countries 40
2.14. Some progress has been made on authorised operators but conditions and benefits vary 41
2.15. Domestic border agency co-operation is progressing for some key functions 44
2.16. but there is considerable scope for improvement 45
2.17. Most progress on cross-border co-operation concerns alignment of working hours 45
2.18. Efforts to deepen co-operation by automation are underway, but incomplete 46
4.1. There is a wide variation in implementation of Single Window initiatives . . 64
4.2. There are also significant gaps to best practice across most indicators 64
4.3. OECD Single Windows indicators: Overall regional performance across selected groups 65
4.4. Institutional aspects and scope: Identifying key challenges 66
4.5. Coverage and scope of Single Windows is strong in ASEAN, but much less so in LAC 67
4.6. Most Single Windows are government financed 67
4.7. Data requirements are largely harmonised to international standards, but electronic processing remains a work in progress 68
4.8. Legal frameworks are generally well-developed, with the exceptions of data sharing and disputes 69
4.9. Progress on establishing technological architecture is mixed 70
4.10. Most systems require secure sign on 71
4.11. With the exception of backup, contingency mechanisms remain a work in progress 71
4.12. Interoperability remains the greatest challenge for Single Windows 72
5.1. Aid for trade facilitation has grown strongly since 2002 82
5.2. LDCs remain the largest beneficiaries of aid for trade facilitation 82
5.3. Aid for trade facilitation goes predominantly to countries in Africa and Asia 83
6.1. Trade cost diagnostics 92
6.2. Implementation of the TFA lowers trade costs for all countries, but especially for lower income countries 94
6.3. Sub-Saharan Africa and Asia stand to gain most from trade facilitation reforms 94
6.4. Some trade facilitation measures are particularly important for cutting trade costs 95
6.5. Trade facilitation can boost participation in GVCs 96
7.1. In the short-term, full implementation of the TFA would increase trade in all sectors 106
7.2. Implementation of the TFA increases trade for countries at all levels of development, especially in intermediates 106

7.3. Implementation of the TFA lowers the costs of inputs for almost all sectors . 107
7.4. By lowering input costs and raising efficiency, trade facilitation increases output across all regions 108
7.5. Manufacturing gains across all regions, but the role of services is increasing 108
7.6. In the long term, production shifts take place within and among regions ... 109
7.7. In the developing world, trade facilitation raises labour income over the longer term 110
7.8. Countries at all levels of development experience welfare gains 111
7.9. Longer term welfare gains are driven by technological changes and utility gains 112
7.10. Over the longer term, welfare increases in all regions 112

Executive summary

Trade facilitation – transparent, predictable and straightforward border procedures that expedite the movement of goods across borders – is becoming ever more important in an increasingly interconnected global economy. In a globalised world, where production is spread across countries and goods cross borders many times before reaching consumers, trade facilitation is essential for lowering the costs of trade. Keeping the costs of trading low is an important part of making trade work for all: trade facilitation helps more – and smaller – firms to participate in trade and more consumers to benefit from lower prices, higher quality and a greater range of goods.

Successive rounds of multilateral trade negotiations have progressively reduced traditional trade barriers, shifting attention to less visible, but often equally costly, measures at and behind the border: these include the procedures, paperwork, and administrative formalities that can add layers of sometimes unnecessary additional costs to goods as they cross borders. Addressing unnecessary costs related to these procedures is essential for firms to be able to take full advantage of new market openings. This is especially the case for micro-, small- and medium-sized enterprises (MSMEs) for whom the costs of trading can be disproportionately large.

The costs of inefficient border procedures for trade are multiplied when goods and components cross borders many times in the course of their production as part of Global Value Chains (GVCs). GVCs have placed a premium on countries' ability to connect seamlessly, rapidly and efficiently with the wider global economy. Trade facilitation is especially critical for trade in perishable agricultural products or high-tech manufacturing components, both of which are highly sensitive to delays. Trade facilitation is also becoming more, not less, important in the digital era. The growing numbers of parcels crossing international borders is both increasing demand, and creating new challenges for, trade facilitation. Moreover, improved transparency, predictability and simplification of trade procedures not only has the potential to reduce trade costs and promote economic efficiency, but also to help remove incentives and opportunities for corruption.

All countries have an interest in promoting good governance and efficient border procedures, whether they are exporters of traditional agricultural products, participating in value chains for high-tech manufactures, or indeed expanding their global presence through online trade. Recognition of this strong commonality of interest, and of the additional gains from all countries acting together, led to the successful negotiation of the World Trade Organization (WTO) Trade Facilitation Agreement (TFA). Given its unique structure which links implementation to the capacities of developing and least developed countries, the TFA is being implemented gradually, with different parts of the agreement implemented earlier than others by countries around the world. This places a premium on understanding well what is actually happening on the ground on trade facilitation.

The OECD Trade Facilitation Indicators (TFIs) are the most precisely targeted instrument in existence today for monitoring and benchmarking country performance on trade facilitation. The TFIs allow the state of play on trade facilitation across more than 160 countries to be captured, and key advances and challenges identified, providing a baseline for monitoring future progress. The TFIs can help to identify and prioritise technical assistance and capacity-building efforts, as well as to support advocacy efforts to build support for trade facilitation reforms.

This book presents key findings from analysis using the TFIs. It presents evidence on the state of trade facilitation reforms around the world at the time of entry into force of the TFA. It highlights progress made, but also key remaining challenges, with an in-depth discussion of the most difficult areas and implications for policy-making. The book makes the economic case for trade facilitation reforms. The main findings are set out below.

Trade facilitation measures are being implemented worldwide, but progress is uneven and some significant challenges remain

Implementation of the TFA is well underway

- Implementation of measures covered by the TFA is well underway, although performance varies across and within all countires in different income groups in most policy areas. There have been early improvements in areas such as automation and streamlining of procedures and engagement with the trade community. By far the biggest challenges are in the areas of domestic and cross-border agency co-operation.
- The introduction and use of information technologies and the establishment of Single Windows are amongst the most expensive elements of trade facilitation, but the biggest challenges can relate to changing attitudes and culture around border procedures, so training is critically important.
- Single Window platforms have gained momentum as a promising avenue for streamlining the flow of trade information and expediting the movement of goods in a reliable and secure way. However, they need efficient border agency co-operation to deliver their full potential. Technological aspects seem to be less challenging, despite their resource requirements. Interoperability is important and the majority of countries are still at an early stage.

Domestic and cross-border agency co-operation remains a critical area for improvement

- Redundant or sequential controls, duplicative documentation requirements and insufficient co-ordination between responsible agencies may exacerbate delays and impose unnecessary costs on traders, decrease efficiency of controls at border crossings, and strain resources at border posts.
- Border agency co-ordination is critical in facilitating legitimate trade. Border agency co-operation is also an important prerequisite for and critical factor in the efficiency of integrated IT systems and Single Window platforms.
- Clear delineation of authority and responsibilities, sound frameworks for sharing data, infrastructure and equipment, and open channels of communication are critical for the day-to-day operation of domestic and cross-border co-operation.

- An explicit and sustained political commitment to ensure effective co-operation among agencies, within and across the border, is a central prerequisite for improving border operations.

Technical and financial assistance is playing an important and supportive role

- The costs of putting in place and maintaining trade facilitation measures are not overly burdensome, and are far outweighed by benefits gained from their implementation. A growing amount of technical and financial assistance to implement trade facilitation measures has been made available to developing countries over the last decade, helping to offset initial costs.
- Country performance in the areas of automation or advance rulings appears to be closely linked to income, suggesting that investments in capacity-building in these areas would yield significant benefits.

Benefits clearly outweigh costs: There is a strong economic case for trade facilitation reforms

Implementing the TFA will reduce trade costs and boost growth, especially in lower income countries

- The TFA is expected to generate trade cost reductions of between 14% and 18%, and increase world trade by 0.6%, boosting global growth. Countries which fully implement the TFA stand to reduce their trade costs by between 1.4 and 3.9 percentage points more than those who take minimalist approaches to TFA implementation. Low and lower middle-income countries enjoy the greatest opportunities for the biggest reductions in trade costs.

Trade facilitation is ever more important in today's highly interconnected world

- Efficient border procedures help firms curb losses on perishables, reduce inventory management costs, better respond to changing consumer preferences, and participate in time-sensitive GVCs. These benefits are felt in exporting and importing countries alike.
- GVCs present new transmission channels for trade facilitation benefits between and within regions. Ambitious reformers will gain the most from faster access to competitively-priced inputs, also becoming more export-competitive in the process.
- Improvements in advance rulings, transparency of fees and charges, automation and streamlining of the border process could lead to increases in value-added trade flows of between 1% and 3.5%. The largest impact is felt on value-added trade in complex manufactures ("high and medium-high tech" sectors).

Trade facilitation brings other economy-wide benefits as well

- Beyond the impacts on trade, trade facilitation positively affects production. Increased competition amongst domestic producers from reduced import-export transaction costs and faster delivery times drives more efficient resource allocation and realisation of economies of scale through global exports.
- Low income countries experience the strongest production effects, followed by lower-middle income and high income countries outside the OECD area. The sectors

benefitting the most are motor vehicles and parts, machinery, and electronic and transport equipment.

- Consumption also increases, spurred by smaller losses at the border and faster delivery times. Consumers derive greater utility from goods received sooner, so are more willing to pay for faster delivery.
- Importantly, trade facilitation also supports good governance, by removing opportunities for bribery and corruption and by removing incentives for trade to occur informally – in turn, facilitating both trade flows and border tax collection.

Chapter 1

Overview

This chapter discusses the role of trade facilitation in the global economy: what it means and why it matters. It introduces the OECD Trade Facilitation Indicators (TFIs), a set of leading edge tools to assist policy makers in identifying, prioritising, and reaching their trade facilitation objectives. It concludes with a short overview of the publication.

Why trade facilitation?

Trade facilitation – transparent, predictable and straightforward border procedures that expedite the movement of goods across borders – is becoming ever more important in an increasingly interconnected global economy. In a globalised world, where production is spread across countries and goods cross borders many times before reaching consumers, trade facilitation is essential for lowering the costs of trade. Keeping the costs of trading low is an important part of making trade work for all: trade facilitation helps more – and smaller – firms to participate in trade and more consumers to benefit from lower prices, higher quality and a greater range of goods.

Successive rounds of multilateral trade negotiations over the years have progressively reduced traditional trade barriers such as tariffs and quotas – the readily measurable costs of trading. This has shifted attention to less visible, but often equally costly measures, at and behind the border: the procedures, paperwork, and administrative formalities that add layers of additional costs to goods as they cross borders. The objective of trade facilitation is to lower these costs to trade by simplifying trade procedures – understood by the World Trade Organization (WTO) as the "*activities, practices and formalities involved in collecting, presenting, communicating and processing data required for the movement of goods in international trade*".

Indeed, addressing costs related to these procedures is essential for firms to be able to take full advantage of the new market openings from reductions in traditional barriers. This is especially the case for Micro, Small and Medium Enterprises (MSMEs) for whom the costs of trading related to cumbersome border procedures can be disproportionately large compared to their relatively low value of exports.

In a world of global production, speed and efficiency matter

The costs of inefficient border procedures for trade are multiplied when goods and components cross borders many times in the course of their production as part of Global Value Chains (GVCs). Falling transport and communication costs have opened new opportunities to enhance and diversify production in GVCs, but also placed a premium on countries' ability to connect seamlessly, rapidly and efficiently with the wider global economy.

Trade facilitation benefits exporters and importers alike by allowing better access to inputs for production and enhancing participation in GVCs. On the supply side, trade facilitation helps reduce business losses resulting from delays of goods at the border. Delays in delivery increase firms' costs for managing inventory and undermine their ability to respond rapidly to changes in consumer preference. On the demand side, faster and more predictable delivery of intermediate goods through the supply chain can reduce firm costs. Trade facilitation improvements are also associated with increased consumer willingness to pay, as consumers derive more utility from goods delivered sooner rather than later.

Trade facilitation is especially critical for trade in perishable agricultural products and high-tech manufacturing components, both of which are highly sensitive to delays as they journey from point of origin to final destination.

Indeed, even beyond time-sensitive GVCs for high-tech and perishable products, trade facilitation is becoming more, not less, important in the digital era. While digitalisation has made it possible to trade services and digital products globally and instantly in digital form over the Internet, it has also enabled growth in traditional trade. Of particular importance in the context of trade facilitation is the explosive growth in parcel trade linked to on-line platforms, where consumers are seeking rapid access to goods from around the world. These platforms are also creating new opportunities for MSMEs to participate in international trade, but realising these opportunities again requires action to lower the costs of trading related to border procedures. The growing numbers of parcels crossing international borders is both raising demand, and creating new challenges for, trade facilitation.[1]

Trade facilitation also supports good governance

The transparency, predictability and simplification of trade procedures not only have the potential to reduce trade costs and promote economic efficiency but they can also help remove the incentives and opportunities for corruption.[2]

Fundamentals of trade facilitation, such as transparent rules, underpin the ability of market participants and stakeholders to fully understand the conditions and constraints for entering and operating in a market. Likewise, the consistent and non-discretionary application of those rules promotes not just efficiency but also integrity in border agencies. The simplification and streamlining of border procedures reduces the discretionary power of Customs and other border agencies and can thus help promote integrity; automation can also provide additional support in harmonising the interpretation and implementation of regulations across all border points.

Moreover, cumbersome and costly trade procedures and the (often related) lack of integrity at the border can increase incentives for trade to occur informally, with large implications for government revenue. Informal trade is often conducted by individual traders and MSMEs to avoid the significantly higher trade transaction costs they face with formal trade, such as import/export duties and taxes, complex and non-transparent regulatory measures and long and inefficient border procedures. Smaller traders may also encounter significant risks of predation, bribery, theft and other "facilitation payments" by Customs officials. This informal trade erodes government revenue, particularly in developing countries where trade taxes may be a significant contributor to state budgets. With trade reforms over the last decades leading to a steady decline in tariff revenue, Customs modernisation measures that ensure more accurate reporting of the value of goods and can detect fraud and tackle smuggling are a major avenue for lowering the fiscal cost of trade liberalisation. Indeed, in some countries, revenue losses from inefficient border procedures are estimated to exceed 5% of GDP, highlighting the potential payoff of enhanced public revenue through trade facilitation measures that provide incentives to formalise (OECD, 2009; De Jong and Bogmans, 2011). Trade facilitation, integrity and promotion of formal trade can thus be mutually supportive.

The WTO Trade Facilitation Agreement

All countries have an interest in promoting good governance and efficient border procedures, whether they are exporters of traditional agricultural products, participating in value chains for high-tech manufactures, or expanding their global presence through online trade. There are thus strong incentives for countries to undertake trade facilitation reforms. However, countries do not only have an interest in their own reforms; while these bring benefits, all countries benefit more when their trading partners also reform their border procedures.

Recognition of this strong commonality of interest, and of the additional gains from all countries acting together, led to the negotiation of the WTO Trade Facilitation Agreement (TFA). Negotiations on the TFA were successfully concluded at the 2013 WTO Bali Ministerial conference. The Agreement entered into force on 22 February 2017, after two-thirds of members had completed their domestic ratification processes.

The core of the TFA is a package of substantial trade facilitation provisions (Section I, Articles 1 to 12) covering measures for expediting the movement, release and clearance of goods, including goods in transit. The Agreement also covers provisions on transparency, administrative simplification, use of information technology for data processing and exchange, as well as provisions on co-operation between customs and other appropriate authorities on trade facilitation and customs compliance issues. It establishes a permanent committee on trade facilitation at the WTO, and requires Members to have a national committee to facilitate domestic co-ordination and implementation of the Agreement (Section I, Article 13).

Uniquely among WTO agreements, the TFA directly links implementation of the Agreement to the capacities of developing and least developed countries (Section II, Special and Differential Treatment). While all developed country WTO Members[3] have to implement the TFA from the date of its entry into force, developing and least-developed countries can determine when they will implement individual provisions of the TFA and are required to implement some provisions only upon receipt of technical assistance and support for capacity building. The TFA is thus being implemented gradually, with different parts of the Agreement implemented earlier than others by countries around the world.

This unique structure of the TFA places a premium on knowing what is actually happening on the ground on trade facilitation. Understanding implementation of the TFA requires detailed information on the state of play on trade facilitation in WTO Members. It requires ongoing insights into where progress is being made and remaining challenges.

The TFIs were developed to support the negotiation and implementation of the TFA and are the most precisely targeted instrument for monitoring and benchmarking country performance on trade facilitation in existence today. As the TFA is gradually implemented, the TFIs allow the state of play on trade facilitation across more than 160 countries to be captured, key advances highlighted and challenges countries will face on the path to full implementation identified, providing a baseline for monitoring future progress on trade facilitation. The TFIs can thus also play a valuable role in helping to identify and prioritise technical assistance and capacity-building efforts. Finally, the TFIs can support advocacy efforts to build support for trade facilitation reforms, as they provide an important analytical tool enabling the potential impact of trade facilitation reforms on trade and the economy to be assessed.

Introducing the OECD Trade Facilitation Indicators

The TFIs are composed of a set of variables measuring the actual extent to which countries have introduced and implemented trade facilitation measures in absolute terms, but also their performance relative to others. The TFIs are tools, not rules: they are not designed to assess country compliance with specific TFA provisions, but rather to help policy makers in developed and developing countries alike to assess the state of their trade facilitation efforts, pinpoint challenges, and identify opportunities for progress.

The TFIs mirror the substantive provisions of the TFA. An additional OECD indicator going beyond the scope of the TFA was added to capture elements of good governance and impartiality of border administrations (Table 1.1).

Table 1.1. **Overall structure of the OECD Trade Facilitation Indicators**

Indicator	Description
(a) Information availability	Enquiry points; publication of trade information, including on Internet
(b) Involvement of the trade community (Consultations)	Structures for consultations; established guidelines for consultations; publications of drafts; existence of notice-and-comment frameworks
(c) Advance rulings	Prior statements by the administration to requesting traders concerning the classification, origin, valuation method, etc., applied to specific goods at the time of importation; the rules and process applied to such statements
(d) Appeal procedures	The possibility and modalities to appeal administrative decisions by border agencies
(e) Fees and charges	Disciplines on the fees and charges imposed on imports and exports; disciplines on penalties
(f) Formalities – documents	Acceptance of copies, simplification of trade documents; harmonisation in accordance with international standards
(g) Formalities – automation	Electronic exchange of data; use of automated risk management; automated border procedures; electronic payments
(h) Formalities – procedures	Streamlining of border controls; single submission points for all required documentation (single windows); post-clearance audits; authorised operators
(i) Internal co-operation	Control delegation to Customs authorities; co-operation between various border agencies of the country
(j) External co-operation	Co-operation with neighbouring and third countries
(k) Governance and impartiality	Customs structures and functions; accountability; ethics policy

Note: The area of governance and impartiality (indicator (k)) is outside the remit of the TFA.

Each TFI indicator is composed of several specific, precise and fact-based variables related to existing trade-related policies and regulations and their implementation in practice. Further information on how the TFIs are calculated is at Annex A.

Data collection

The TFI database covers 163 countries, including economies at all income levels – 28 low income countries (LICs), 42 lower middle income countries (LMICs), 40 upper middle income countries (UMICs), 19 high income economies outside the OECD area (HICs non-OECD) and 34 OECD countries – as well as all geographic regions (namely, Asia-Pacific, Europe and Central Asia, Latin America and the Caribbean, Middle East and North Africa and Sub-Saharan Africa). Full lists of countries by income and regions can be found in Annex B.

The TFIs are based on a detailed questionnaire, with the aim of ensuring factual information that is geographically comparable and consistent over time (the questionnaire is at Annex C). Data is collected from three types of sources: a) publicly available information included in the websites of Customs and other relevant border agencies, official publications such as Customs Codes, annual reports, or public databases;[4] b) direct submissions from countries; and c) factual information from the private sector – in particular express industry associations[5] and companies operating worldwide (Figure 1.1). Discrepancies are verified by the OECD, and completed country datasheets are sent to capitals for validation.[6]

Figure 1.1. **TFIs data collection process**

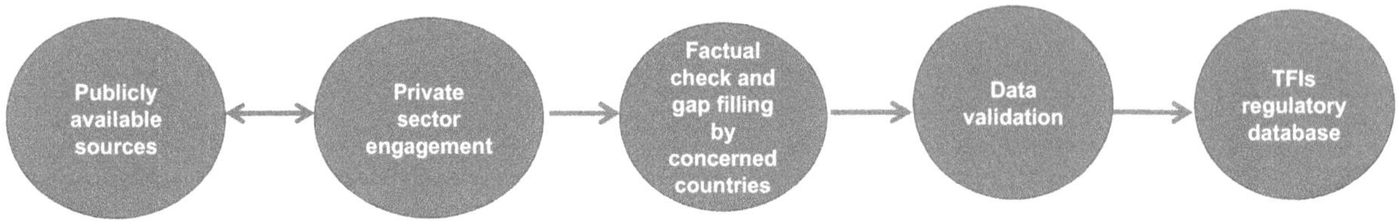

The process aims to ensure accuracy and to combine applicable regulation with a practitioner's account on how things work on the ground, while keeping the resource requirements manageable.

Using the TFIs

The TFIs dataset allows for comparisons by income group, geographical group and among regional grouping members; for examination of the state of play by individual trade facilitation measure; and for assessment of the evolution of performance over time. Interactive online tools have been developed to help countries make the most of the TFIs as a tool for informing reform strategies (Box 1.1).

Box 1.1. **Interactive online TFI tools**

Two interactive tools are available through the TFIs internet page (*www.oecd.org/trade/facilitation/indicators.htm*):

- **Compare your country:** Allows users to access individual country profiles which display an overview of trade facilitation performance. The tool allows comparison, in a dynamic way, of a selected country with other countries belonging to the same income group or region. The user can also visualise progress made by the selected country across all TFI areas.
- **Policy simulator:** Allows the user to quickly obtain an overview of the indicators and the key measures driving the overall performance of a selected country and to compare the selected country with other countries. It also allows for the simulation of potential policy reforms: by modifying the data in specific policy areas, the user obtains an "edited" performance bar, showing the impact of policy modifications on the overall performance of the selected country and on its relative performance in comparison to other countries. The information obtained can be shared, referenced or downloaded.

The TFIs can also be used as an evaluation tool to assess the economic impact of trade facilitation reforms and in particular of implementation of the TFA (Figure 1.2).[7] These analyses can range from quantitative analysis in order to disentangle the channels through which trade facilitation reform can benefit the global economy, as well as national economies, to estimates of the impact of specific reforms on the demand and the supply sides of GVC activity. Testing the TFIs against various economic variables also enables estimation of the impact at the macro level of specific reforms to the trade procedures of given countries, as well as providing an indication of the net benefits of specific reforms at the micro level. Further details on the methodology for these analyses is found in Annex A.

Figure 1.2. **TFIs as an evaluation tool**

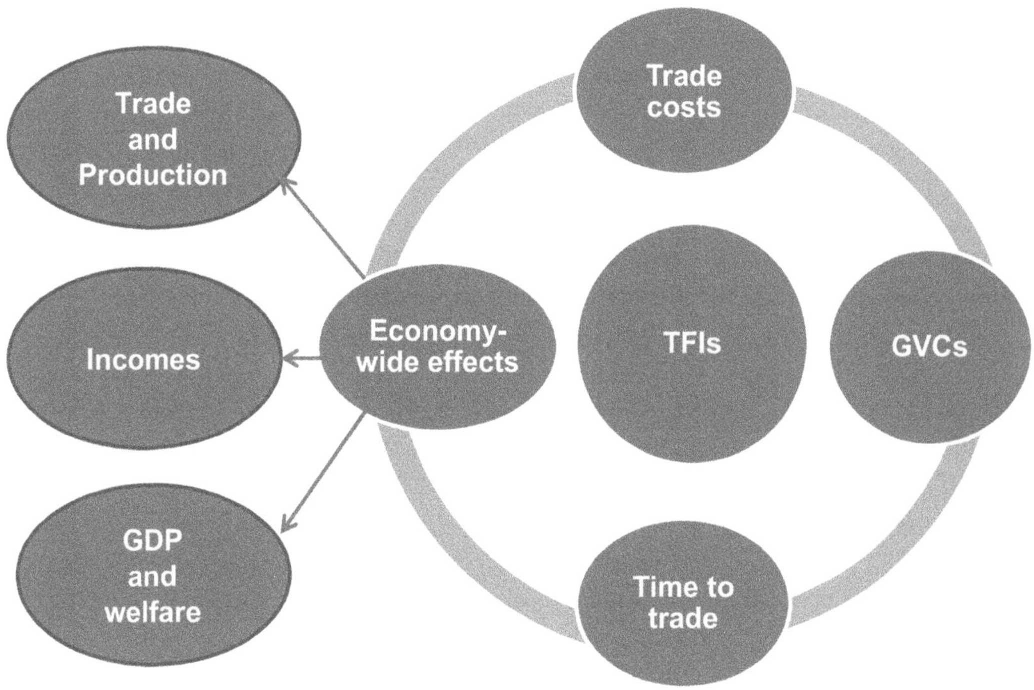

Overview of this publication

Against this background, the rest of this publication discusses the progress made on trade facilitation, the remaining challenges, and measures the economic gains that trade facilitation reforms bring in the context of both trade in GVCs and the economy as a whole.

This publication has two parts. Part I focuses on implementation, drawing on the TFIs to take a global view of trade facilitation reforms and more specific analysis on the most challenging areas. Part II uses the TFIs to analyse and measure the economic benefits from trade facilitation reforms, underscoring the compelling case for action on trade facilitation.

Part I opens with evidence from the 2017 update of the OECD TFIs on the state of play of trade facilitation for 163 countries worldwide (Chapter 2). The OECD TFIs offer a snapshot of trade facilitation at the time of the entry into force of the TFA, providing a baseline for future progress. This chapter presents the results of trade facilitation reforms covered by the mandatory provisions of the TFA, with detailed breakdown of progress and challenges by country income grouping and region. It highlights the areas where most progress has been made, but also those areas that countries still need to address to implement the Agreement.

Chapters 3 and 4 then dive deeper into two areas which have proven most challenging for trade facilitation reforms with a view to providing insights for policy makers on how progress could be made.

Chapter 3 focuses on border agency co-operation, both at the domestic level among the various agencies with responsibility for trade-related regulation, and at the international level between neighbouring countries. In both these areas, it draws on evidence from the TFIs, as well as international best practice and country experience to highlight key lessons for policy makers on the most important factors for success in achieving effective border agency co-operation. At both the domestic and international levels, it highlights the importance of focusing not only on changes to procedures, but also to working culture and the importance of strong and sustained political commitment to building trust and enhancing co-operation among agencies.

Chapter 4 examines the related issue of Single Window platforms. It provides detailed evidence from the OECD TFI focused on Single Windows to discuss progress in 23 economies across various regions. In particular, it draws lessons from the experience of the Association of South East Asian Nations (ASEAN) in implementing a Single Window to highlight key implications for success and challenges for policy makers.

Part I concludes with a look at the costs and challenges of implementing trade facilitation reforms (Chapter 5). It highlights the growing role that Aid for Trade has played in supporting trade facilitation reforms, and draws on experience from 24 developing and emerging economies to present evidence on the nature of the costs incurred in trade facilitation reform and how they compare with the benefits received.

Part II then explores further the economic case for trade facilitation reforms. Chapter 6 explores how specific border measures affect trade and the functioning of global supply chains and what policy makers can do to optimise their operation. Drawing on analyses from the TFIs, it presents quantitative evidence on which reforms have the greatest impact on reducing trade costs and enhancing trade flows, and which reforms matter most for boosting a country's participation in global supply chains. Moreover, as trade facilitation benefits both importers and exporters, analysis focuses on the impact of trade facilitation reforms on both the supply and demand side of value chains.

Chapter 7 concludes by stepping back to examine the global economic benefits from trade facilitation. While quantifying the gains from trade facilitation reforms can be challenging, this analysis takes an innovative approach drawing on the TFIs and the OECD's METRO model to document the channels through which trade facilitation reforms can benefit the global economy. It discusses the distribution of those potential benefits across country groupings and sectors, over the short and longer term, and explores the impact on labour income and employment, as well as welfare over the longer term.

Notes

1. Trade facilitation and growing trade in parcels is the subject of ongoing OECD work, as is deeper analysis of which trade facilitation reforms matter most for MSMEs.
2. The relationship between trade facilitation and integrity is also the subject of ongoing work at the OECD.
3. In the WTO, Developing Member status is self-selected. Least Developed Countries are defined with reference to the United Nations classification of LDCs.
4. These include other international databases, repositories and reports such as: United Nations Regional Economic Commissions (UNRCs) released results of the latest Global Survey on Trade Facilitation and Paperless Trade; the World Bank Logistics Performance Index; the World Bank Doing Business Trading Across Borders data; World Economic Forum (WEF) Global Competitiveness Report (GCR); WTO Trade Policy Reviews.

5. The Global Express Association (GEA) has developed questionnaires in an attempt to compile reports on market access and customs barriers in a large set of developed and developing countries. The objectives of the survey, among others, are to identify national laws and policies that make it difficult for express delivery companies and other transport companies to serve a particular country in an efficient manner as well as to identify capacity building needs in the country's customs administration. The GEA survey questions (within the Customs Capabilities Report) cover three key areas: transparency, customs efficiency and post-release processes.
6. Country datasheets are sent for validation with the assistance of WTO Permanent Delegations in Geneva, the World Customs Organisation (WCO) and the ASEAN Secretariat for economies outside the OECD membership.
7. Calculation of the potential impact of the TFA is based on two scenarios: a) "full" implementation, where countries implement all the options contained in the Agreement, including those formulated on a "best endeavours" basis; and b) "limited" implementation, where countries implement only the mandatory provisions, but taking into account that some of the best endeavours measures have already been implemented by some countries. These two scenarios provide upper and lower bounds of potential trade cost reductions likely to be obtained by implementing the TFA.

Bibliography

De Jong, E. and C. Bogmans (2011), "Does Corruption Discourage International Trade?", *European Journal of Political Economy*, 2011, Vol. 27, pp. 385-398.

OECD (2009), *Overcoming Border Bottlenecks: The Costs and Benefits of Trade Facilitation*, OECD Publishing, Paris, *http://dx.doi.org/10.1787/9789264056954-en*.

PART 1

Trade facilitation, a growing global footprint

PART 1

Chapter 2

Trade facilitation around the world: The state of play

This chapter provides an update, at the entry into force of the Trade Facilitation Agreement (TFA), of trade facilitation efforts worldwide, using the OECD Trade Facilitation Indicators (TFIs). The TFIs offer a snapshot of trade facilitation actions on the ground for over 160 countries, drawing on comparative data to shed light on emerging successes, opportunities, and challenges for countries worldwide.

The entry into force of the TFA brought new momentum to trade facilitation efforts

The entry into force of the WTO Trade Facilitation Agreement (TFA) on 22 February 2017 reinforced the centrality of trade facilitation on the global trade agenda. Uniquely among WTO agreements, the TFA directly links implementation of the Agreement to the capacities of developing and least developed countries. While all developed country WTO Members[1] have to implement the TFA from the date of its entry into force, this special and differential treatment (SDT) allows developing and least-developed countries to determine when they will implement individual provisions of the TFA and to only implement some provisions upon receipt of technical assistance and support for capacity building (Box 2.1). The TFA is thus being implemented gradually, with different parts of the Agreement implemented earlier than others by countries around the world.

The unique structure of the TFA means that understanding its implementation requires information on the state of play on trade facilitation around the world, on the main advances being made and on the remaining challenges that countries will need to address.

The 2017 update of the OECD Trade Facilitation Indicators (TFIs) provides, at the time of entry into force of the TFA, a precise and comprehensive overview of the strengths and weaknesses of national border-process mechanisms for more than 160 countries around the world. The updated TFIs not only show progress achieved since 2013, they also provide a baseline for monitoring future progress. Analysis of the TFIs also helps identify areas where domestic reform and investment in technical assistance and capacity building are likely to yield significant benefits.

This chapter begins with an overview of implementation across all countries covered in the TFIs, including a breakdown by income group, followed by snapshots of regional performance (regional groupings are set out in Annex B). The chapter then digs deeper into what the TFIs tell us about the implementation of areas covered by the TFA, and the remaining challenges.

Box 2.1. **Implementing the WTO Trade Facilitation Agreement**

A unique feature of the WTO TFA is that developing and least developed WTO Members categorise and notify each provision according to their capacity for implementation. Provisions are identified as those to be implemented upon entry into force of the TFA (*Category A*); to be implemented after a transitional period (*Category B*); and to be implemented upon the receipt of technical assistance and support for capacity building (*Category C*).

Six developing and least developed WTO Members[1] have committed to implementing the entire TFA as of the date of its entry into force, while another ten have committed to fully applying over 90% of the Agreement as of that date.[2]

Box 2.1. **Implementing the WTO Trade Facilitation Agreement** *(cont.)*

Of the approximately 36 notifiable measures under the TFA almost 80% are indicated for immediate implementation by over 50% of developing and least developed country Members. More than 70% of those Members also designated a quarter of all measures as Category A (that is, to be implemented as of the date of entry into force of the Agreement or within the following year). For 40% of those WTO Members, almost 95% of TFA measures were designated as Category A (Neufeld, 2016).

Of the 93 Category A notifications received as of February 2017, the most frequently notified measures tend to relate to quite specific or narrow issues. The most frequently notified category A measure is pre-shipment inspection (Article 10.5), followed by the use of Customs brokers (Article 10.6), and provisions (Article 9) related to the movement of goods intended for import under Customs control. The next most frequently notified Category A provisions are also very specific, relating to detention (Article 5.2) and temporary admission of goods and inward and outward processing (Article 10.9).

Broader provisions follow next, including those related to the application of common Customs procedures and uniform documentation requirements for the release and clearance of goods throughout a Member's territory (Article 10.7); return of rejected goods (Article 10.8); transit of goods (Article 11); procedures for appeal or review (Article 4); penalties (Article 6) and use of international standards (Article 10.3). Measures relating to making information available (Article 1) are also increasingly notified under Category A.

The least frequently notified measures are for Single Windows (Article 10.4, Category A in less than 30% of notifications); Authorised Operators (Article 7.7); measurement and publication of average release time of goods (Article 7.6); test procedures (Article 5.3); and advance rulings (Article 3).

By region, those countries indicating the earliest implementation timeframes are in Europe (with an average of over 80% of category A commitments), followed by the Middle East (78%). Latin America and the Caribbean ranks equal third with Asia and the Pacific with average Category A designation rates of 57%, while Central Asian countries (50%) and those in Africa (36%) indicate longer timeframes.

1. Hong Kong, China; Israel; Korea; Mexico; Singapore; and Chinese Taipei.
2. Chile, Colombia, Costa Rica, the former Yugoslav Republic of Macedonia, Malaysia, Qatar, Saudi Arabia, Turkey, and Uruguay.

Source: Neufeld (2016) and Trade Facilitation Facility Notifications Database (2017), *www.tfadatabase.org/*.

The big picture: Current state of play on trade facilitation globally

The TFIs show that implementation of measures falling under the scope of the TFA was already well underway at the time of its entry into force in February 2017 (Figure 2.1). The TFIs also indicate that good progress has been made on many of the substantive provisions of the TFA that developing and least developed WTO Members committed to apply from the date of entry into force or within the following year (termed by the Agreement as *Category A provisions*).

Worldwide performance is even in a number of areas, but others pose challenges for lower-income countries

While there are some differences in implementation amongst countries including by both income and geography, worldwide performance was relatively even in a number of areas, in particular in relation to areas covered by the TFA disciplines on border fees and charges and streamlining of border procedures.

Across the board, the most challenging areas for implementation relate to co-operation of border agencies, both within a country and across the border. Domestic and cross-border co-operation among the agencies responsible for border controls remain a work in progress around the world, but encouraging steps have been taken by countries at all levels of development.

In terms of aggregate performance by income group, progress on automating the border process appears to be closely correlated with income, with less advanced economies faring less well than more advanced ones. This suggests that automation is an area where capacity building may yield significant benefits. Indeed, measures such as risk management or Single Windows feature heavily among the provisions WTO developing and least-developed country Members designated for implementation after a transitional period and for which technical assistance and support for capacity building would be required (*Category C provisions*).[2] Income-related differences in performance are less marked for the streamlining of border procedures, possibly reflecting the extensive capacity building undertaken on Customs matters in recent years.

Low income countries (LICs) appear to face particular challenges in areas such as consultations with concerned stakeholders, advance ruling mechanisms and the availability and operation of appeal procedures. Their performance gap in these areas is quite significant compared to a relatively homogeneous average performance for other country income groups. This is also the case for governance and impartiality measures (which are included in the TFIs but are beyond the scope of the TFA). The distance of LIC performance from implementation of the full set of mandatory TFA provisions on advance rulings is consistent with their low number of *Category A* notifications for these provisions.[3] This is less the case, however, for appeal procedures.

In general, more advanced economies perform better than countries at lower levels of development (Figure 2.1). For most policy areas, there is a significant difference between the performance of OECD countries and that of other groups. The largest disparities are found in areas beyond the mandatory provisions of the TFA, such as external border agency co-operation. The relationship between performance and income is also underscored by the distance of developing and emerging economies from the top 25% performers in the world (Figure 2.2). That said, there are also several areas where the gap is relatively small, such as for fees and charges, procedures or external border agency co-operation.

Performance among countries within income groups is far from homogeneous, with high and low performers in every group. Policy areas showing a wider variation appear to be those that are inherently more challenging to implement. Among LICs, more pronounced disparities in implementation occur in the areas of automation, advance rulings, appeal procedures, and involvement of the trade community, with most of the better performers coming from the top income quartile. Among lower middle income countries (LMICs) and upper middle income countries (UMICs), there are also wide variations in implementation of areas covered by the TFA disciplines on fees and charges and simplification and harmonisation of documents. High income countries outside the OECD area (HICs non-OECD) display the widest disparities in implementation across all areas. This reflects the fact that they are a very heterogeneous group, ranging from very high performers in Asia to less strong performers in the Middle East and North Africa

(MENA) region. Performance is more consistent across OECD countries, with the exception of practices around documents and border agency co-operation.

Figure 2.1. **Implementation of areas covered by the TFA is underway worldwide**

TFIs, 2017: Full sample snapshot, income groupings

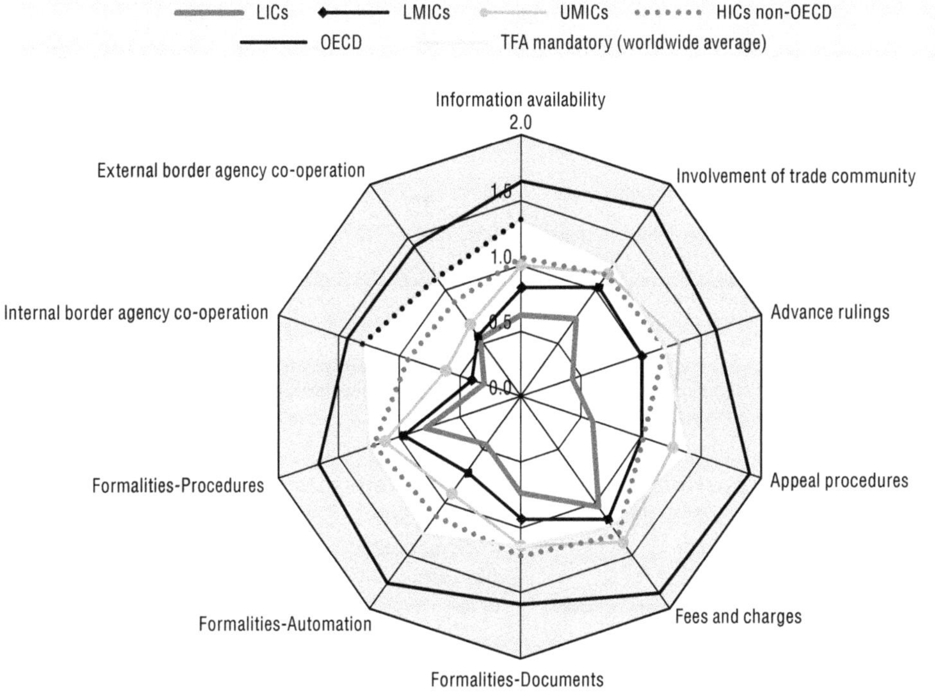

Note: The shaded area depicts measures that go beyond the mandatory provisions of the TFA and are to be implemented on a best endeavours basis. The dotted portion of the grey line highlights the fact that all TFA provisions for external border agency co-operation are "best endeavours". The averages account for the economies where all indicators are available.
Source: TFIs (2017), *www.oecd.org/trade/facilitation/indicators.htm*.

Comparison of the 2015 TFIs to the 2017 update confirms the positive momentum generated by the negotiation and adoption of the TFA for all groups of countries (Figure 2.3). Several important trends are evident: while there were improvements in the overall performance of the LICs, LMICs and OECD groupings, the average performance of UMICs and high income non-OECD economies in 2015-17 only improved marginaly in some areas, such as in the involvement of the trade community, automation, and streamlining of procedures. The LICs and LMICs groupings also experienced improvements in information availability, advance rulings and governance and impartiality.

Implementation varies significantly across regions

Regional averages confirm the picture from income group averages. Once again, the greatest challenges relate to the co-operation of border agencies within a country and across the border. The streamlining of formalities (harmonisation of documents, automation of the border process and simplification of procedures) and the availability of trade-related information also present continuing challenges across all regions (Figure 2.4). Performance on the streamlining of procedures and on consultations with stakeholders was relatively homogeneous across regions; this was much less the case for the availability

Figure 2.2. **In general, more advanced economies perform better**

Distance to top 25% of performers

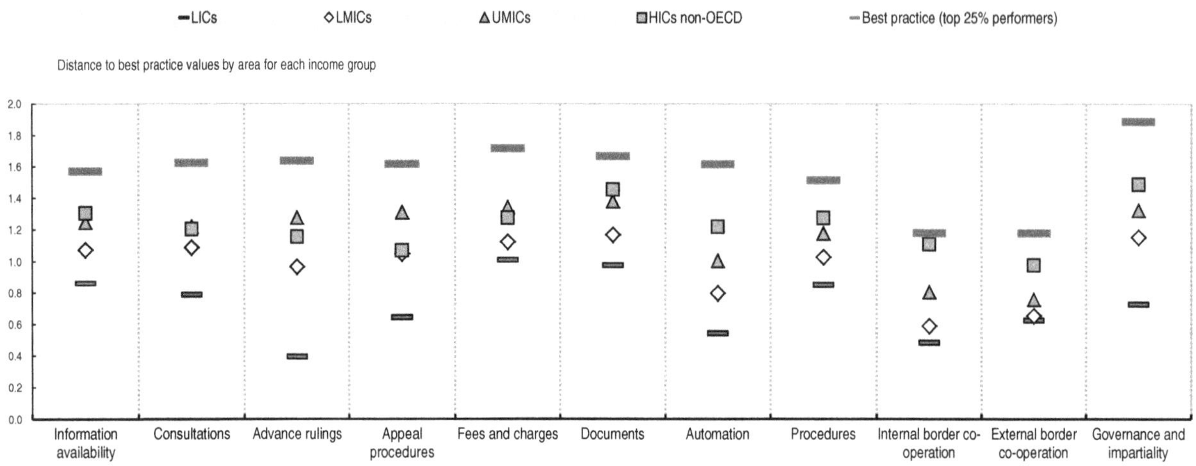

Note: The figure shows the average gap between a group average's performance for a selected area and the performance level of the top 25% countries for each area covered. OECD members' performances are in the top quartile (best) performance for the overall sample.

Source: TFIs (2017), *www.oecd.org/trade/facilitation/indicators.htm*.

Figure 2.3. **But there is positive momentum on implementation for all countries**

TFIs: Income groups, 2015 and 2017

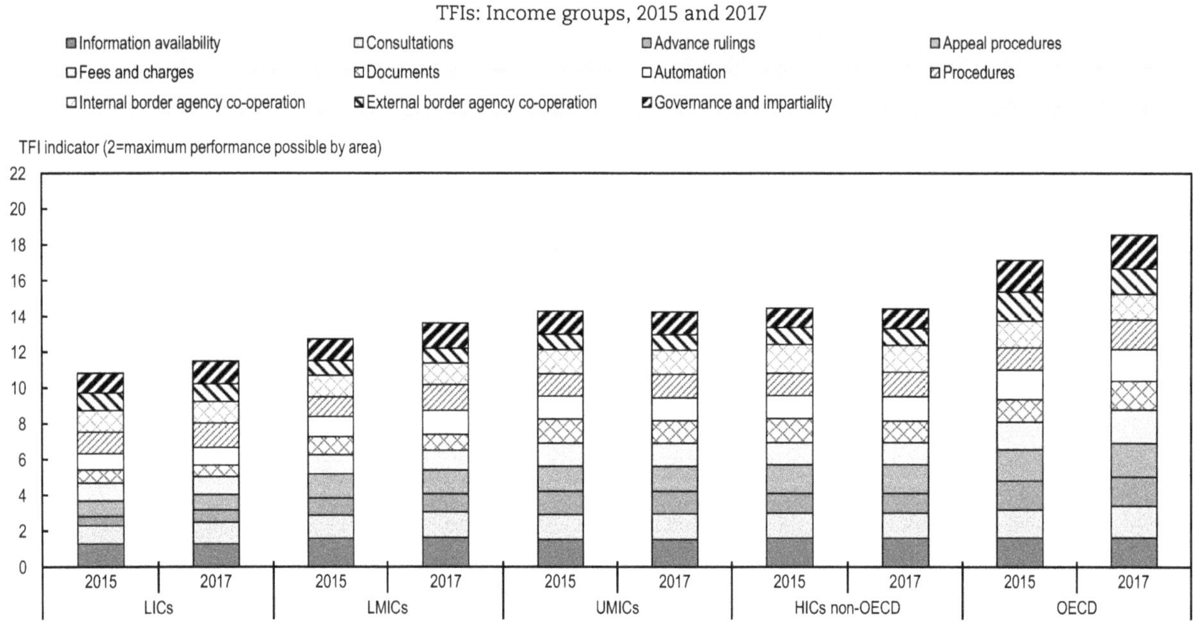

Source: TFIs (2017), *www.oecd.org/trade/facilitation/indicators.htm*.

of information, automation of the border process and harmonisation of trade documents. The widest disparities across regions occur in the operation and performance of advance ruling mechanisms, the availability and operation of appeal procedures and governance and impartiality. The relatively strong performance of Europe and Central Asia is largely driven by European Union members, while that of the Asia-Pacific region is driven by several East Asian high performers. The Sub-Saharan Africa (SSA) region is the weakest performer across the board, due mainly to lower performance in the areas of information availability, advance ruling mechanisms and automation, as well as governance and impartiality.[4]

Figure 2.4. **TFIs 2017: Full sample snapshot, regional groupings**

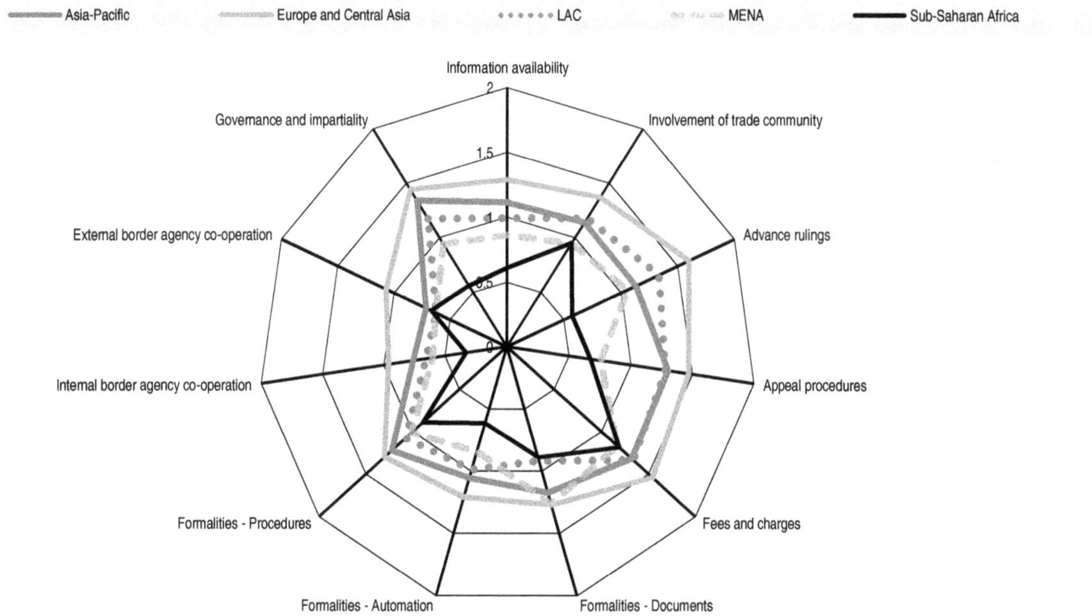

Note: The geographical groupings include OECD members. The averages account for the economies where all indicators are available.
Source: TFIs (2017), *www.oecd.org/trade/facilitation/indicators.htm.*

To a much larger extent than within income groups, performance variations are also notable across regions, particularly with regard to consultations with stakeholders, advance ruling mechanisms, availability and operation of appeal procedures, simplification and harmonisation of documents, automation of the border process, and inter-agency co-operation. Within-group disparities are most marked for the Asia-Pacific and Europe and Central Asia regions. In the Asia-Pacific region, wider disparities can be seen in the areas of consultations, advance rulings, and automation; the widest disparities in Europe and Central Asia concern automation, advance rulings, and appeal procedures.

A closer look: Key challenges in relation to the TFA

Transparency and predictability

Articles 1 to 6 of the TFA include provisions aimed at enhancing the transparency and predictability of the import, export and transit processes. Measures covered by these Articles are a first step in providing greater certainty and reliability in the transaction chain. These measures are reflected in variables in the first five TFIs, namely Information availability, Involvement of the trading community, Advance rulings, Appeal procedures, and Fees and charges.

Information availability measures in TFA Article 1 (*Publication and availability of information*) refer to web-based and other forms of publication about Customs and border-related rules and procedures, as well as transparency mechanisms such as enquiry points.

TFI data shows that the kinds of requirements falling under Article 1.1 are already quite widely implemented (Figure 2.5). Among the types of information listed in Article 1.1, countries across all income groups publish relatively widely the basic steps of importation, exportation and transit procedures (1.1.a) and applied rates of duties and taxes (1.1.b). LICs and UMICs also make available information regarding classification and valuation rules (1.1.d), appeal procedures (1.1.h) and agreements with third countries (1.1.i). This information is generally made available through paper publications, with online publication still lagging across country groupings. An increasing number of countries provide specific webpages for advance rulings; however, most do not have an interactive interface allowing online filing of advance ruling requests.

Figure 2.5. **Availability of information provisions are already widely implemented**

TFA Article 1: Publication and availability of information

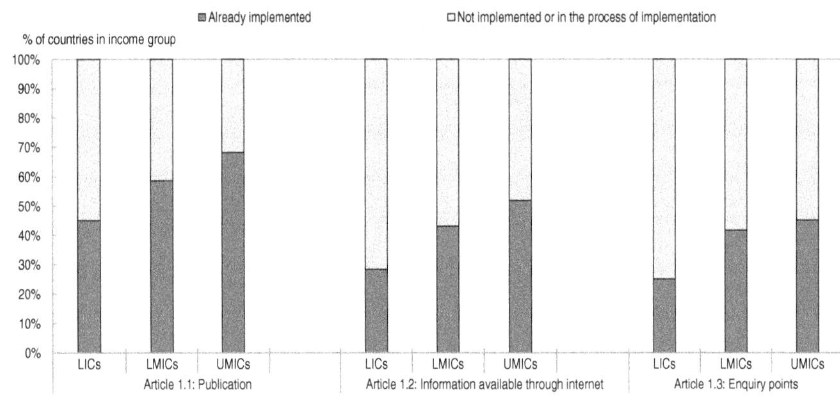

Source: TFIs (2017), *www.oecd.org/trade/facilitation/indicators.htm.*

There has been relatively little progress in providing documents and forms directly for download on the Customs website, especially among LICs and LMICs. Moreover, new web functionalities – such as the existence of a specific page for professional users or the publication of user manuals – are currently in place only in some UMICs, high-income non-OECD economies, and OECD countries.

Significant progress has been made since 2012 in recognising the efficiency-enhancing potential of enquiry points (1.3): the majority of LMICs and UMICs and 60% of surveyed LICs maintain one or more enquiry points and offer the possibility to submit questions about Customs-related issues, either by phone or via an online form. However, timeliness of response from enquiry points appears to be problematic: less than 30% of developing countries had hours of operation fully aligned with commercial needs, or service charters establishing a standard response time to enquiries.

TFA Article 2 (*Opportunity to comment, information before entry into force and consultations*) seeks to ensure the involvement of the trade community in the design and everyday operation of border-related policies and procedures. The Article also refers to the scope, contents and outcomes of such consultations between traders and governments. In 2017, 50% of surveyed countries (mainly middle income and high income countries) hold regular consultations with traders – a share that has risen from 40% in 2015. Developing countries now appear to have well-established guidelines and procedures in place to govern the public consultation process (Figure 2.6). The scope of consultations has also been widened, with new stakeholders enjoying access to consultations; about 55% of developing and emerging economies seek to involve at least four stakeholder groups.

Figure 2.6. **Dialogue with the private sector is progressing but modalities remain challenging**

TFA Article 2: Opportunity to comment, information before entry into force, and consultations

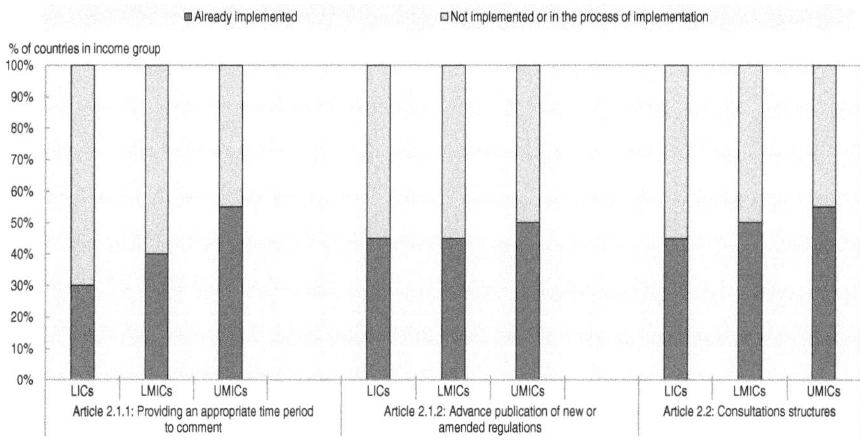

Source: TFIs (2017), *www.oecd.org/trade/facilitation/indicators.htm.*

That said, the content and outcomes of consultations remain challenging for many countries. Less than half of surveyed countries consistently provide opportunities to comment (2.1.1), or allow an interval between the publication and entry into force of all new or amended trade related laws and regulations (2.1.2). Drafts are available before the entry into force of a rule and stakeholder comments are possible in 29% of LICs and 57% of UMICs, but only 14% of developing countries involve the trading community during the drafting stages of new trade-related legislation.

While general notice-and-comment procedures appeared to be in place across the countries surveyed, outside the OECD grouping these are not always used in the context of trade and border issues. Moreover, while public comments received during consultations appeared to be taken into account across 53% of the countries surveyed, administrations rarely provide explanations of how such comments were ultimately addressed, or to what extent.

TFA Article 3 (*Advance rulings*) addresses key mechanisms for providing traders with greater certainty about Customs requirements and duty liabilities and can play a particularly important role in facilitating trade (Box 2.2). Advance information can also be fed into Customs risk management machinery. While in more than 80% of countries across all income groups, Customs issues binding advance rulings (3.1 and 3.5), implementation of other provisions – relating to validity (3.3), refusal to issue or revocation (3.4), timely issuance (3.6), review (3.7) and publication of advance rulings of general interest (3.8) – varies considerably by country group (Figure 2.7). Upgrading advance rulings systems remains a work in progress for most countries.

TFA Article 4 (*Procedures for appeal or review*) addresses basic characteristics of the appeal system such as transparency, fairness, accessibility, and timeliness and effectiveness of applicable rules and outcomes. A well-functioning appeals mechanism ensures transparent and accountable application and enforcement of legislation by Customs and related agencies. Although the right to appeal (4.1) now appears more widely available than in the period 2012-15, measures concerning the timeliness (4.4) and communication of the reasons for administrative decisions (4.5) are in place in only half of

Figure 2.7. **Binding advance rulings are generally available, but other aspects remain a work in progress**

TFA Article 3: Advance rulings

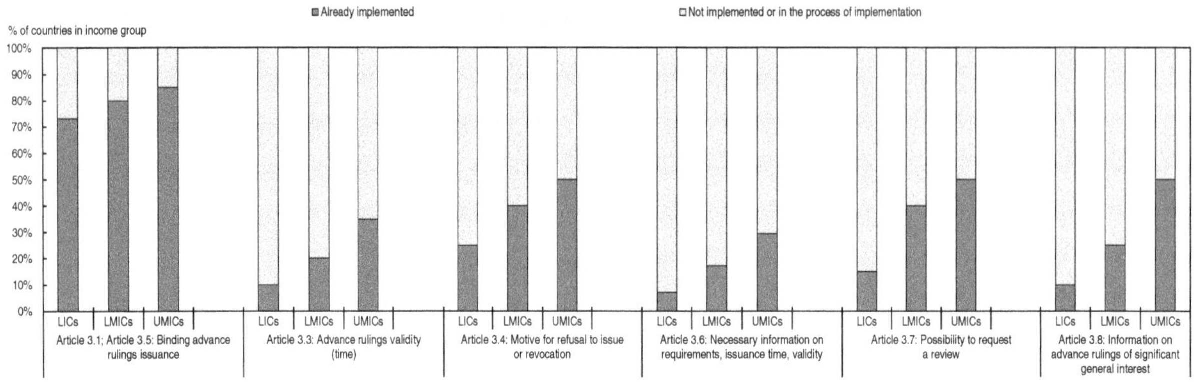

Source: TFIs (2017), *www.oecd.org/trade/facilitation/indicators.htm.*

Box 2.2. **Do advance rulings increase trade flows?**

Advance rulings are issued in relation to, for example, the tariff classification, valuation, and country of origin of goods, or duty drawback provisions.[1] In those countries issuing them, typically more than 90% of advance rulings relate to classification, followed by advance rulings on the origin of the good.

Analysis using the TFIs shows a positive correlation between the TFI score in relation to advance rulings and the volume of trade flows, in particular for OECD and UMICs. This raises the question of whether trade volumes drive the demand for advance rulings or whether predictability from advance rulings reduces trade costs and thus increases trade volumes. In the OECD area, while a number of the largest traders issue the highest number of advance rulings (United States, Japan and Germany), several smaller traders, including Norway, Australia, Switzerland and the Netherlands issue only marginally fewer such rulings than the large traders in absolute terms.

Analysis undertaken using the US CROSS (Customs Rulings Online Search System) database also indicates that the main predictors of the number of advance rulings, in order of importance, are: average tariff levels; the number of tariff lines; the percentage of trade entering under a preference program; and the number of importers. In sum, the overall volume of trade does impact advance rulings, but only modestly and in selected sectors.

Per Article 3 of the TFA, the TFI on advance rulings covers governance and efficiency of these mechanisms, as well as efforts to encourage compliance through increased communication between Customs administrations and traders. Countries scoring highest issue rulings quickly, post rulings for public review, keep rulings valid until revoked and allow importers to request a review of an advance ruling.

In addition to the efficiency of the mechanism, other aspects that may influence the demand for advance rulings include the length of validity of advance rulings (fewer requests are necessary when the ruling is valid for longer); or the applicable tariff (the higher the tariff, the more useful an advance ruling). Equally, advance rulings may not be in high demand in less complex trading environments (where, for instance, tariff classifications do not go beyond the six digit level[2]).

Box 2.2. **Do advance rulings increase trade flows?** *(cont.)*

In sum, it is not trade volumes that drive the demand for advance rulings but advance rulings that increase trade volumes by improving predictability and reducing costs and delays, in particular in complex trade regimes.

1. Refunding import duties and fees for a product upon its re-exportation.
2. In the Harmonised System, which includes product classification at the 6 digit level while national classifications can be at 8 and 10 digit levels.

Source: Moïsé et al. (2011).

surveyed countries (Figure 2.8). Overall, aspects related to timing for appeals – including sufficient time to contest a decision, to prepare and lodge an appeal, and avoidance of undue delays in the rendering of decisions – appear to be particularly challenging for LICs and LMICs.

Figure 2.8. **The right to appeal is widely available but timeliness and communication of processes varies**

TFA Article 4: Appeal or review procedures

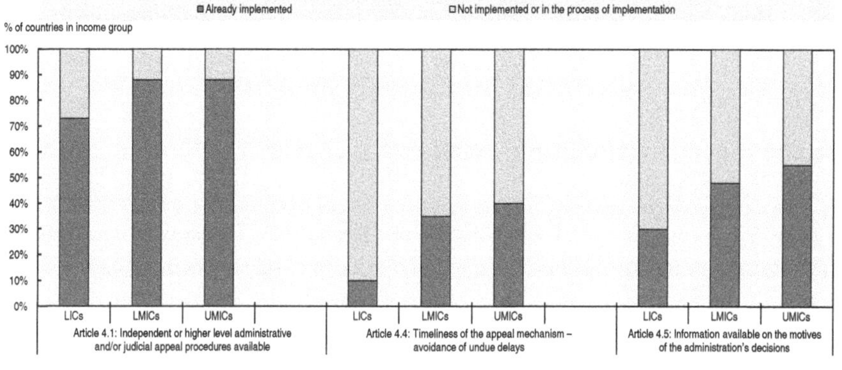

Source: TFIs (2017), *www.oecd.org/trade/facilitation/indicators.htm.*

TFA Article 6 promotes transparency and predictability of *fees, charges and penalties*. Provisions relating to penalties (6.3) were covered for the first time in the 2017 update of the TFIs.[5] Performance around periodic reviews of fees and charges (6.1.4), information published on fees and charges (6.1.2), and limitation of fees and charges to the approximate cost of services rendered (6.2) all display significant variations by income group (Figure 2.9). They appear to be especially challenging for LICs.

Accessible, publicly available data on fees and charges remains limited. With the exception of OECD countries and some high-income non-OECD economies, only a few developing countries (mainly UMICs) have a dedicated page covering fees and charges on their Customs websites.

In many of the developing countries surveyed, Customs administrations apply fees for services during normal working hours. Where countries charge fees for answering enquiries, in only about 65% of countries are these limited to the approximate cost of the services rendered. A further issue is the absence of periodic reviews of fees and charges. Time periods between the publication of new or amended fees and charges and their entry

Figure 2.9. **Implementation of disciplines on fees and charges is modest and varies by income**

TFA Article 6: Disciplines on fees and charges imposed on or in connection with importation, and exportation and penalties

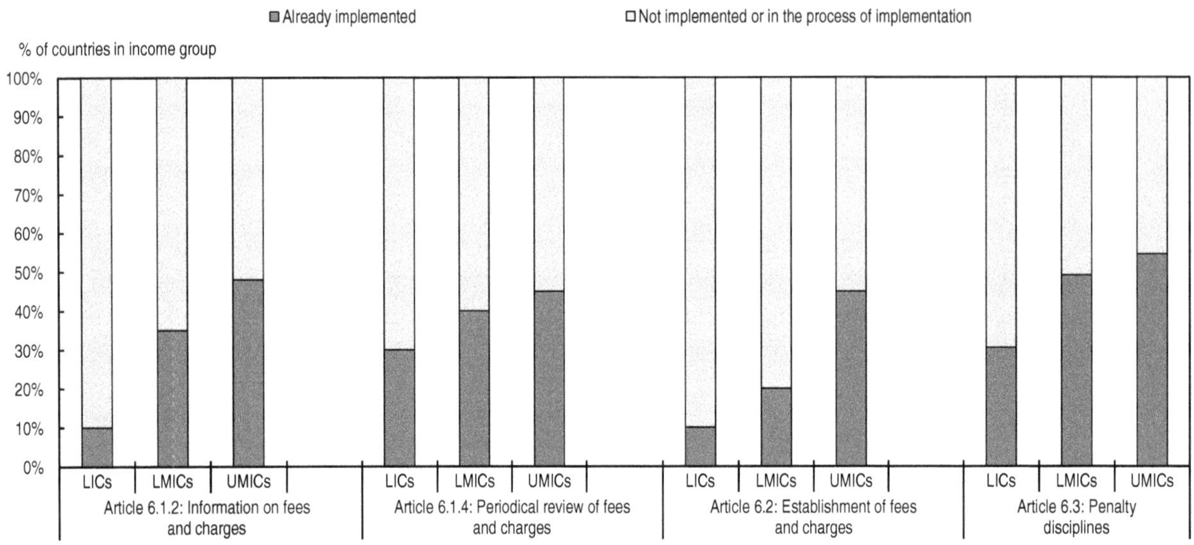

Source: TFIs (2017), *www.oecd.org/trade/facilitation/indicators.htm.*

into force also remain insufficient in many cases, with about 65% of countries providing adequate advance notice to traders.

TFA Article 6.3 requires that administrative penalties imposed by Customs take into account the facts and circumstances of the case and be commensurate with the degree and severity of the breach. The Article also requires avoidance of conflicts of interest in the assessment and collection of penalties and duties; written explanations of penalties imposed and of the applicable legal provisions; and adjustment of penalties when a breach is voluntarily disclosed.

Implementation appears to be relatively homogeneous among LMICs and UMICs with regard to penalties for breach of Customs laws or regulations, procedural requirements for transparency and proportionality, and procedural guarantees (i.e. providing an explanation in writing, specifying the nature of the breach and the applicable regulation). However, LICs are still facing challenges, with implementation in only about a third of the grouping. Conflicts of interest in the assessment and collection of penalties and duties are still a significant problem: in only around half of the countries surveyed is remuneration of Customs officials independent of any penalties or duties they assess or collect. There is also scope for further progress on voluntary disclosure, with less than 30% of developing countries surveyed considering this to be a mitigating factor for the purposes of establishing penalties (Figure 2.10).

Streamlining of formalities

Articles 7 and 10 of the TFA seek to minimise the number and complexity of import, export and transit formalities. Article 10 specifically addresses formalities and documentation requirements related to importation, exportation, and transit, while

Figure 2.10. **Implementation of disciplines on penalties is relatively homogenous among MICs, but remains problematic for LICs**

TFA Article 6.3 snapshot: Disciplines on penalties

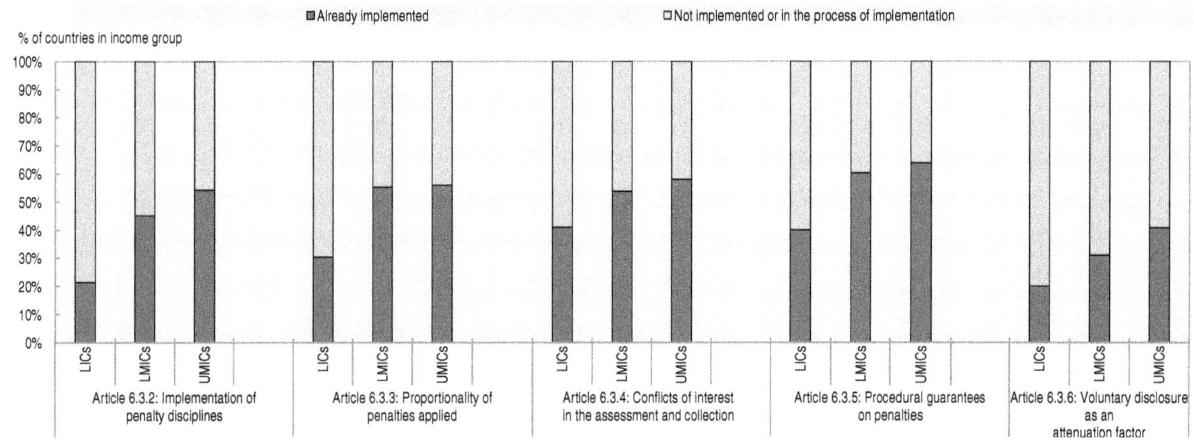

Source: TFIs (2017), *www.oecd.org/trade/facilitation/indicators.htm.*

Article 7 covers the release and clearance of goods, including processes and requirements relating to perishable goods. These Articles are covered by the three TFIs on Formalities, namely Documents, Automation, and Procedures discussed below. Transit, a key issue for landlocked developing countries, is discussed in Box 2.3.

TFI variables relating to documentation requirements refer to the extent that trade documents are harmonised with international standards, and documentation requirements simplified, through use of copies and reduction in the number and complexity of required documents. Compliance with international standards[6] (10.3) has improved among the surveyed countries over the past five years: as of 2017, about two-thirds of developing countries had ratified[7] at least two of the relevant International Conventions (Figure 2.11).

Figure 2.11. **Progress has been generally good on trade formalities**

TFA Article 10: Formalities connected with importation and exportation

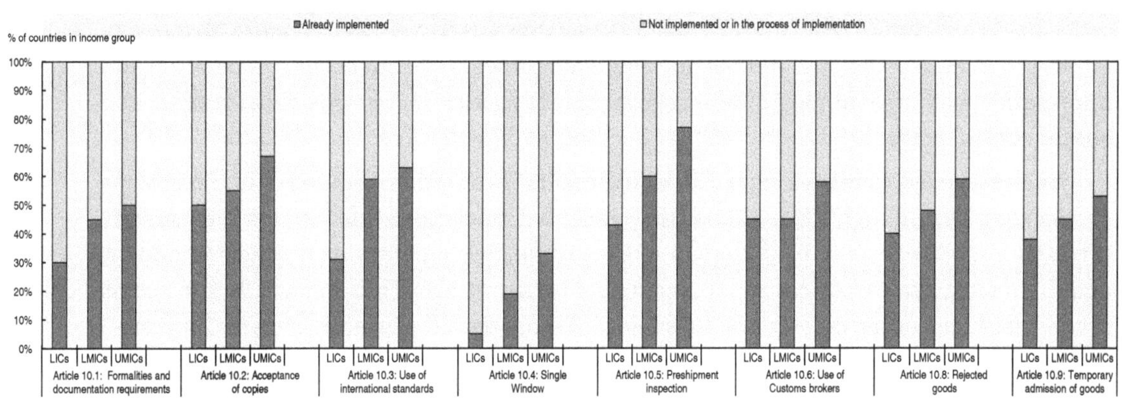

Source: TFIs (2017), *www.oecd.org/trade/facilitation/indicators.htm.*

The review and simplification of formalities and documentation requirements (10.1) remains a work in progress across all income groups. LICs lag significantly behind MICs in terms of reducing both the number of documents necessary for exporting and importing, and the average time required for the preparation of such documents. Periodic reviews of documentation requirements and discontinuation of those no longer needed are rare in practice: only 10% of LICs ensure that unnecessary requirements are discontinued as a result of such reviews (for UMICs, the figure is 40%).

In contrast, noticeable progress has been made on acceptance of copies (10.2); agencies in about 60% of developing and emerging countries accept copies when another government agency holds the original. However, even in those countries, copies are not accepted in all cases; only 8% of LICs and MICs accept copies without exceptions (related to the type of good, the circumstances or the agency) and the original may still need to be presented upon request.

Harnessing the power of information technology (IT), an increasing number of MICs, as well as HICs non-OECD, appear to be clearing import and export procedures electronically. That said, very little information is available on the actual percentage of import and export procedures that allow for electronic processing in LICs, LMICs and UMICs. By contrast, in the OECD area at time of publication the figure was 99.2%.

Article 10 provisions relating to pre-shipment inspection (10.5) and the use of Customs brokers (10.6) appear to be relatively widely implemented, although not without challenges for several LICs and LMICs (Figure 2.11). Countries still applying pre-shipment inspection are principally LICs, although similar arrangements can be found in some MICs. In some cases, pre-shipment inspection appears to have been eliminated only fairly recently: while half of the countries in Sub-Saharan Africa for which data were available were applying pre-shipment inspections in 2015, that share seems to have fallen to 43%.

Provisions on rejected goods (Article 10.8) and temporary admission of goods for inward and outward processing (Article 10.9) also show significant worldwide implementation.

The introduction and operation of Single Windows (Article 10.4) remains one of the most important challenges among TFA provisions, and the policy area where the least progress has been achived in particular for LICs. Around one-third of HICs non-OECD, UMICs and LMICs and only 10% of LICs appear to have a fully operational mechanism[8] in place. This share appears to be higher for OECD economies (60%). Information on progress on IT and Electronic Data Interchange (EDI) systems (see below), suggests that a key remaining challenge for operationalising Single Windows is the quality of co-operation and information exchange among different government agencies, Customs departments, and border control posts.

Most surveyed countries state that a Single Window is either planned or in the process of implementation, highlighting the importance that countries attach to this mechanism. Given its importance, and the limited progress to date, implementation of Single Windows, and the related issue of co-operation among border agencies both domestically and across borders (also discussed below), are the subject of more detailed investigation in Chapters 3 and 4.

For the majority of surveyed countries, IT systems capable of EDI – essential for simplifying documentation requirements and reducing the complexity of document submission – are either being implemented or are already functional. IT systems in most LMICs and UMICs are ready for EDI, with most LICs indicating that implementation of such systems is already underway. Moreover, around-the-clock automated processing for

Customs agencies is available in 60% of developing countries, up from 45% in 2015. The large majority of countries implementing around-the-clock automated processing are UMICs, high income non-OECD economies, and OECD countries.

Other challenges remain in automated border procedures, including pre-arrival processing (7.1) and its application in an automated environment; the existence of a system for the electronic payment of duties, taxes, fees and charges (7.2) and its integration with the automated declaration/cargo processing system; and the acceptance of digital certificates and signatures. While such features appear to be in place in half of MICs, implementation remains much lower in LICs (Figure 2.12).

Figure 2.12. **Automating border procedures remains a challenge**

TFA Article 7: Release and clearance of goods

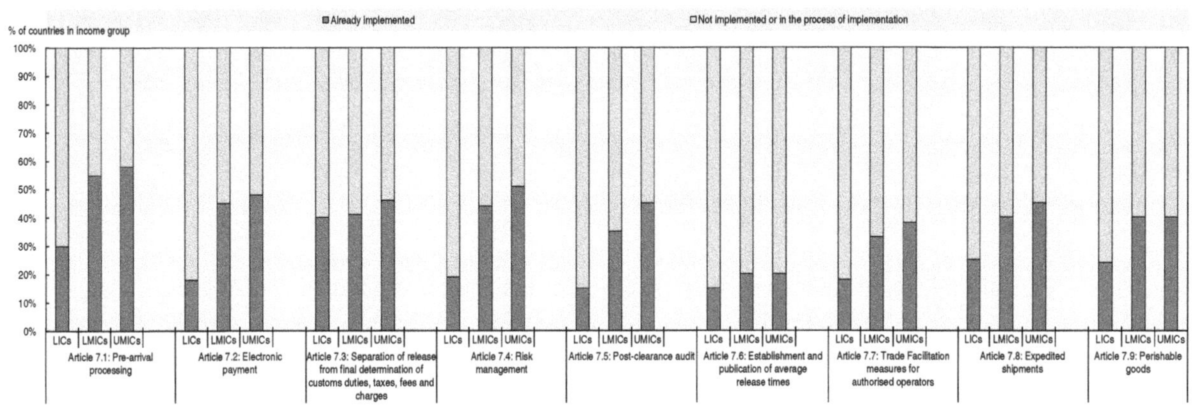

Source: TFIs (2017), *www.oecd.org/trade/facilitation/indicators.htm.*

Even where automation is in place, more information would be required to determine whether it works reliably. The availability and reliability of connectivity and electricity for example, can greatly influence the reliability of automated systems, in particular for remote border posts in some developing countries. In many developing countries surveyed, access by public services such as Customs to reliable energy remains low and average electricity transmission and distribution losses remain very high (Moisé and Sorescu, 2013).

Risk management to improve the efficiency and reduce the burden of Customs controls (7.4) seems to have been successfully implemented and to be currently operating in an automated environment in 35% of surveyed countries – essentially UMICs, high income non-OECD economies and OECD countries. This is a notable improvement over previous years, when this was the case for only a quarter of the sample. Other countries surveyed (largely LMICs and LICs) either do not have such a system or are in the process of introducing one. For the large majority of HIC non-OECD, UMICs, LMICs and LICs, border controls other than Customs are not yet supported by a risk management system or the system is yet to be fully implemented (Figure 2.13).

On balance, risk management efforts seem to have stalled at the single-agency (Customs) stage and have yet to achieve their full potential. Making risk management more comprehensive and integrating trusted trader programs, post-clearance controls, input from all border agencies and mutual recognition could bolster efficiency at the border and further sustain interagency co-operation. The deployment of risk management beyond Customs could be a useful area for future capacity-building efforts.

Figure 2.13. **Implementation of risk management has significantly improved, but mostly in higher income countries**

Risk management implementation

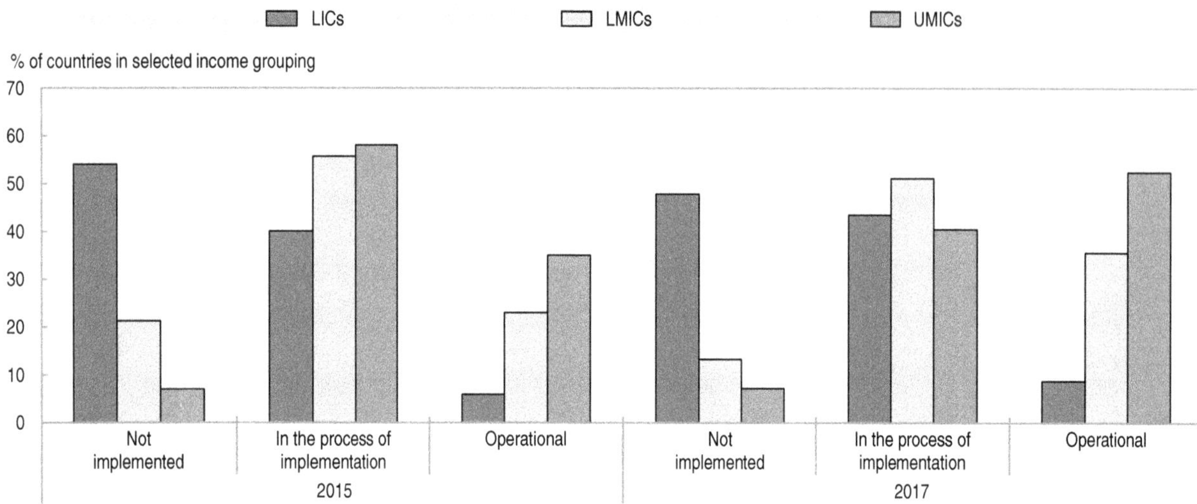

Source: TFIs (2017), *www.oecd.org/trade/facilitation/indicators.htm.*

Remaining challenges for measures falling under the provisions of TFA Article 7 lie at a more operational level. For instance, only 20% of the countries surveyed, mostly in the UMICs and HICs groupings, appear to calculate and publish average release times (Article 7.6). By contrast, the separation of release from clearance (7.3) appears unrelated to income level, and is available in around 40% of LICs, LMICs and UMICs.

Adoption of measures for perishable goods (7.9), whether relating to physical inspections, storage conditions or the separation of release from clearance, is underway but incomplete across all income groupings. That said, progress is notable among UMICs: more than half of surveyed countries that treat perishable goods differently from non-perishable goods across the clearance process were in this grouping. In general, border agencies in LMICs and UMICs give appropriate priority to perishable goods when scheduling required examinations, but do not generally allow for the clearance of these goods outside normal business hours.

TFA Article 7.5 calls for the adoption or maintenance of post-clearance audits (PCAs). Post-clearance auditing is one of the most effective trade facilitation strategies available to border agencies as it enables the immediate release of imported cargo through the subsequent use of audit-based regulatory controls to check compliance with relevant regulations. However, while most countries seem to allow for PCAs, in practice they seem to be seldom used and to lack standard policies and procedures to ensure transparent and risk-based implementation. This is an area where there remains considerable scope for improvement.

TFA Article 7.7 refers to mechanisms for identifying and offering better treatment to traders who meet specific criteria. Traders meeting criteria related to good management, solvency, security and compliance records – termed Authorised Operators (AOs) – can be offered additional trade facilitation measures related to import, export, and transit formalities. Many such initiatives are underway at both national and regional levels (Figure 2.14). OECD countries have progressed considerably in enlarging AO coverage and expanding the participation of SMEs, but equivalent information is scarce for the rest of the surveyed countries.

There are wide disparities in the transparency of the criteria for qualifying as an AO, as well as in procedures for submission and review of applications for AO status; the timeliness with which such a certification is granted; and the number and types of benefits granted to AOs. Across programs surveyed in HICs non-OECD, UMICs, LMICs and LICs, benefits granted to AOs mainly cover the deferred payment of duties, taxes, fees and charges, and rapid release times. More mature AO programs in OECD countries also cover reduced documentary and data requirements, use of reduced guarantees, and clearance of goods at AO premises. Across the sample, the least granted benefit is a single Customs declaration valid for a given period.

Figure 2.14. **Some progress has been made on Authorised Operators but conditions and benefits vary**

Authorised Operators programmes

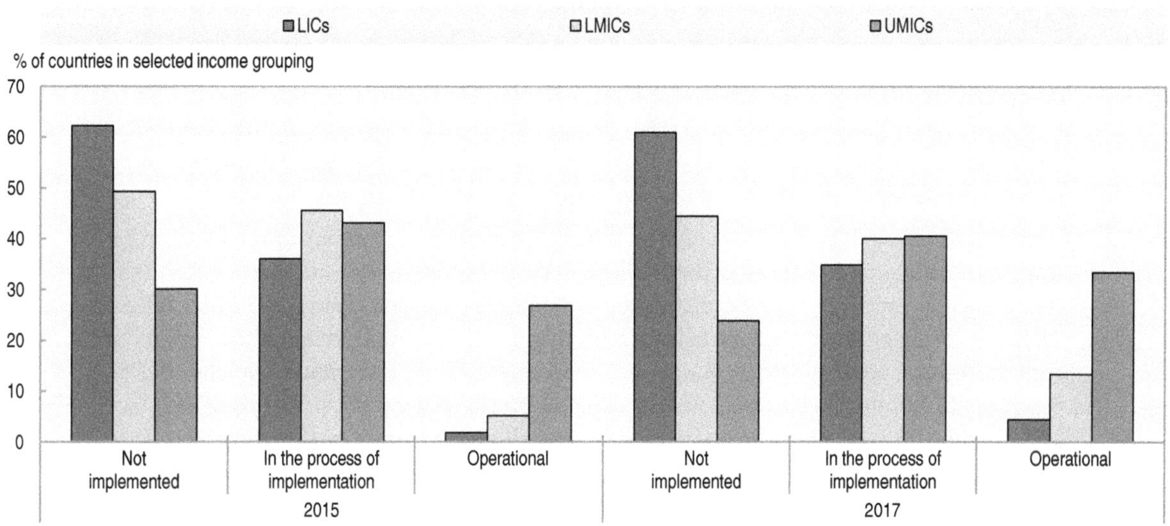

Source: TFIs (2017), *www.oecd.org/trade/facilitation/indicators.htm.*

Information on expedited shipments and associated release procedures (7.8) shows that, in 65% of surveyed countries, goods may benefit from expedited release to persons meeting certain criteria. But this benefit is limited to certain types of goods, generally either those entering through air cargo facilities or of low value. Only in very few (mostly OECD) economies does expedited release apply to all goods, irrespective of type, weight or value.

The development and implementation of PCAs, AO programs, and expedited release procedures are intrinsically linked. PCAs can help detect potential high-risk traders, but can also identify low-risk traders eligible for "fast-track" permissions and simplified procedures available under AO and other time and cost-saving compliance recognition-based programs.

Border agency co-operation: Institutional and operational challenges

Co-ordination among domestic border agencies aims to increase operational efficiency and facilitate legitimate trade by removing redundant or sequential controls and duplicative documentation requirements. TFA Article 8 calls for agencies to "co-operate

Box 2.3. **Transit facilitation remains challenging across most regions**

The TFA addresses the important issue of transit in Articles 7 and 10 (which focus on rationalisation and simplification of transit formalities) but also in Article 11 (Freedom of Transit), which prohibits unnecessary requirements, delays, restrictions, charges or discrimination against traffic in transit. These provisions are particularly important for landlocked and transit countries, which face significant administrative, technical and logistical difficulties.

Estimation of separate, statistically robust transit indicators presents considerable challenges, including a narrower sample of landlocked and transit countries; the scarcity of reliable data on implementation; and the need for specific bilateral transit data, for which there is no publicly available database depicting actual flows. Early in the development of the TFIs, four transit-specific indicators were developed to try to capture the particular challenges affecting landlocked countries. Collaboration with the USAID Trade Hubs for West Africa and Southern Africa and with UNESCAP allowed data to be collected in 2012 for selected African and Asian countries.[1] The main findings from this exercise are set out below.[2]

Streamlining of transit formalities and the existence of transit agreements and co-operation seemed to be the major factors influencing transit trade in goods and in particular manufactures. Landlocked countries' exports were strongly influenced by the availability of transit guarantees, as well as by the rationalisation and simplification of import and export formalities and the availability of trade-related information.

Only half of the countries surveyed in the 2012 transit study published information on transit fees and charges, either in publications or on the Customs website. Among the many fees associated with the cross-border movement of goods, the most opaque were escort fees. These cover the cost of an official vehicle escorting individual trucks through the country of transit in order to ensure that goods in transit from the port are not off-loaded before reaching the border. No information was available on the method of calculating transit fees and charges for countries in Asia, while the majority of countries in Africa seemed to be calculating such fees and charges *ad valorem*. Transit fees and charges were periodically (annually or more frequently) reviewed by only a third of the surveyed countries.

Information on transit formalities appeared to be available in African countries. Relevant documents and procedures were reviewed periodically, but less frequently than for fees and charges (every two years at best). West African countries had physically separate transit facilities at all entry points, while in the Southern African sub-region there were either no physically separate border crossing facilities, or they were present only at large transit entry points. In Asia, separate border-crossing facilities for transit were available in half of the surveyed countries.

Physical inspections on transit goods were generally limited in Asia thanks to risk assessment; however, a third of surveyed Asian countries applied the same quality controls and technical standards to transit goods as on imported goods, while another third applied controls only to hazardous materials and high risk cargos. In Africa, transit trade goods were subject to frequent physical inspections, as a risk-based system was not used or used only on a limited basis, but quality controls and technical standards were generally not applied to transit trade. Electronic data submission did not seem to be widely used for transit trade. Pre-arrival processing seemed to be available in half of the surveyed countries but applied only partially, for selected importers/goods/entry points/modes of transport. Half the surveyed countries – and only one in Africa – seemed to have at least partially established a Single Window for transit trade.

Box 2.3. **Transit facilitation remains challenging across most regions** *(cont.)*

Transit guarantees were accepted in one or more non-monetary forms in the majority of surveyed Asian countries and in half of the African countries; the other half of African countries did not accept transit guarantees in any form. The lack of banking infrastructure and financial markets able to support the issuance of such guarantees often led transit countries to require the deposit of full duties and taxes to cover the transit operation. Limited information was available on the average number of days necessary for full release of guarantees for the countries surveyed. For several of the surveyed countries, the guarantee system was covered by different regional agreements implementing systems similar to the *Transports Internationaux Routiers* (TIR) guarantee system.[3]

Transit agreements and co-operation, including the ASEAN Framework Agreement on the Facilitation of Goods in Transit; the *Transit Routier Inter-Etats* (TRIE) transit system developed in the Economic Community of West African States (ECOWAS); or the transit systems that have been developed by members of the Southern African Customs Union (SACU) and the Southern African Development Community (SADC), can promote unencumbered and cost-effective access to sea ports for landlocked countries. However, they frequently suffered from lack of enforcement due to overlapping and multiple membership or because national regulations took precedence in practice. Co-operation to simplify documentation requirements seemed to be stronger in the Southern Africa region, and much weaker in West Africa. For most of the surveyed Asian countries there was some co-operation between the agencies involved in transit, albeit varying in nature and intensity. The situation was relatively similar in Africa, with limited co-operation in West Africa and somewhat stronger co-operation covering procedural and legal dimensions for most countries in Southern Africa.

1. Analysis on transit was based on data covering Azerbaijan, Bangladesh, Benin, Bhutan, Burkina Faso, Cambodia, the People's Republic of China, Côte d'Ivoire, Ghana, India, Indonesia, Kyrgyz Republic, Malaysia, Mozambique, Namibia, Nepal, Pakistan, Philippines, Russian Federation, Senegal, Singapore, South Africa, Sri Lanka, Tanzania, Thailand, Togo and Viet Nam.
2. Given the limited availability of trade data on an ongoing basis, it was decided not to continue separate data collection and analysis on transit beyond this initial exercise.
3. TIR is an international transit system, based on the TIR UN Convention and implemented at global level in public-private partnership. With TIR, goods are contained in sealed load compartments, and the contents are detailed in a TIR Carnet, accompanying the driver and the cargo along its journey. Customs simply verify the Carnet and that the seals are intact, rather than opening the container and physically checking the load.

Source: United Nations Office of the High Representative for the Least Developed Countries, Landlocked Developing Countries and Small Island Developing States (2007); West Africa Trade Hub (2010); Moïsé and Sorescu (2013).

with one another and co-ordinate their activities in order to facilitate trade" at the national level (8.1), and provides five illustrative cross-border co-operation activities (under 8.2). Newly-elaborated variables included in the 2017 TFI series aimed to shed light on how agencies can best achieve these goals.[9]

In 2015, co-operation among various border agencies within the same country (8.1) seemed to be relatively well-established for around half of countries surveyed. The 2017 data explores more specific implementation challenges in: the institutional and legal and regulatory frameworks; the procedures for co-operation; communication and information exchange; and infrastructure and equipment. A significant number of surveyed countries have in place a general co-operation framework for co-ordination, exchange of information and mutual assistance across domestic agencies involved in the management of trade.

Explicit co-ordination strategies are present in more than half of OECD economies and non-OECD HICs, but in only 13% of UMICs. A significant number of countries appear to have also established inter-agency co-ordination bodies, but detailed information about their operation remains scarce.

Day-to-day implementation challenges can be successfully addressed through systems connectivity and open communication amongst relevant agencies, bolstered by clear delineation of authority and responsibilities and clear frameworks for sharing data, infrastructure and equipment. In OECD countries, domestic inter-agency co-ordination mechanisms meet regularly to develop strategy and oversee implementation of border agency co-operation. They also promote the sharing of inspection and documentary control results, sharing of infrastructure, and delegation of controls from other border agencies to Customs. These practices are also gaining ground in the rest of surveyed countries, in particular in UMICs and non-OECD HICs (Figure 2.15).

Figure 2.15. **Domestic border agency co-operation is progressing for some key functions**

Domestic border agency co-operation: Key strengths

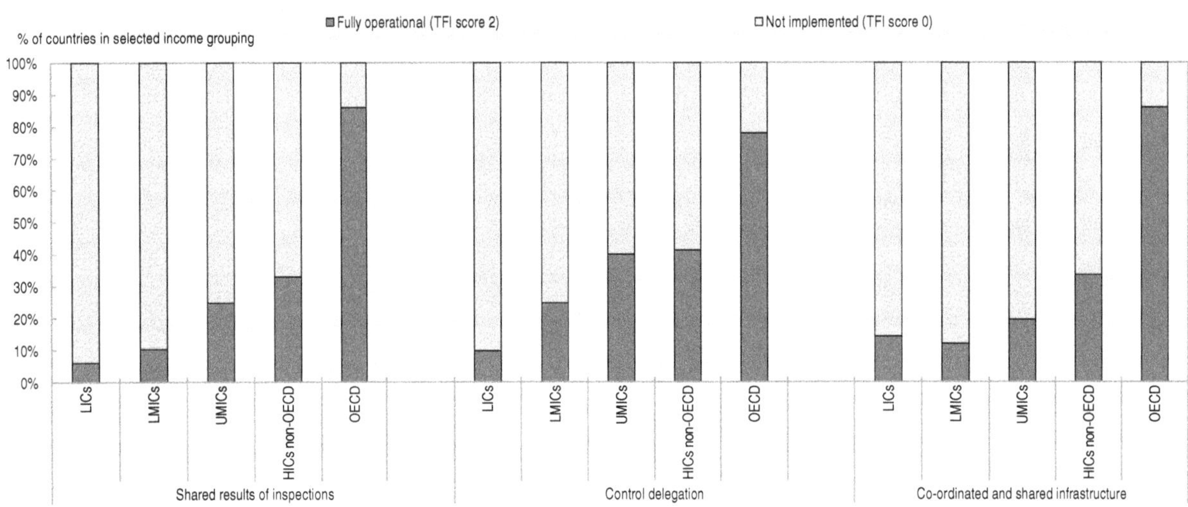

Source: TFIs (2017), *www.oecd.org/trade/facilitation/indicators.htm.*

There remains considerable scope for improvement, however. While border agencies around the world may be progressively sharing inspection and control results, co-ordination of these processes and requirements is underway in only approximately 40% of countries surveyed. Development of interconnected or shared computer systems and real time availability of pertinent data, as well as interagency collaboration on the certification of AOs, also remains incomplete across all groups, including OECD countries (Figure 2.16).

Co-operation with border agencies in neighbouring and third countries is even more challenging than domestic border agency co-operation. Between 2015 and 2017 most progress was made on the alignment of working days and hours, with the best performers found among OECD countries and LICs. Good progress was also made on alignment of procedures and formalities, which is under implementation in most surveyed countries, but which is not yet fully operational outside the OECD area (Figure 2.17).

Figure 2.16. **But there is considerable scope for improvement**

Domestic border agency co-operation: Key challenges

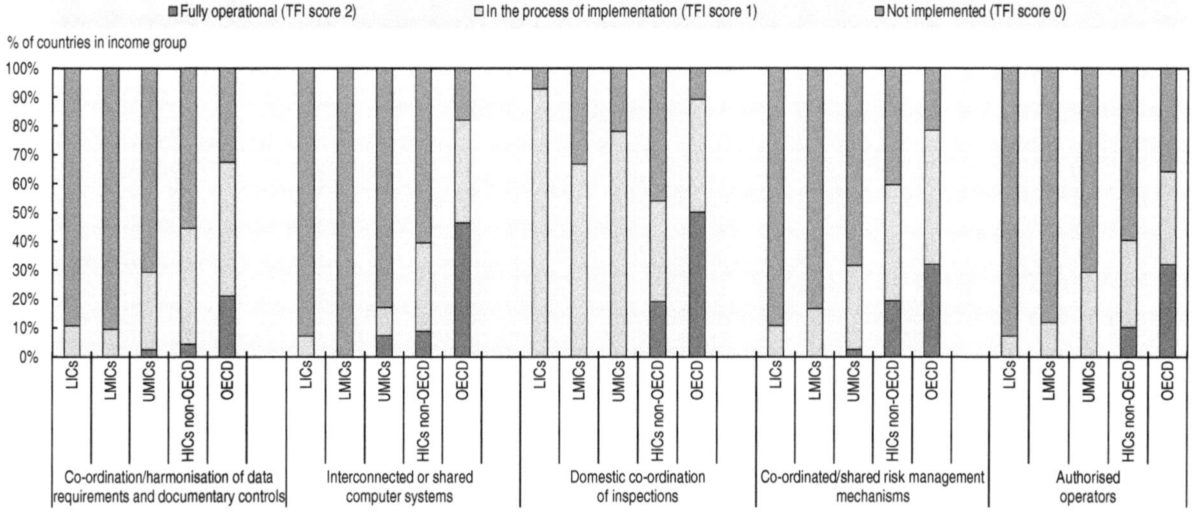

Source: TFIs (2017), *www.oecd.org/trade/facilitation/indicators.htm*.

Figure 2.17. **Most progress on cross-border co-operation concerns alignment of working hours**

Cross-border agency co-operation: Streamlining of procedures

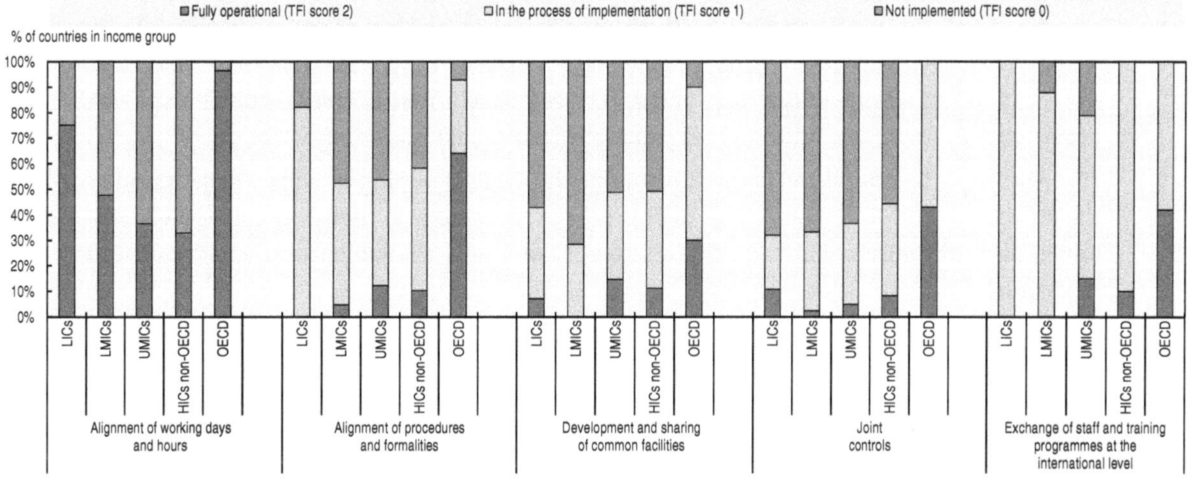

Source: TFIs (2017), *www.oecd.org/trade/facilitation/indicators.htm*.

Development and sharing of common facilities is fully operational in only 30% of OECD countries. One-Stop Border Posts (OSBPs) are operational in only a few developed economies and are in various stages of progress at several borders in Africa. OSBPs require significant infrastructure investment, as well as high levels of co-operation and trust.

Efforts to deepen cross-border agency co-operation through automation are underway, but remain incomplete. Advances have been made mainly in OECD countries and mostly in co-ordination/harmonisation of data requirements and documentary controls. In other areas, such as co-ordination/harmonisation of different computer systems, risk management co-operation and systematic sharing of control results among neighbouring countries, implementation by OECD countries is again significantly more advanced than in other countries surveyed (Figure 2.17).

Figure 2.18. **Efforts to deepen co-operation by automation are underway, but incomplete**

Cross-border agency co-operation: Automation tools

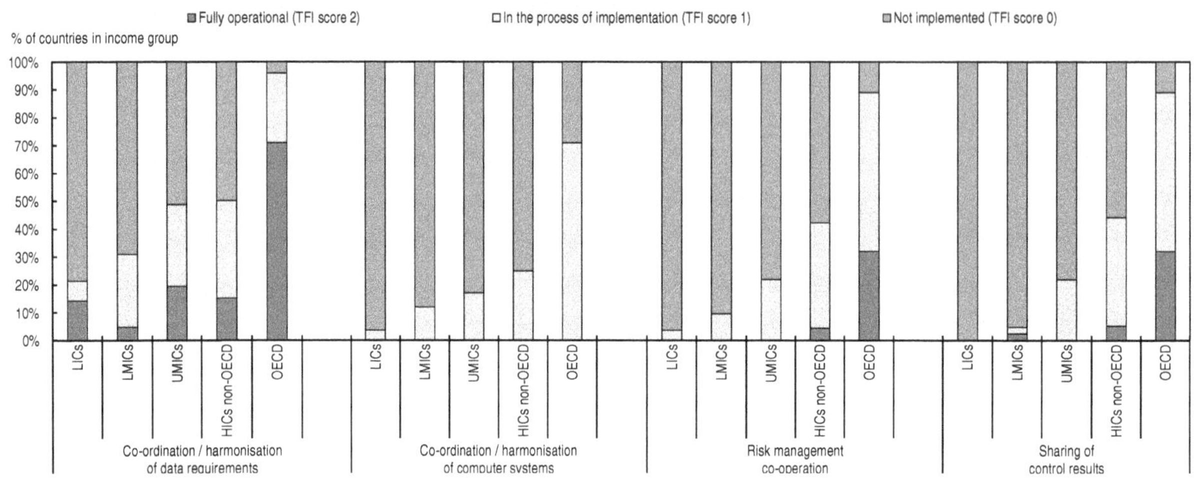

Source: TFIs (2017), *www.oecd.org/trade/facilitation/indicators.htm.*

Governance and impartiality

The final TFI indicator, for additional good governance practices, goes beyond the scope of the TFA. It covers clearly established and transparent structures and functions; the existence of a Code of Conduct and an ethics policy; internal audits, and transparent provisions for financing; and internal sanctions in the Customs administration.

Around 60% of surveyed countries outside the OECD grouping provide a description of the structures and functions of the Customs administration on their respective websites; however, information about the financing of Customs is available in only 25% of these countries.

Notable progress has been made in implementing internal audit systems and in communications strategies making Codes of Conduct available to all employees, but less in establishing a help desk or a special body to guide staff on ethical issues. Only limited information on the implementation and transparency of sanctions against misconduct is found in Customs Codes.

Information on the publication of annual Customs reports is available for half of the countries surveyed. A third of the developing and emerging economies surveyed (mainly UMICs and HICs non-OECD) publish annual Customs reports and make them publicly available. But the large majority of countries provide only limited information on Customs activities, with little information on budget, duties collected, complaints or efficiency indicators.

For OECD countries, significant improvements have been made in areas such as internal communication of policies and procedures, transparency and proportionality of disciplinary provisions, existence of clear provisions for the financing of the Customs administration, and inclusion of sufficient information in annual reports on Customs activities. However, significant disparities persist across the OECD in terms of the transparency and proportionality of non-compliance penalties for border agency staff.

Way forward: Paving the way for full implementation of the TFA

Analysis from the TFIs shows that, in countries around the world, efforts to improve trade facilitation are underway and have been further galvanised by the entry into force of the WTO TFA. Solid progress is evident in a number of areas since the previous TFIs covering the period 2012-15.

Implementation of some provisions, notably risk management and automation, appears to be correlated with income, but good progress on many areas covered by the WTO TFA is occurring across countries at all levels of development. There is also significant variation within country income and regional groupings, with strong performers found in all regions and income levels.

Strongest progress has been made on consultations and border formalities, underscoring that TFA implementation need not require costly investment. For all countries, co-operation among border agencies, both domestically and with neighbouring and third countries remains a significant challenge. These areas are the subject of further investigation in the following chapters.

Notes

1. In the WTO, developing Member status is self-selected. Least Developed Countries are defined with the reference to the United Nations classification of LDCs.
2. As notified to the WTO up to February 2017.
3. As notified to the WTO up to February 2017.
4. This is however outside the purview of the TFA.
5. The provisions on penalties were not included in previous iterations of the OECD TFIs due to scarcity of related data.
6. This variable covers the ratification of the following International Conventions: Facilitation of International Maritime Traffic (2005); International Civil Aviation (2006); Temporary Admission of Goods (Istanbul Convention, 1990); Harmonized Commodity Description and Coding System (International HS Convention, 1986); and Simplification and Harmonisation of Customs procedures (Revised Kyoto Convention, 1999, General Annex).
7. Nonetheless, scoring for the "international standards compliance" variable should be interpreted with caution; ratification of a treaty does not automatically mean its full and immediate implementation, while some countries in the sample may have not ratified such conventions, but are already applying some of the provisions in practice.
8. The scope and ambitions of these mechanisms can vary widely. The variable on Single Windows does not investigate the scope and characteristics of the surveyed mechanisms.
9. The 2012 and 2015 TFI indicators (i) and (j) mirrored the coverage of WTO TFA Article 8, which does not specify the most appropriate way of ensuring border agency co-operation. New variables added in 2017 reflect the main factors seen as critical for efficient border agency co-operation in existing international agreements or recommendations and the literature, complemented by case studies of countries with relevant experience. In so doing, they seek to measure effective interagency co-operation based on worldwide best practice, not to assess what might be needed for country compliance with TFA provisions.

Bibliography

Lesser, C. and E. Moïsé (2009), "Informal Cross-Border Trade and Trade Facilitation Reforms in Sub-Saharan Africa", *OECD Trade Policy Working Papers*, No. 86, OECD Publishing, Paris, *http://dx.doi.org/10.1787/225770164564*.

Moïsé, E., T. Orliac and P. Minor (2011), "Trade Facilitation Indicators: The Impact on Trade Costs", *OECD Trade Policy Papers*, No. 118, OECD Publishing, Paris, *http://dx.doi.org/10.1787/5kg6nk654hmr-en*.

Moïsé, E. and S. Sorescu (2017), "Single Window and Border Agency Co-operation: Expanding Selected OECD Trade Facilitation Indicators", TAD/TC/WP(2016)14/FINAL.

Moïsé, E. and S. Sorescu (2013), "Trade Facilitation Indicators: The Potential Impact of Trade Facilitation on Developing Countries' Trade", *OECD Trade Policy Papers*, No. 144, OECD Publishing, Paris, *http://dx.doi.org/10.1787/5k4bw6kg6ws2-en*.

Neufeld, N. (2016), "Implementing the Trade Facilitation Agreement: From Vision to Reality", *WTO Working Paper ERSD-2016-14*, Geneva, September.

OECD (2017), "Economy-wide Effects of Trade Facilitation: A METRO Model Simulation", TAD/TC/WP(2016)15/FINAL.

OECD (2015), "Implementation of the WTO Trade Facilitation Agreement: The Potential Impact on Trade Costs", *www.oecd.org/tad/tradedev/WTO-TF-Implementation-Policy-Brief_EN_2015_06.pdf*.

TFA Facility (2017), TFA notifications database, *www.tfadatabase.org/*.

United Nations Office of the High Representative for the Least Developed Countries, Landlocked Developing Countries and Small Island Developing States (UN-OHRLLS) (2007), "Trade, Trade Facilitation and Transit Transport Issues for Landlocked Developing Countries", United Nations Office of the High Representative for Least Developed Countries, Landlocked Developing Countries and Small Islands Developing States.

West Africa Trade Hub (WATH) (2010), "ETLS Gap Analysis ECOWAS Free Trade Area", Country reports (Benin, Burkina Faso, Cote d'Ivoire, Ghana, Mali, Nigeria, Senegal, Togo), West Africa Trade Hub.

PART 1

Chapter 3

Border agency co-operation

Border agency co-operation is critical for increasing operational efficiency, facilitating legitimate trade and reducing traders' costs at both the domestic and cross-border levels. Yet significant implementation challenges remain. This chapter explores progress to date on border agency co-operation, both domestically in terms of co-ordination among all agencies involved in the trade process at the border and across the border between agencies in neighbouring countries, whether in the form of logistics or procedural harmonisation, or integrated controls under a One-Stop Border Post. The chapter draws lessons from country experience and case studies to help identify for policy makers key challenges and factors for success.

Co-operation among agencies, including across borders, matters

The benefits of a country's trade facilitation reforms will be greatly enhanced if its trading partners undertake similar reforms and if border agencies from different countries are able to work together to ensure the smooth flow of goods. Equally, the efficiency with which goods are able to cross borders in any one country can depend not only on the efficiency of Customs, but also on all the agencies with responsibility for trade-related regulation. Hence border agency co-operation, often termed Integrated Border Management (IBM) or Coordinated Border Management (CBM), includes both a domestic dimension, relating to co-ordination and co-operation among national agencies involved in border controls, and an international dimension, relating to co-operation between agencies of States with common borders.

Article 8 of the Trade Facilitation Agreement (TFA) calls on agencies to "*co-operate with one another and co-ordinate their activities in order to facilitate trade*" and sets out requirements for both national level co-ordination (8.1) and cross-border co-operation (8.2). The Article does not specify the most appropriate way of ensuring such co-operation, but sets out five illustrative co-operation activities. Other international agreements and recommendations, as well as country experience, also offer insights into the key factors for efficient border agency co-operation. Analysis of all these factors enabled the development of the TFI indicators on border agency co-operation. These indicators go beyond simply what might be needed to satisfy the requirements of the TFA, and focus on measuring performance in relation to worldwide best practice.

The Trade Facilitation Indicators (TFIs) show that border agency co-operation remains a significant implementation challenge for countries at all levels of development. This chapter identifies the key elements of effective domestic and cross-border agency co-operation. Drawing on insights from case studies, it also highlights concrete steps that policy makers can take to make border agency co-operation, both domestic and international, work.

Measuring effective domestic border agency co-operation

At the national level, Article 8 of the TFA on Border Agency Co-operation calls on each Member to "*ensure that its authorities and agencies responsible for border controls and procedures dealing with the importation, exportation and transit of goods co-operate with one another and co-ordinate their activities in order to facilitate trade.*" This recognises that the border process involves not only the determination and collection of Customs duties and other government revenue, but also operations to enforce national legislation on health and safety, security, environmental protection, immigration, consumer protection, and commercial policy. In addition to Customs agencies, various other governmental agencies and private entities, often also represented at the border, undertake document and physical controls of goods, vehicles and people.

Redundant or sequential controls, duplicative documentation requirements, and insufficient co-ordination among different agencies at the border can cause delays, complicate compliance by traders and strain border post resources. Border agency co-ordination aims to increase operational efficiency, reduce compliance costs for traders and enforcement costs for authorities, and facilitate legitimate trade. Addressing border agency co-ordination failures, already important for trade flows of finished goods, is essential for the smooth operation of global and regional value chains.

Domestic border agency co-operation has been high on the trade facilitation agenda for many years, not only as an important element of the WCO 1999 Revised Kyoto Convention (RKC)[1] and the 2005 SAFE Framework of standards,[2] but also as a key foundation of several donor-supported border reform projects.[3] While the terminology has changed several times over the years, from Integrated Border Management (IBM) to Collaborative, to Coordinated Border Management (CBM),[4] the key concept has remained the same: the simplification, integration and automation of national border processes and procedures in order to enhance the free flow of goods across the border, while at the same time protecting national security and collection of government revenues.

Key elements of effective domestic border agency co-operation

Border agency co-operation shifts the focus beyond the traditional Customs-specific trade facilitation agenda to a new and more comprehensive "whole-of-government" approach to reform. This new approach relies less on institution-specific reform and more on a wider trade supply chain approach designed to tackle the major issues traders face in navigating regulatory requirements. Country experience shows that the first step in promoting domestic border agency co-operation is mapping the current situation across all key management aspects; undertaking a thorough gap analysis and needs assessment; and preparing an inventory of all ongoing and planned activities in the area of domestic border management. Important supporting features include the creation of inter-agency working groups, exchanges of liaison officers among agencies, and establishment of a co-operation culture by sharing intelligence, carrying out joint risk assessments, or maintaining joint specialist task forces.

The TFI on internal border agency co-operation captures the key elements of Article 8.1 of the TFA, supplemented by additional factors identified in the literature and country experience as supporting efficient domestic agency co-operation.[5] These additional factors aim to capture six key management areas of domestic border agency co-operation: the institutional framework; the legal and regulatory framework; procedures for co-operation; communication and information exchange; infrastructure and equipment; and human resources and training. These are discussed briefly below.

Institutional framework

Border agency co-operation can be implemented through different governance frameworks and levels of co-ordination. These range from simple consultative mechanisms to align office hours; co-operation on a voluntary and *ad hoc* basis at the border; mutual administrative assistance and sharing of information on infringements;[6] to establishing a legal framework for the exchange of information[7] and sharing of control functions amongst agencies, through to the setting up of a new agency incorporating the responsibilities of some or all of the previously existing agencies.[8]

These changes and frameworks involve varying degrees of organisational transformation which can be challenging to implement. Any re-organisation requires political will and clear leadership, as well as incentives and drivers to bring about changes in the institutional culture. These can be provided by a new agency incorporating the responsibilities of previously existing border agencies or, where that is not pursued, a body entrusted with defining the national inter-agency co-operation strategy and its implementation may be needed to lead the process. Such a body should be composed of the key stakeholders in border management (including relevant ministries, institutions and agencies) and provided with the necessary political, administrative and financial support.

Legal and regulatory framework

The legal and regulatory framework provides the necessary legal basis for the implementation of structures for co-ordination and information exchange, and defines the responsibilities and roles of agencies to ensure that they are appropriately empowered to fulfil their mandate. A clear determination of authority, tasks and responsibilities at central, regional and local levels is important to avoid conflicting or overlapping responsibilities or, on the contrary, gaps in the attribution of responsibility.

Successful inter-agency co-operation is based on a legal framework (including laws and regulations and administrative or standing instructions and formal agreements) that fits all border agencies' operational needs and clearly defines the key elements of co-operation. These include: the responsibilities and tasks of each agency; the powers and authorities vested in agencies to implement their tasks; offences, actions and penalties, along with clarity on jurisdiction; records (databases) of each agency and access to information (databases) of other agencies; and delegated responsibilities (that is, which tasks can be carried out by other agencies).

Co-operation procedures

Co-operation procedures set out how the work of each agency is done, identifying responsibilities and giving step-by-step descriptions of how specific tasks are to be implemented. To ensure streamlined and better co-ordinated procedures, the existing workflows of each agency must first be described and analysed at the head office, regional and local levels with a view to identifying overlapping mandates. This is especially true of responsibilities, sequencing and processing times at land border posts. Joint efforts to resolve identified overlaps and delays and to amend relevant procedures help sustain improved co-ordination over the longer term.

An important factor in cementing inter-agency co-operation is the development of a common risk strategy, which enhances control efficiency and greatly facilitates the flow of goods at the border. All concerned agencies need to work together to define priorities and establish common risk profiles. This common strategy can be supported by specific activities, such as identifying inland control points on major transit routes or joint mobile units of Customs officers and border police.

Importantly, contingency and emergency plans should clarify the division of responsibilities in case of imminent threats to national security or public health, or extreme situations such as natural disasters, pandemic diseases, mass influx of irregular migrants or refugees, terrorist activities or major accidents and fires in the border zone. These plans should be developed at the national level, but be adjusted at the regional and local level to ensure that each border post is fully informed about the distribution of responsibilities and tasks in maintaining service delivery in these situations.

Communication and information exchange

Standardised and efficient communication and information exchange between the different agencies is critical for ensuring effective and sustainable co-operation. A formal agreement among all participating agencies can clarify which information will be shared and with whom, how the information will be exchanged, and how it can be tracked and traced. An effective early warning system, be it through a system of contact points in individual agencies or through IT solutions, can greatly enhance information exchange efficiency.

Sharing of infrastructure and equipment

The sharing of infrastructure and equipment supports co-ordination and co-operation at all levels. An overall border-related investment strategy that includes equipment standards can help avoid capacity disparities among agencies. Investment plans at the national level, applying to all relevant agencies, also ensure that adequate infrastructure and equipment can be procured in a timely manner, and can permit economies of scale in the context of limited budgets. Standards and investment plans should be aligned with the volume and nature of traffic at specific border posts; not every border post needs to be equipped in the same way.

A co-ordinated but tailored strategy requires regular assessments of existing facilities and equipment, as well as feedback from other stakeholders, such as ministries of transport and freight operators. Additionally, in some countries, border post infrastructure is neither owned nor under the direct control of border management agencies, necessitating contracts to formalise the terms of their use, maintenance, and cost coverage. Finally, consultations with neighbouring countries can also be helpful in order to take into account their border post development plans.

Human resources and training policies

The above pillars need to be enforced through well-targeted human resources and training policies. Border management tasks are highly specialised and need to be treated as such in training plans, but a common border agency co-operation curriculum and joint training courses can also help foster a corporate culture of co-operation. Joint training activities ideally involve staff from all border management agencies, promoting confidence-building and information exchange as well as more efficient use of training resources.

Making domestic border agency co-operation work

Drawing on the above elements and the Costa Rican experience (Box 3.1), the key factors for efficient design and implementation of domestic border agency co-operation are:

- An explicit co-ordination strategy with strong political backing, led at a senior level.
- An institutionalised mechanism to support inter-agency co-ordination (e.g. an inter-agency co-ordination body).
- Regular meetings to develop strategy and oversee implementation of border agency co-operation.
- Co-ordination and/or harmonisation of data requirements and document controls, for example through common data definitions and types of information requested, as well as mechanisms to ensure timely exchange of information.

- Interconnected or shared computer systems and real time availability of pertinent data.
- Co-ordination of inspections.
- Co-operation in terms of risk analysis, data sharing, and risk profiling of goods.
- Explicit strategies to harmonise the requirements for, co-ordinate the certification and inspection of, and manage the follow-up for Authorised Operators.
- Co-ordinated and efficient sharing of infrastructure and equipment.

Box 3.1. **Domestic border agency co-operation in practice: Costa Rica**

Costa Rica embarked upon the modernisation of its main land border crossings in an effort to optimise implementation of its FTAs, streamline Customs and international trade procedures, improve border efficiency and promote trade facilitation. Efficient border agency co-operation is an essential part of this endeavour, particularly in view of the expected increase in transactions at the border posts undergoing modernisation. The efforts undertaken to improve co-ordination among agencies with responsibilities for the border process, in particular at the border crossing of Las Tablillas, highlight important success factors, as well as challenges. These include:

- Sustained political commitment is essential to support inter-agency co-ordination bodies in their early years of operation. This is particularly the case when practices vary significantly among agencies, or where particular agencies are reluctant to relinquish control or change modes of operation to adopt the new, co-ordinated approaches.
- The extent of momentum on trade facilitation reform provided by an inter-agency strategy and working group depends on the commitment of the dedicated Secretariat, and its ability to co-ordinate research and analysis on key policy issues, to monitor action plan implementation, and to encourage participation by the private sector.
- Building a strong corps of well-trained border officials that value trust and collaboration with other border authorities is essential for the success of institutional reforms, and system and infrastructure investments.
- The legal framework should define the organisation, mission and functions of each agency within a collaborative framework. Manuals containing standard operating procedures and guidelines should be developed by the inter-agency working groups and made available to all staff present at border posts.
- The complexity and fragmentation of information systems can create knowledge gaps and undermine performance. The interoperability of information systems can benefit from the support of an expert group, tasked with addressing legal, technical and operational questions, including the necessity, technical feasibility and proportionality of available options and their data protection implications.
- Implementation of joint operational processes among border agencies and co-ordinated inspection systems also benefits from regular meetings and upgraded IT solutions and platforms. Communication and information exchange needs to be not only structured, but also timely.
- Domestic co-ordination of inspections needs to be based on a solid legal framework establishing control delegation, and include regular monitoring of processes at the border and co-ordination with the national steering body at a policy level. This chain of activity is key to ensuring the predictability and transparency of border processes.

Source: Moisé and Sorescu (2017).

Measuring effective cross-border agency co-operation

If effective co-operation among domestic border agencies sharing common language, culture and government poses challenges, this is even more the case for co-operation among border agencies across countries.

In recognition of these greater challenges, TFA Article 8.2 on cross-border co-operation includes greater flexibility, providing that "*Each Member shall, to the extent possible and practicable, co-operate on mutually agreed terms with other Members with whom it shares a common border with a view to co-ordinating procedures at border crossings to facilitate cross-border trade*". The Article suggests five possible features of such co-operation, such as alignment of working days and hours; alignment of procedures and formalities; development and sharing of common facilities; joint controls; and establishment of One-Stop Border Post (OSBP) control.

Key elements of effective cross-border agency co-operation

These five features are all reflected in the OECD TFI on external border agency co-operation, supplemented by a number of additional factors identified in the literature and country experience as supporting the aims of TFA Article 8.2.[9]

These factors aim to capture the institutional and legal framework enabling co-ordination, as well as main areas for co-ordination and exchange. They include exchange of data and harmonisation of requested documentation; joint, co-ordinated, delegated or mutually recognised processes and procedures, inspections and controls; mutually recognised Authorised Operator schemes; cross-border sharing of resources and infrastructure; and well-established communication amongst the agencies.

TFA Article 8.2 identifies progressively more ambitious approaches to trade facilitation, ranging from co-ordination of logistics, to procedural harmonisation supported by the sharing of resources, to the sharing of responsibility,[10] culminating in integrated controls in the framework of a OSBP. Each of these presents its own implementation challenges; however, many of these could be eased or even eliminated thanks to reforms undertaken subsequent to other provisions of the TFA.

For example, alignment of working days and hours may require some adjustments in internal operations, although changes may be more limited where these are already designed to reduce the time and cost of compliance for traders. Similarly, the alignment of procedures and formalities between cross-border partner countries might also call for some procedural reengineering, although again, this task may be greatly facilitated where countries are already bringing procedures into line with relevant provisions of the TFA. This may be the case, for example, with implementation of provisions on the use of international import, export or transit standards, or on pre-arrival processing of documents or electronic payment of duties.

The development and sharing of common facilities may require significant infrastructure investments; however, this challenge is recognised by development co-operation partners and financial assistance for infrastructure related to trade facilitation focuses increasingly on co-operative cross-border projects.

Joint controls and OSBPs (Box 3.2) require increasing levels of mutual co-operation and trust, particularly in view of the need to exchange information for joint actions. However, this information exchange can also support more effective risk management that can in turn positively impact revenue collection.

Indeed, while cross-border co-ordination and co-operation clearly facilitate trade and expedite border crossings by minimising lag time, avoiding duplicative requirements and reducing the number of stops and participating agencies, they are also essential for addressing risks and threats. These range from Customs fraud and smuggling, to sanitary risks and criminal activities and terrorism. In particular, intelligence sharing among agencies across the border allows better targeting of offending goods while minimising the burden on legitimate flows.

In a OSBP, the border authorities of one party are authorised to perform all Customs checks and formalities applicable to import, export and transit on behalf of the authorities of the other party, enabling a one-stop process at the border (usually upon entering a country). Thus, each border post handles incoming traffic only, with exit and entry procedures completed in the same building. Such an arrangement already exists between Norway and Sweden,[11] and Norway and Finland, and is in progress at borders in Africa (e.g. between Zambia and Zimbabwe). OSBPs can be implemented using juxtaposed facilities, or a common facility located in the territory of one of the countries.

Making cross-border co-operation work

Drawing on the above elements and the experience of Switzerland and the European Union (Box 3.2), the key factors for efficient design and implementation of cross-border agency co-operation are:

- Sustained political will to champion required changes through all relevant agencies on both sides of the border.
  - This is an essential condition, but also a significant challenge, as it requires clarifying and sharing policy and control objectives. Establishing an effective national strategy for cross-border co-operation can help both ensure the sustainability of efforts at the working level and address potential issues of trust and responsibility. The degree of trust among partnering countries is key in determining the extent of cross-border co-operation. Close cultural and historical links help with building trust, but open communication channels are also required for common endeavours and shared responsibilities.
- Ensure clear linkages to national trade and economic priorities.
  - Political will is more readily sustained when co-operation is linked to broader national economic and trade development strategies. Likewise, a clear focus on areas of strategic national (or regional) importance should guide implementation efforts. For example, in countries where food exports are important, special co-operation arrangements for operating hours and phytosanitary inspections may be a priority.
- Foster a regional approach to cross-border co-operation.
  - Transit necessarily involves the agreement of several countries and a comprehensive co-operation framework, offered for instance by membership in, or association with, a regional economic community (REC), which will be more efficient than separate arrangements with each country. For Switzerland and the European Union, cross-border integration is supported by common membership of the European Economic Area (EEA).
- Seek the backing of all major stakeholders, including the business community.
  - The Swiss-EU experience shows the benefits of this engagement taking place at the outset. Ideally, this involves creation of a team to undertake regular consultations and

Box 3.2. **Cross-border agency co-operation in practice: Switzerland and its EU neighbours**

Switzerland has an extensive cross-border co-operation programme with its EU neighbours across all areas identified in Article 8.2 of the TFA. The programme draws extensively on the strong legal framework within which Swiss Customs operates, including international trade agreements, a series of bilateral agreements with the European Union, and individual bilateral agreements with EU countries bordering Switzerland.

The programme's success is attributed in part to the use of standard trade facilitation systems and adherence to global conventions such as the World Customs Organization's Revised Kyoto Convention, which enables the use of similar processes at the borders between Switzerland and the European Union. Highly efficient transit procedures significantly reduce waiting times at the border and facilitate simplified approaches for companies, such as the authorised consignor or consignee programme. Likewise, use of international data standards for trade documentation and data exchange has facilitated interoperability. That said, beyond the transit procedure, there is currently no exchange or harmonisation of data between Switzerland and the European Union and duplication still exists between the procedures on either side of the border.

Swiss Customs works closely with other agencies involved in inspections at the border and even undertakes inspections on behalf of other agencies. This eases co-ordination, and builds trust between Swiss Customs and its clients.

The use of risk management as a basic Customs strategy and the collaboration between Switzerland and the European Union in defining security risk profiles support the low level of documentation-related or physical controls of goods crossing the border. In addition, the existence of a common security zone between Switzerland and the European Union reduces the number of necessary checks. Finally, the high level of automation of Customs in Switzerland and its EU neighbours and the use of juxtaposed Customs offices at the main border crossings, with shared facilities and co-ordinated procedures, minimises the amount of time a truck spends at the border.

In view of the significant cross-border co-operation already in place at the Swiss-EU borders further steps in the direction of co-ordinated border management are within reach. Cutting edge measures based on the interoperability of Customs systems and procedures, real time availability of data on both sides of the border and new, jointly designed processes ultimately leading to the implementation of OSBPs could further reduce costs, reinforce integration into regional and global value chains and enhance the competitiveness of the Swiss and the EU economies.

Source: Moisé and Sorescu (2017).

garner ongoing feedback from border posts. Full engagement of all stakeholders is also critical for change management. Support and training is essential during the introduction of enhanced cross-border co-operation, particularly to allay fears and uncertainties associated with the introduction of new systems and procedures. In the absence of adequate support and training, new systems can be introduced, but old habits and practices will remain.

- Establish a comprehensive legal framework to support cross-border co-operation and security.
  - This requires not only the negotiation of bilateral and multilateral agreements, but also the reorganisation of processes and procedures. The use of existing conventions and agreements, such as the transit conventions of NCTS (New Computerised Transit System) and the TIR (*Transports Internationaux Routiers*)[12] can help. The legal framework should also include mutual recognition of facilitating arrangements, such as Authorised Operator programs.
- Manage sensitivities to enable the greatest possible co-operation and data exchange.
  - Empowering national agencies to conduct controls pursuant to national law outside their territory, and allowing control officers of the adjoining state to conduct border controls pursuant to their national laws within the host state's territory can be an important challenge. Exchange of data can raise similar sensitivities. Transit declarations are usually not contentious, but transfer of information that has a commercially sensitive content often encounters strong opposition. Co-operation in risk management can be equally sensitive; however, experience has shown that the exchange of risk profiles can greatly enhance the operation of a risk management system and increase mutual security. All these areas depend critically on the level of trust established among the partnering countries. To draw the greatest benefits from their co-operation, countries should work towards the maximum level of data exchange, within the boundaries of national sensitivities.
- Develop and maintain effective infrastructure and clear allocation of resources and responsibilities.
  - Infrastructure development includes both the management and maintenance of juxtaposed or OSBP facilities, and the development of ICT infrastructure to ensure efficient connectivity between partner countries' systems. Development of ICT architecture must be based on a thorough business process analysis of existing practices and on consultations with key stakeholders on the desired future scenario.
- Use international tools and standards.
  - Use of international tools and standards from the outset can reduce the cost and increase the flexibility of information exchange among the partnering, and other neighbouring, countries. For example, all UN data and trade document standards and tools, such as those developed by the UN Centre for Trade Facilitation and Electronic Business (UN/CEFACT),[13] are available free of charge. These data standards are used extensively throughout the world, facilitating interoperability and scalability, at the national, regional and global level.[14]
- Maintain open communication channels to address day-to-day implementation challenges.
  - Frequent meetings at the strategic and operational level between the parties help preserve the goodwill necessary for effective cross-border co-operation. Training of officers on both sides of the border can also greatly increase knowledge of each other's procedures and systems and help avoid confusion or grey areas, especially in juxtaposed or OSBP operations. Joint training also generates a greater sense of camaraderie among the officers of the different jurisdictions and helps increase co-operation and mutual assistance.

- Build on domestic co-ordination among the various border agencies within each partner country.
  - Strong and effective domestic inter-agency co-operation is a powerful enabler, facilitating and simplifying co-operation across the border. Ideally (as in the case of Switzerland), Customs acts on behalf of all other government agencies at the border. Failing that, strong co-ordination and integration among domestic agencies is necessary to facilitate cross-border co-operation. The existence of an efficient Single Window mechanism, for example, would normally indicate enhanced integration of domestic agencies and inspections.
- Regular reporting by working level authorities to the political level about progress and challenges.
  - Achieving cross-border co-operation presents a range of challenges, and political support is critical in sustaining change. While efforts across a range of areas are needed to make cross-border co-operation work, success can bring many benefits to both sides.

Notes

1. See in particular its transitional standard 3.35: *If the goods must be inspected by other competent authorities and the Customs also schedules an examination, the Customs shall ensure that the inspections are co-ordinated and, if possible, carried out at the same time.*
2. The SAFE Framework of Standards to Secure and Facilitate Global Trade was adopted in 2005 to promote end-to-end management of goods across borders, and has been regularly updated since. In June 2015, a third Pillar was added, covering co-operation between Customs and other border agencies, calling on governments to "*foster mutual co-operation between their Customs administration and other competent government agencies*" (Pillar 3, Standard 1). A series of technical specifications cover co-operation with aviation, maritime and port security, as well as with land transportation authorities and postal operators.
3. See, for example, World Bank Collaborative Border Management (McLinden, 2012).
4. The evolution from "integrated" to "collaborative" or "co-ordinated" border management" sought to avoid the "threatening connotations of the organisational integration" arising from the term of "integrated border management (IBM)" (Doyle, 2011). One of the reasons organisational integration is treated cautiously is because it requires a "significant organisational change" and may create problems "as various entities struggle to retain their identities and protect their mandates and resources" (Doyle, 2011).
5. See indicator (i) in Annex B. As noted above, this aims at measuring trade facilitation endeavours in relation to international best practice, rather than assessing country compliance with the TFA.
6. As on the basis of the WCO Johannesburg Convention.
7. This needs to specify the conditions for sharing and use of information in respect of national legislation on data protection and data privacy.
8. Examples of institutional integration of border functions under a single roof with a particular focus on security (especially anti-terrorism) and border protection are the US Customs and Border Protection (US CBP), the Canada Border Services Agency (CBSA), and the Australian Customs and Border Protection Service (CBPS), while in New Zealand the Border Sector Governance Group was established in order to oversee the implementation of CBM (the Group comprises the chief executives from the New Zealand Customs Service, Department of Labour, Department of Internal Affairs, Ministry of Transport, Ministry of Agriculture and Forestry and Food Safety Authority).
9. See indicator (j) in Annex B. As noted above, this aims at measuring trade facilitation endeavours in relation to international best practice, rather than assessing country compliance with the WTO TFA.
10. See sub-paragraphs i, ii, iii, and iv respectively.

11. As described in the 2005 Communication from Norway to the WTO Negotiating Group on Trade Facilitation, the agreement between Norway and Sweden allows the national border authorities of each country to "provide services and exercise legal powers not only on behalf of their home state, but on behalf of their neighbouring states as well". When goods are exported from Norway to Sweden, Swedish customs may take care of all paperwork and formalities related to the Norwegian export and Swedish import process, and vice-versa for Swedish exports to Norway. Norway considers this arrangement both cost-efficient and administratively effective. Customs officers from both countries meet on a regular basis to review the operation of the agreement, provide training, and update each other on any changes to legislation or procedures. Senior official meetings are held at least once per year. Swedish and Norwegian customs officials have the same access to each other's systems as the country's own officers and can review and perform the necessary Customs procedures.
12. *www.unece.org/tir/welcome.html.*
13. *www.unece.org/cefact.*
14. UN/CEFACT's EDI standard UN/EDIFACT is the leading data interchange standard globally.

Bibliography

Aniszewski, S. (2009), "Coordinated Border Management – A Concept Paper", World Customs Organization, *www.wcoomd.org/en/topics/facilitation/activities-and-programmes/?/media/WCO/Public/Global/PDF/Topics/Research/Research%20Paper%20Series/cbm.ashx.*

Doyle, T. (2011), "The Future of Border Management", in McLinden, G., E. Fanta, D. Widdowson and T. Doyle (eds), *Border Management Modernization*, IBRD/World Bank, Washington, DC.

Kieck, E. (2010), "Coordinated Border Management: Unlocking Trade Opportunities Through One-Stop Border Posts", *World Customs Journal*, Vol.4, No.1.

Inter-American Development Bank (IDB) (2013a), "Border Integration Program of Costa Rica: Loan Proposal", Washington, DC.

IDB (2013b), "Support to the Border Integration Program of Costa Rica and the Modernization of its Border Crossings: Las Tablillas (Costa Rica) – San Pancho (Nicaragua) Border Post", Washington, DC.

McLinden, G. (2012), Collaborative Border Management: A New Approach to an Old Problem, PREM Note No. 78, *http://siteresources.worldbank.org/EXTPREMNET/Resources/EP78.pdf*

Moïsé, E. and S. Sorescu (2017), "Single Window and Border Agency Co-operation: Expanding Selected OECD Trade Facilitation Indicators", TAD/TC/WP(2016)14/FINAL.

OECD (2016), *Market Openness Review of Costa Rica*, TAD/TC/ACS(2015)3/FINAL.

Oliver, J. and R. Arce (2013), "Facilitating Trade Through Effective Border Control: Costa Rica's Challenging Reform Agenda", SAIS, John Hopkins University.

Pitakdumrongkit, K. and M.T. Anna Robles (2014), "Assessing the Progress of AEC Projects: A New Approach", *RSIS Working Paper* No. 280.

Polnar, M. (2011), "Coordinated Border Management: From Theory to Practice", *World Customs Journal*, Vol. 5, No. 2.

Southern African Development Community (SADC) (2011), "Draft Guidelines for Coordinated Border Management: A Practical Guide on Best Practices and Tools for Implementation", August.

WCO (2005), *WCO SAFE Framework of standards to secure and facilitate global trade*, WCO, Brussels.

World Bank, World Development Indicators (2016), Costa Rica, viewed at: *http://data.worldbank.org/country/costa-rica.*

Trade Facilitation and the Global Economy

PART 1

Chapter 4

Single Window systems

Implementation of Single Windows remains one of the most important challenges among all the areas covered by the TFA. This chapter draws on Single Window indicators in the TFIs to assess implementation of Single Windows in 23 economies across various regions. It identifies key implications for policy makers, and in addition draws lessons from ASEAN's experience with creating a regional Single Window.

Single Windows bring benefits, but are challenging to design and implement

For firms and traders, Single Windows epitomise the gains they would like to see from trade facilitation: a single point of entry for trade procedures and formalities, cutting time and costs, and easing access to trade for even the smallest firm.

Single Windows are formally defined as "facilities that allow parties involved in trade and transport to lodge standardised information and documents with a single entry point to fulfil all import, export, and transit-related regulatory requirements".[1] They can take the form of a single authority or single automated system serving as the sole point for the collection and dissemination of information. Though existing Single Windows do not necessarily cover all aspects of border agency co-operation, they can support it by facilitating exchange of data and operation of integrated procedures.

A well-functioning Single Window provides traders with transparent and consistent application of rules and more predictable clearance procedures. More efficient use of human and financial resources may in turn generate improvements in productivity and competitiveness for both traders and the economy as a whole. For the public sector, Single Windows can bring improvements in risk management and in transparency and accountability, as well as more accurate revenue collection through greater trader compliance. Lastly, neighbouring countries also benefit from enhanced prospects for regional collaboration, integration and exchange of trade information (UN/CEFACT, 2005).

However, for Single Windows to operate efficiently and deliver their full potential, the border agency processes included in the platform need to have been sufficiently synchronised and co-ordinated beforehand. This may be one reason why, despite their significant benefits, implementation of Single Windows remains one of the areas where least progress has been made among the provisions of the TFA.

This chapter draws on specific Single Window indicators developed under the TFIs to assess implementation of Single Windows for 23 economies around the world, highlighting the implications for policy makers. It concludes by drawing lessons from the experience of ASEAN in creating a regional Single Window.

Indicators on Single Windows in the TFIs

There is no single model for Single Windows; they are tailored to specific national or regional requirements. Single Windows can also provide a wide variety of services and facilities, depending on their design and coverage. That said, a number of standards, tools and guidelines have been developed by intergovernmental agencies and international organisations[2] – to ensure that the Single Windows developed across countries and regions are more likely to be compatible with each other, and to support exchange of information.

Drawing on this body of work, five specialised OECD indicators have been developed to build a shared understanding of Single Windows and a systematic approach to tracking their implementation. These indicators seek to capture common design and operational features of Single Windows going beyond the basic concept set out in the TFA.[3] These include: institutional aspects and scope (indicator A); data content and structure (indicator B); legal framework (indicator C); technological architecture and scope (indicator D); and interoperability (indicator E).[4]

The indicators aim to offer a state-of-the-art tool to assist economies in the design and implementation of national and regional Single Windows.[5] Data gathered over 2015-16 using the indicators identified key achievements and challenges in designing, implementing, and operating Single Windows in 23 economies across some of the most advanced regional Single Window initiatives: the Inter-American Network of International Trade Single Windows in the Latin America and the Caribbean (LAC), the Asia-Pacific Economic Co-operation (APEC) and the Association of Southeast Asian Nations (ASEAN) (Table 4.1). Some economies participate in more than one Single Window initiative.

Table 4.1. **Economy groupings**

Latin America and the Caribbean (LAC)	Asia-Pacific Economic Co-operation (APEC)	Association of Southeast Asian Nations (ASEAN)
Argentina	Australia	Indonesia
Brazil	Canada	Malaysia
Chile	Chile	Philippines
Colombia	Indonesia	Singapore
Costa Rica	Japan	Thailand
Honduras	Korea	Viet Nam
Mexico	Malaysia	
Paraguay	Mexico	
Peru	New Zealand	
Trinidad and Tobago	Peru	
Uruguay	Philippines	
	Singapore	
	Chinese Taipei	
	Thailand	
	Viet Nam	

The overall picture

Amongst these initiatives, there is a wide variation in how key dimensions of Single Windows are currently implemented (Figure 4.1). The technological architecture of Single Windows (indicator D) is the area where there is least variation in – and the best overall – performance, perhaps because it is relatively more straightforward to implement, subject to resource availability. In contrast, indicators (A) institutional aspects and scope; (B) data content and structure; and (C) legal framework display a greater variation, linked to the wide-ranging political and organisational challenges (including related to vested interests) involved in their implementation. There are also significant gaps between current performance and best practice in these three areas (Figure 4.2). It is also perhaps not surprising that the most notable difference in average performance across the selected groups, and where all economies are still at an early stage, is in the challenging area of interoperability (indicator E).

The three country groupings surveyed also display significant differences in their average performance. LAC lags behind best practice, as well as behind the average performance of all the economies explored, and of APEC and ASEAN, on all indicators except that for technological architecture (indicator D) (Figure 4.3). The LAC performance gap is particularly significant in the area of data content and structure.

Figure 4.1. **There is a wide variation in implementation of Single Window initiatives**

OECD Single Windows Indicators: Full sample snapshot, selected regions

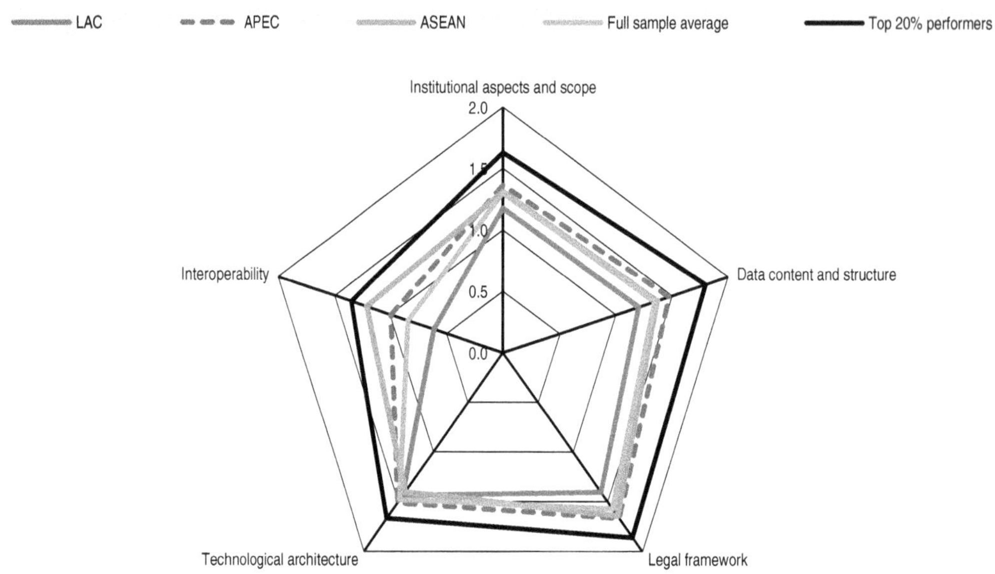

Source: OECD Single Windows Indicators estimates (2015-16).

Figure 4.2. **There are also significant gaps to best practice across most indicators**

Average performance gap to top 20% performers in the full sample

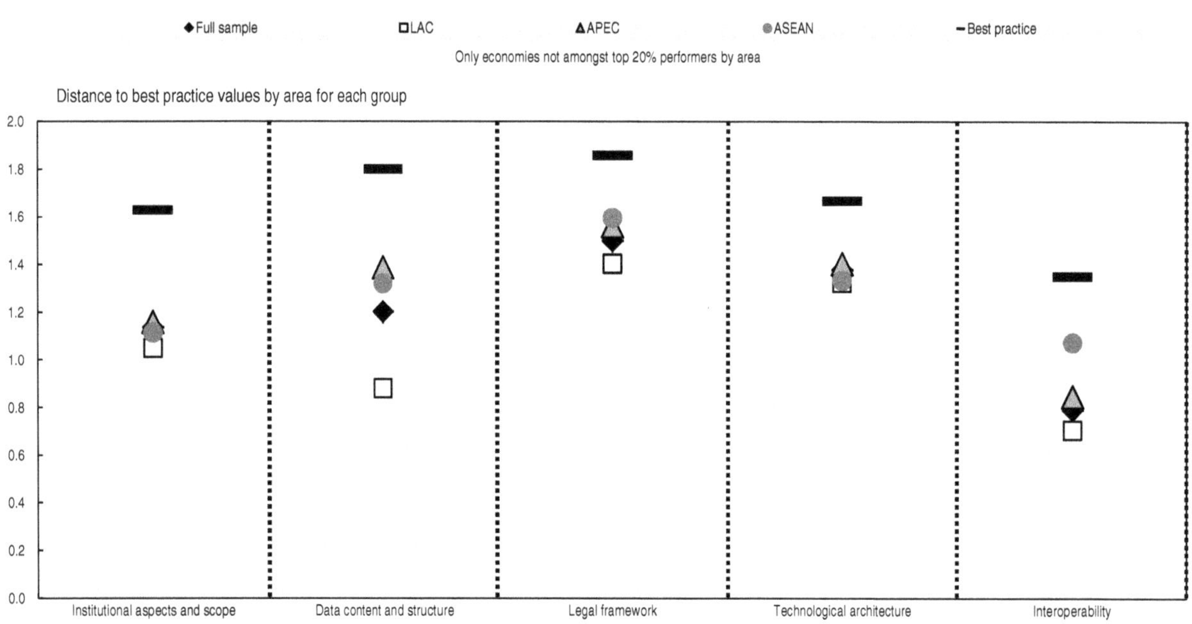

Source: OECD Single Windows Indicators estimates (2015-16).

APEC and ASEAN both perform very close to the average across all economies (Figure 4.3). The overall average is also closer to best practice, thanks to some strong performers within their ranks, and to the momentum provided by the ASEAN Single Window initiative (discussed further below). This initiative is also the main factor explaining ASEAN's near-best practice performance in the area of interoperability.

How each selected group performs across each indicator is discussed in the following section.

Figure 4.3. **OECD Single Windows indicators: Overall regional performance across selected groups**

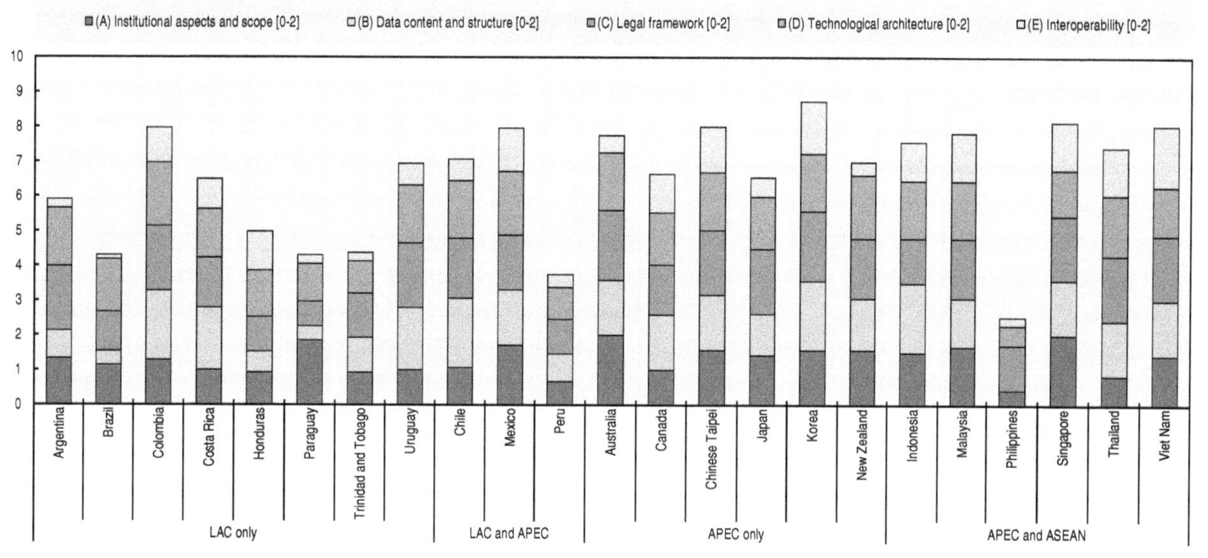

Source: OECD Single Windows Indicators estimates (2015-16).

Institutional aspects and scope

Indicator A (institutional aspects and scope) monitors progress towards building a comprehensive Single Window across two broad dimensions: the number of public and private entities included, and their relevance and impact; and the functioning and effectiveness of the Single Window in relation to the structure, funding and array of services offered. The ultimate success of a Single Window depends critically on the involvement, commitment and readiness of the parties to ensure that the system becomes a regular feature of their business processes. A snapshot of all the economies surveyed (Figure 4.4) shows that, across the systems surveyed, key challenges lie in:

- the extent of trade transactions covered by the Single Window;
- incorporation of functionalities enabling the calculation and payment of relevant duties, taxes and fees;
- mechanisms for the co-ordination of controls and inspections (other than document controls) by various government agencies; and
- comprehensiveness of the coverage of border agencies and related regulatory requirements.

The number of public and private agencies involved in import, export and transit currently included in the Single Window differs between and within groupings, with the highest variations observed within LAC (Figure 4.5). The same is true for the level of import, export, and transit regulatory requirements or functionalities currently covered by Single Window systems. ASEAN Single Windows have, on average, the highest coverage of the most important regulatory requirements and functionalities by volume of export, import and transit transactions.[6] This again attests to the ongoing efforts of ASEAN countries to put in place comprehensive Single Window mechanisms.

Figure 4.4. **Progress on institutional aspects is mixed**

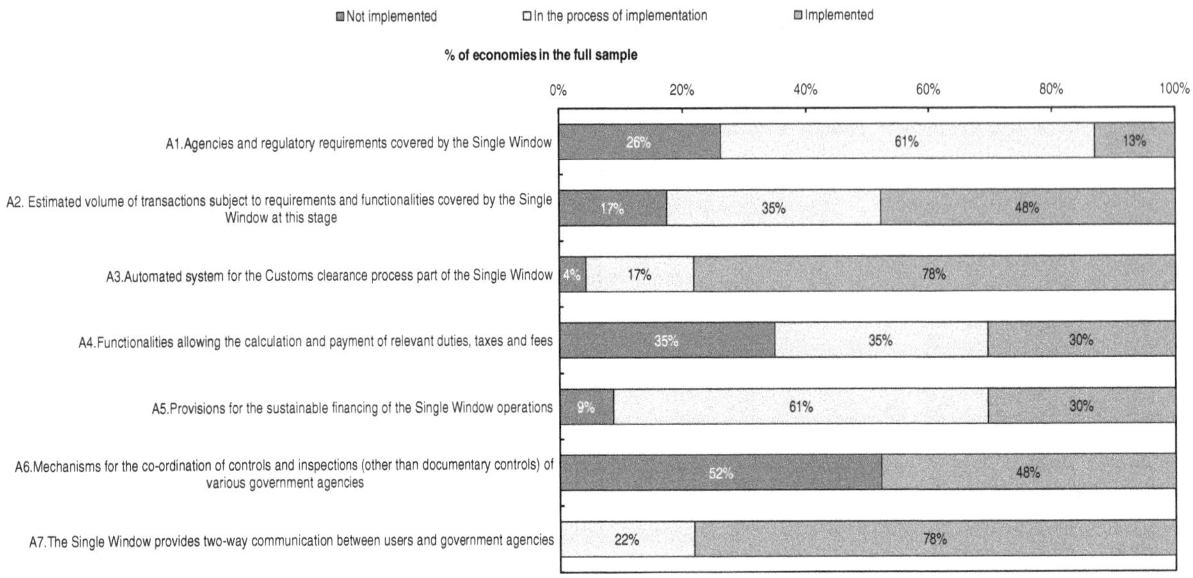

Source: OECD Single Windows Indicators estimates (2015-16).

Single Windows differ in scope and approach across the surveyed countries. Many economies start with a smaller scope and gradually expand the coverage of the Single Window, with further incorporation of government agencies and private sector stakeholders planned for the longer term. In over two-thirds of the economies surveyed, Single Windows also provide for two-way communication between users and government agencies.

An automated Customs clearance process is either already part of the Single Window (the large majority of surveyed economies, at 78%) or in the process of implementation (17% of economies surveyed). In view of its key role in the border process, across all economies surveyed, Customs is usually either the hosting agency or one of the participating agencies for the Single Window, and the lead agency in many economies.

Mechanisms for the co-ordination of controls and inspections of various government agencies, other than for documents, are not yet widespread: 52% of economies surveyed have not yet taken initial steps in this direction. Functionalities enabling the calculation and payment of relevant duties, taxes and fees are even less common, being included in only one third of systems.

More than 90% of the Single Windows surveyed already incorporate, or are in the process of implementing, provisions for sustainable financing of their operations over the medium- and long-term.[7] Government financing is the most widely used mechanism, followed by self-funding through service fees. Public-private partnerships and concession agreements do not appear to be widely used (Figure 4.6).

Data content and structure

Indicator B (data content and structure) covers the use of data in the Single Window and the degree of harmonisation aimed at minimising repetition and costs; the contribution of the Single Window to reducing duplicative or unnecessary data-related

Figure 4.5. **Coverage and scope of Single Windows is strong in ASEAN, but much less so in LAC**

Agencies and regulatory requirements covered

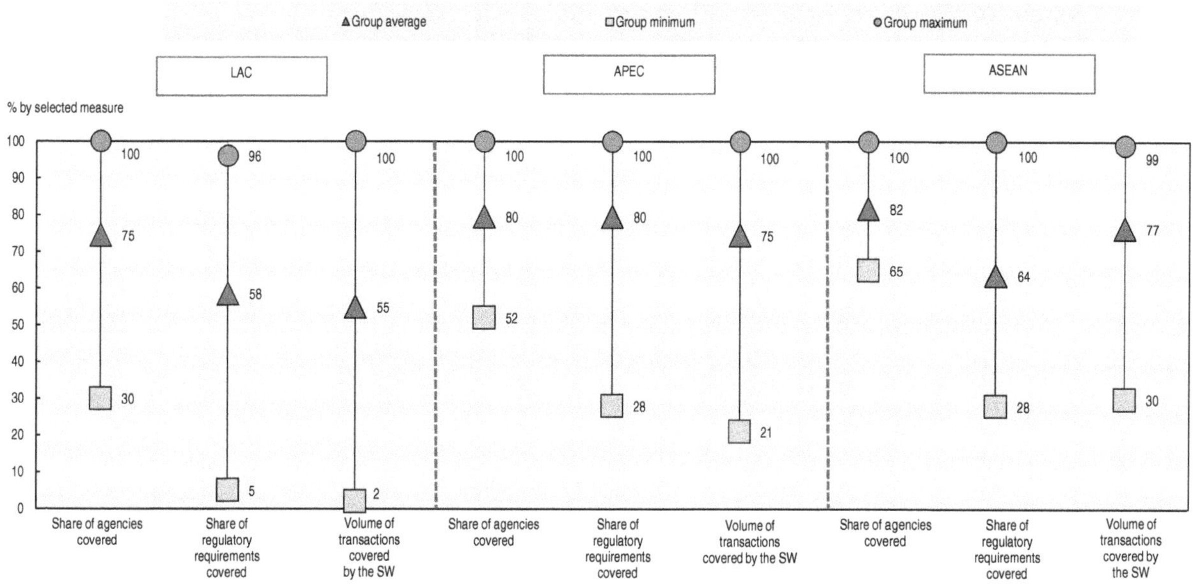

Source: OECD Single Windows Indicators estimates (2015-16).

Figure 4.6. **Most Single Windows are government financed**

Provisions for the sustainable financing of the Single Window operations

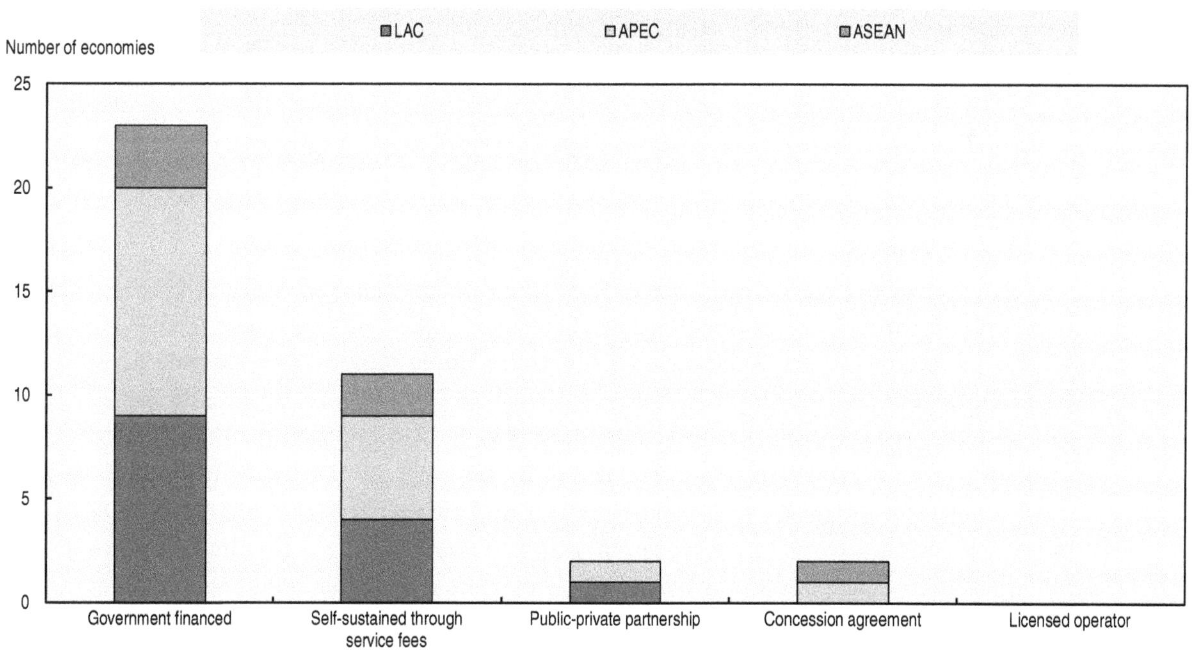

Source: OECD Single Windows Indicators estimates (2015-16).

formalities; and the interactivity of the Single Window and its support to paperless and virtual procedures.[8] Comprehensiveness, stability, and compliance with international norms for electronic data exchange should guide the selection of data standards within a

Single Window. Across the full range of economies surveyed (Figure 4.7), key data-related challenges currently lie in:

- all-electronic processing of import, export and transit transactions;
- use by all government agencies of data submitted through the Single Window, rather than requiring separate submissions;
- one common dataset covering data for import, export and transit for all agencies involved; and
- compatibility of Single Window data requirements, design and work plans with those of other border management and user platforms.

Figure 4.7. **Data requirements are largely harmonised to international standards, but electronic processing remains a work in progress**

Data content and structure: Identifying key challenges

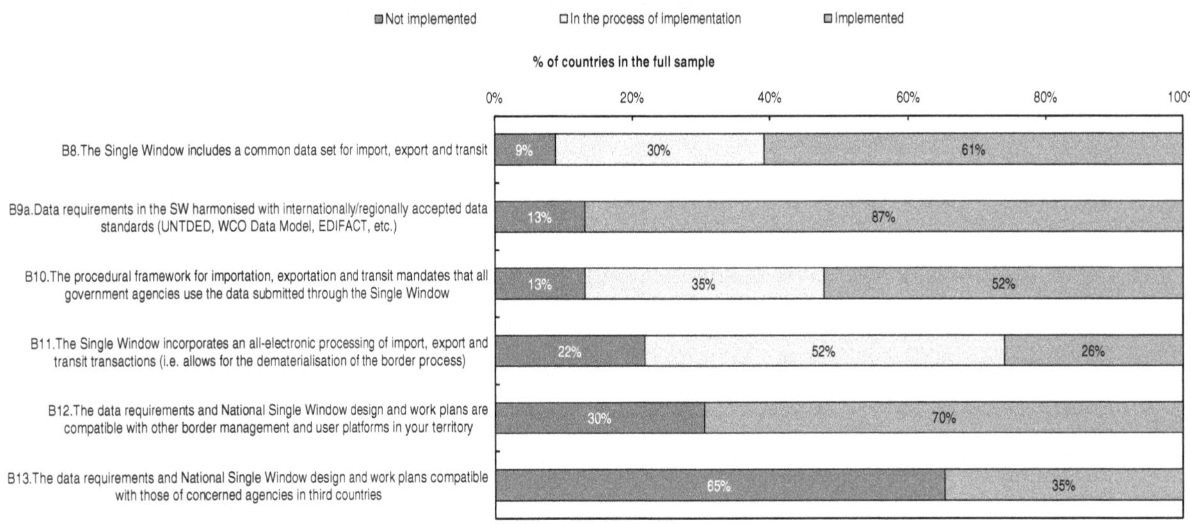

Source: OECD Single Windows Indicators estimates (2015-16).

In only half of the economies surveyed are all government agencies required to use data submitted through the Single Window. This could potentially be linked to the low level of transactions currently submitted through the Single Window (see variable A2 in Figure 4.4). In contrast, across 87% of economies surveyed, data requirements in the Single Window are harmonised with internationally and/or regionally accepted data standards.

All-electronic processing of import, export and transit transactions via Single Windows remains a work in progress: only 26% of systems allow for the complete dematerialisation of the border process. Even here, users may still submit documents in paper form when use of the Single Window is not mandatory.

For more than two-thirds of the Single Windows surveyed, data requirements, design and work plans are currently compatible with other national border management and user platforms. This allows the Single Window systems to interact with domestic port or cargo community systems or service provider platforms where they are not already part of the Single Window, increasing the reach of the Single Window for trade and economic activities.

Compatibility with the data requirements, design and work plans of agencies in third countries, an important building block for Single Window interoperability, is much less advanced. It is currently implemented in only one third of the economies surveyed, with no significant progress in the other economies.

Legal framework

Indicator C (legal framework) looks at how effectively the Single Window addresses privacy and confidentiality, data protection, definition of liabilities and dispute resolution. Creating the legal enabling conditions is one of the key tasks for economies establishing a Single Window or seeking to exchange information with other Single Windows. This is a complex process, requiring a thorough review of the existing practices governing the flow of trade-related information, and changes and clarifications to the data exchange process and related laws and regulations. Implementation is most challenging across the following areas (Figure 4.8):

- availability of recourse in case of a dispute with the Single Window process;
- legal constraints on sharing data;
- mechanisms to handle inaccurate or incomplete data transactions; and
- capacity for electronic archiving and establishing audit trails.

The establishment of laws and regulations on electronic data submission and exchange, as well as on ensuring confidentiality and data protection, is well advanced in most of the Single Windows surveyed. Moreover, 78% of the Single Windows surveyed accept electronic (digital) signatures. However, legal constraints on sharing data among participating agencies remains a significant hurdle, with more than half of the economies surveyed either having taken no action on, or still in the process of addressing, this issue.

Figure 4.8. **Legal frameworks are generally well-developed, with the exceptions of data sharing and disputes**

Legal framework: Identifying key challenges

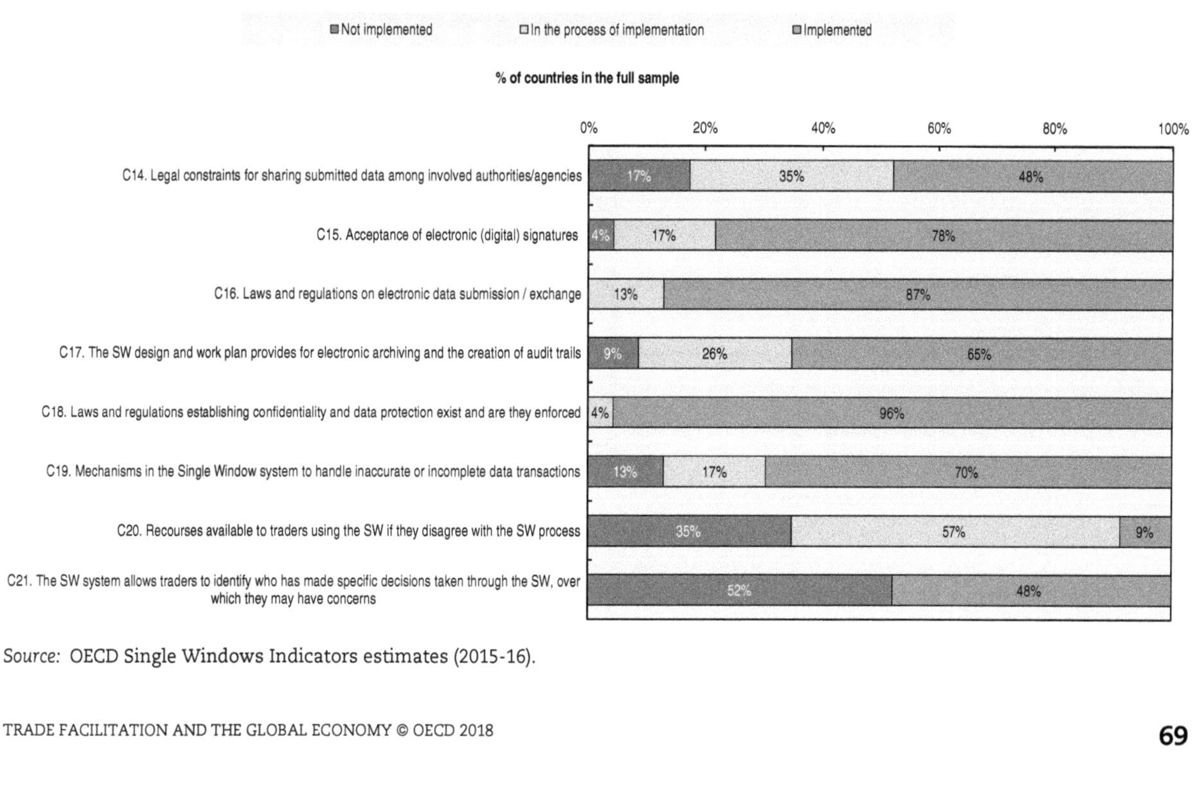

Source: OECD Single Windows Indicators estimates (2015-16).

Finally, 65% of Single Windows surveyed provide for electronic archiving and audit trails, while for 26% this remains under implementation.[9] This feature is generally accompanied by mechanisms to handle inaccurate or incomplete data transactions (operational in 70% of Single Window systems surveyed). However, in general, users lack recourse in case of any dispute with the Single Window or its participating agencies: for the majority of economies (57%) this remains a work in progress, while more than one-third of economies have not yet taken any action in this area. Moreover, 52% of the systems surveyed do not allow traders to identify who under the Single Window has taken a specific decision, about which they may have concerns.

Technological architecture

Indicator D (technological architecture) explores how the Single Window addresses the identification and authentication of users, and whether the system is easy to use, fail-proof and capable of handling future developments. It reviews software and hardware development and deployment in the Single Window, particularly as it affects the achievement of policy objectives, and given their important role in underpinning trust in the Single Window by both participating agencies and users. To that end, the following should be a priority (Figure 4.9):

- mechanisms to help verify the identification and authentication of individual transactions;
- mechanisms to secure integration with the systems of agencies that feed information into the Single Window; and
- contingency mechanisms.

Figure 4.9. **Progress on establishing technological architecture has been good, but some challenges remain**

Technological architecture: Identifying key challenges

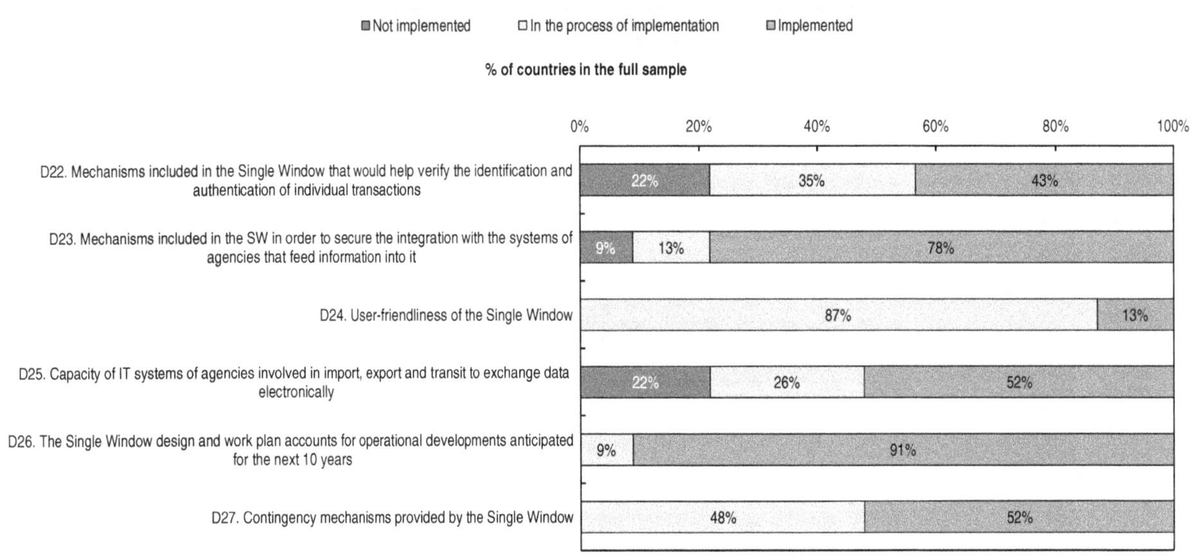

Source: OECD Single Windows Indicators estimates (2015-16).

Only 43% of Single Windows surveyed include mechanisms aimed at verifying the identification and authentication of individual transactions, such as through logins and passwords, digital certificates, or electronic signatures. That said, 78% of systems are already integrated with those of other agencies, through mechanisms such as a single sign on, digital certificates for establishing an encrypted channel or Internet Protocol (IP) control. Figure 4.10 highlights how these different mechanisms are currently used across the regional groupings.

The capacity of IT systems of participating agencies to exchange data electronically remains limited in half of the economies surveyed. Likewise, the incorporation of contingency mechanisms[10] in case of system failure remains a work in progress for an important share of economies (Figure 4.11). User-friendliness[11] is an ongoing process, with 87% of economies still making additional functionalities available in the system.

Figure 4.10. **Most systems require secure sign on**

Incorporation of mechanisms facilitating Single Window transactions

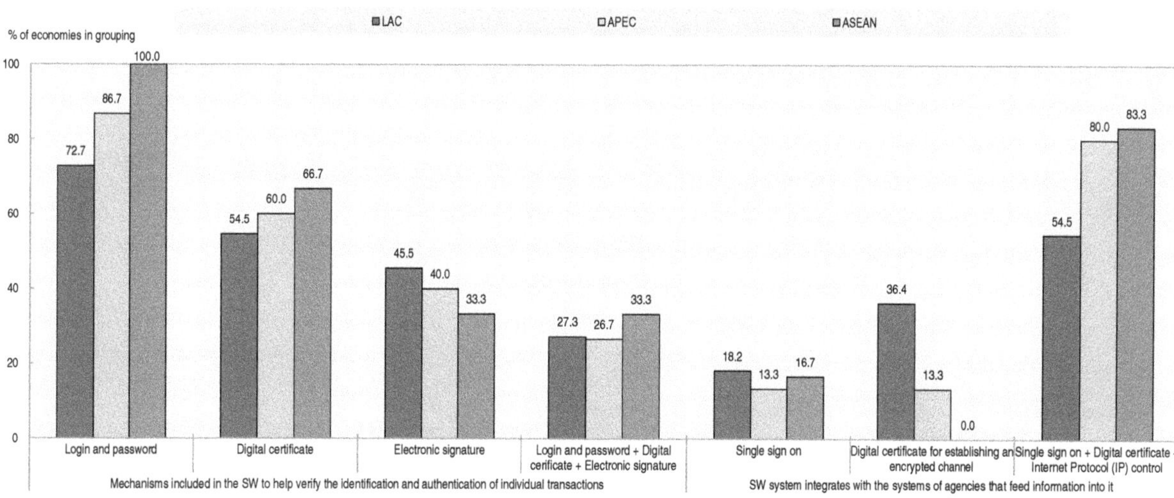

Source: OECD Single Windows Indicators estimates (2015-16).

Figure 4.11. **With the exception of backup, contingency mechanisms remain a work in progress**

Incorporation of contingency mechanisms

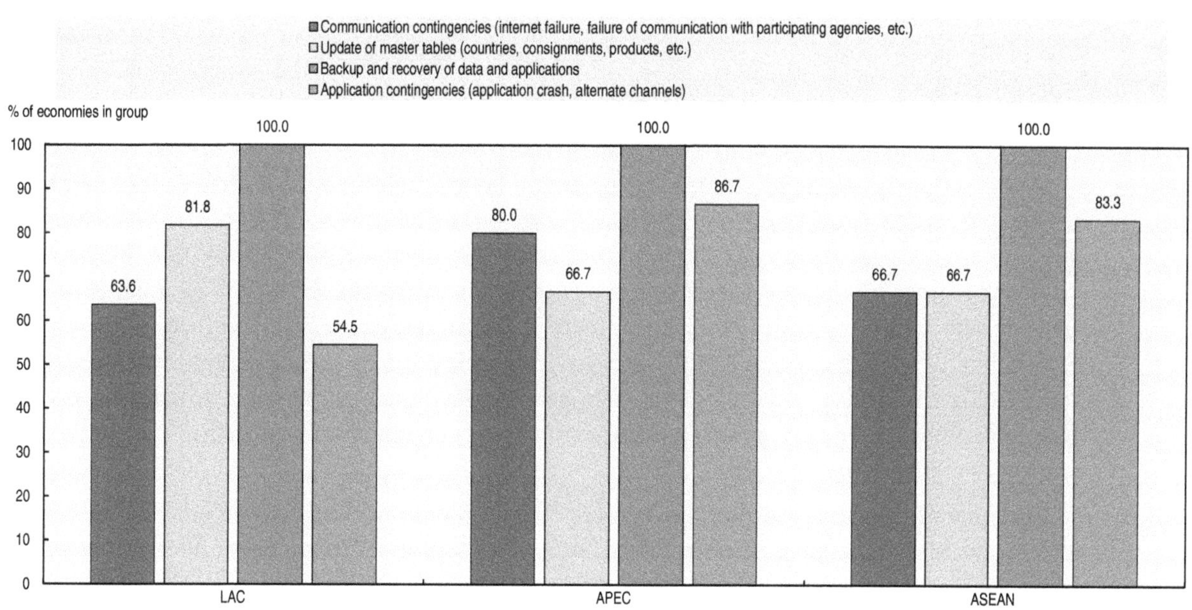

Source: OECD Single Windows Indicators estimates (2015-16).

Lastly, policy makers have recognised the need to develop interfaces able to adapt to future technological advances and increases in data volume. Across 91% of systems, the design and work plan account for operational developments covering the next decade, including: the capacity of both hardware and software to evolve; ease of upgrading the software base (operative system, data motor base, etc.); and the possibility of adding more users to the system and more functionalities to the existing application.

Interoperability

Indicator E (interoperability) assesses the capacity of the system to interact with those of private service providers and neighbouring and third countries. All Single Window initiatives surveyed recognise the importance of international interoperability, as well as the use of international standards to enable the seamless sharing of information to facilitate legitimate trade and increase supply chain security. Yet interoperability remains by far the most challenging dimension of Single Window implementation (Figure 4.12).

Figure 4.12. **Interoperability remains the greatest challenge for Single Windows**

Interoperability: Identifying key challenges

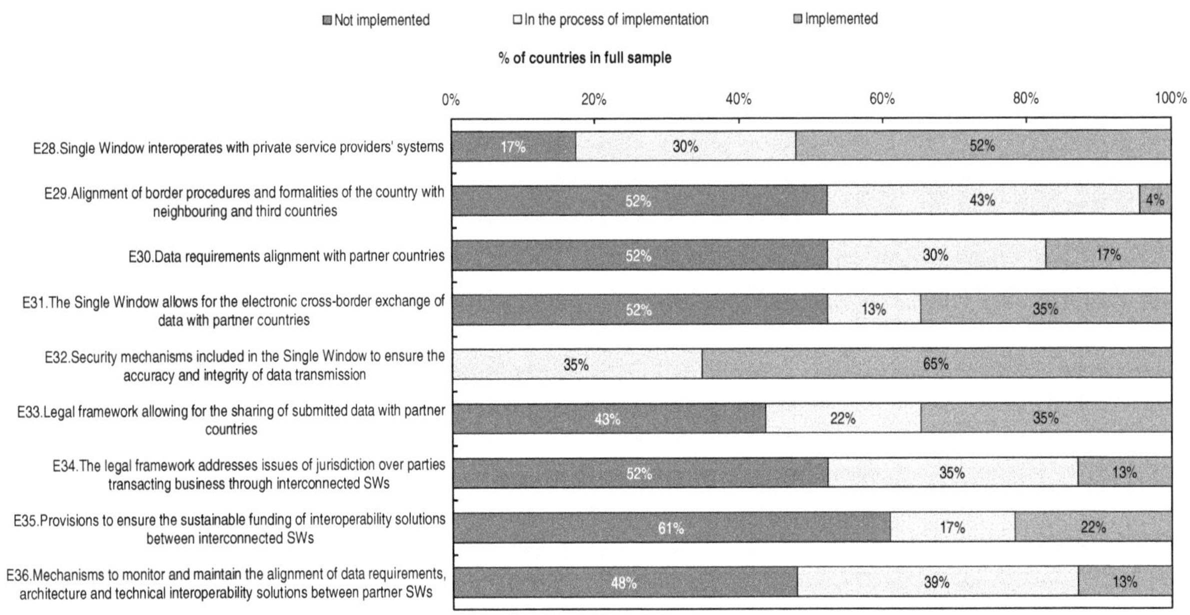

Source: OECD Single Windows Indicators estimates (2015-16).

Most progress has been made on the incorporation of different security mechanisms ensuring the accuracy and integrity of data transmission.[12] This is followed by interoperability with the systems of private service providers: 52% of Single Windows are interoperable with those of both logistics service providers (including freight forwarders, Customs brokers, shipping agents) and financial service providers, allowing for the payment of relevant duties, taxes and fees.

Very few of the surveyed economies have full alignment of their border procedures and formalities with neighbouring and third countries. This refers to the general Customs and border procedures and is not limited to Single Window-related procedures; the challenges related to this dimension have already been highlighted in Chapter 3. Progress is similarly limited on alignment of data requirements with those of partner countries[13] and on allowing the electronic cross-border exchange of data with partner countries.

In only one-third of economies do legal frameworks allow for sharing of submitted data with partner countries and appropriate protection of confidential commercial information. Moreover, even when permitted, in only very few systems is sharing of data backed by appropriate cyber-security measures, such as mutual recognition of electronic documents and data messages; definition of the required level of encryption; or secure data storage. In many of the surveyed economies, the legal framework also currently fails to address jurisdiction over parties conducting business transactions through interconnected Single Windows: 52% of the economies surveyed do not address this issue and for a further 35% it remains a work in progress.

Lastly, only 22% of systems provide for the sustainable funding of interoperability solutions between interconnected Single Windows. Mechanisms to monitor and maintain the alignment of data requirements, architecture and technical interoperability solutions between partner Single Windows are fully implemented in only 13% of systems surveyed.

Creating a regional Single Window: The experience of ASEAN

In 2005, ASEAN agreed to implement the ASEAN Single Window (ASW)[14] to fully integrate National Single Windows (NSWs) of ASEAN member economies, drawing on internationally accepted standards, procedures, documents, technical details and formalities.

The ASW involves direct exchanges of data between ASEAN Member States which are then synchronised across the region.[15] This allows data and information to be submitted only once, and avoids duplicative decision-making for Customs, but makes an effective ICT platform essential. The ASW is composed of three networks: the regional (or central) domain, which allows communication among NSWs, supports the secure electronic transfer of information and tracks transaction statistics; the national domain, which represents the network infrastructure hosted by each Member; and the external networks used by the trading community, which only have direct access to national domains to preserve data confidentiality. While data is directly exchanged between NSWs, it is not retained centrally.[16]

The ASW is overseen by the ASW Steering Committee (ASWSC), which reports directly to ASEAN Directors General of Customs and ASEAN Senior Officials. The ASWSC is assisted by technical (TWG) and legal (LWG) working groups. These groups consulted the private sector on development of the ASW and priorities for data exchange, and studied options for the governance, business model and financial sustainability of the ASW. The TWG and LWG also undertook awareness raising and capacity building at the regional level on business process analysis, data harmonisation and legal aspects, and at the national level on use of software applications.

A pilot evaluation, including a cost-benefit analysis, was launched in 2011, involving seven of the ten ASEAN Members.[17] The pilot tested the technical architecture[18] and sought to streamline and standardise data, explore efficient business processes, strengthen partnerships with stakeholders and raise public awareness. The ASW web portal was launched in 2013 upon successful completion of the pilot, which had seen over a million messages exchanged. A Legal Framework agreement regulating the cross-border exchange of electronic data was concluded in 2015 and is undergoing ratification by members. Indonesia, Lao PDR, the Philippines and Viet Nam have also conducted legal gap analyses on their NSWs.[19]

Although the original intention was to incorporate the ASEAN Customs Declaration into the ASW, this proved too complicated, including due to standardisation and confidentiality issues. Countries focused instead on the ASEAN preferential certificate of origin, which was important to the private sector, raised no confidentiality issues, and for which a standard operating procedure was already in place. Indonesia, Malaysia, Singapore, Thailand and Viet Nam have initiated bilateral pilots on certificate exchanges and discussions are underway about a broader pilot involving as many ASEAN countries as possible. The intention is also to incorporate commercial and transport documents for goods, as well as documents required for the release and clearance of goods. It is also intended to progressively analyse other government-to-government data, such as phytosanitary, veterinary and health certificates, as well as business-to-business data, such as bills of lading, air waybills, packing lists and invoices with a view to their inclusion. However, these steps are some way off, as the initial stages are only now gaining momentum.

Expected benefits of the ASW include improved risk management and compliance, enhanced track-and-trace capabilities, smoother pre-arrival clearance and better supply chain integration. Importantly, the creation of the ASW has also generated significant impetus for the creation and improvement of NSWs.[20] It has also spurred efforts to harmonise data and procedures among members, including beyond those required for the ASW, such as conformity assessment or phytosanitary policies, thereby supporting broader policy harmonisation efforts.

Finally, by seeking compatibility with international open communication standards, the ASW ensures that each Member can exchange data securely and reliably with third parties.[21] In the long run, the ASW could serve as a platform for all sorts of cross-border data exchange, from the ASEAN Customs Transit System, currently under preparation, to information about assistance goods and equipment shipped by NGOs in case of disasters, as well as providing a basis for monitoring ASEAN economic integration (Benjelloun et al., 2012).

Factors of success and challenges

A first observation is that commitment by Heads of State, economic and trade ministers, and finance ministers, along with pressure from the private sector, has been critical to the ability of ASEAN countries to address challenges related to the ASW.

As ASEAN is not a Customs Union, there were no standard services, forms or processes among NSWs and no harmonised legal frameworks at the outset.[22] This made the initial (technically simpler) suggestion for an ASW in the form of a central portal too ambitious, including politically.[23] A second observation is that it is important for any Single Window endeavour to have ambitious but realistic objectives and a clear vision from the political level of what the mechanism is supposed to accomplish.

While there have been significant achievements, the ASW remains a work in progress. Budget limitations forced countries to scale-down the original technical solutions, but these were not the most challenging issues: ASEAN countries extensively harnessed public-private partnerships, as well as donor funding at both the regional and national level. Current challenges relate to commitment, confidence and overcoming legal hurdles.

While the ASW started slowly as technical issues were resolved, this gave more time to Members to develop their own NSWs, and increase collaboration among their experts.

Effective NSWs are critical for the ASW, but this remains a significant challenge. The original deadline for completing NSWs for some ASEAN members (Brunei Darussalam, Indonesia, Malaysia, Philippines, Singapore and Thailand) was 2008, while others (Cambodia, Lao PDR, Myanmar and Viet Nam) had until 2012 (these timelines have been pushed to 2012 and 2015 respectively).[24] A third observation is that while the ASW provided useful momentum for developing NSWs, the fact that NSWs were not in place or substantially under way when the regional mechanism was initiated greatly complicated its establishment.

A fourth observation is that disparities among ASEAN members with regard to the quality of infrastructure, systems automation, or personnel have also slowed implementation. For instance, NSWs' compliance with information security standards is still uneven, affecting the reliability of sensitive data protection, as all data is retained at the national, not the regional, level. This in turn undermines the confidence of operators in the ASW. Numerous complementary measures are also needed at the national level to support paperless clearance in ASEAN, including a Single Window-ready legal environment, risk management systems, pre-arrival processing mechanisms and Authorised Economic Operator programs.

A fifth observation is the need for domestic co-ordination to underpin regional efforts: insufficient domestic co-ordination between Customs administrations, relevant agencies and economic operators has also slowed progress of the ASW. Moreover, in most participating countries, risk management is undertaken only by Customs, not other border agencies, complicating future discussions about the incorporation of non-Customs documents and procedures.

Legal challenges, including relating to mutual recognition of digital signatures, equivalence of paper and electronic documents, data confidentiality and liability, were also significant. A sixth observation is that legal gap analysis at the national level, but also for cross-border exchanges, needs to start as early as possible, as issuing new or amended legislation can be a lengthy process. Single Window interoperability also faced domestic laws that did not allow the exchange of national data, or which required the consent of the trader.[25] Even for the preferential certificate of origin, which raised no confidentiality or process standardisation challenges, the existing certification procedures had to be adapted to allow e-copies. Given the time required for reviewing, mapping and addressing regional legal impediments, these challenges should be dealt with as early as possible.

The ASW has provided an important opportunity for ASEAN to promote a trade facilitation agenda, both in the form of gradually strengthening NSWs and in analysing and reengineering basic trade documents and processes. While this has been a slow and complicated process, the learning and problem-solving process is already yielding benefits for the region's trade.

The process of developing the ASW also provides important insights for other regions on important factors in establishing a Single Window. In sum, these are:

- The importance of sustained political commitment.
- The need for ambitious but realistic objectives and a clear vision from the political level of what the Single Window is supposed to accomplish.
- Regional Single Windows can provide momentum for developing national Single Windows; however, the absence of established National Single Windows greatly complicates the establishment of a regional Single Window.

- Disparities among parties in terms of the quality of infrastructure, systems automation, or personnel can negatively affect implementation.
- Co-ordination at the domestic level among Customs administrations, relevant agencies and economic operators agencies is needed to underpin regional efforts.
- Given the lead times for crafting and introducing changes, legal gap analysis at the national level, but also for cross-border exchanges, needs to start as early as possible.

Notes

1. UN/CEFACT Recommendation 33. This is the most known definition of the Single Window concept.
2. These include the United Nations Economic Commission for Europe, the United Nations Conference on Trade and Development, the World Customs Organization, the International Maritime Organization, the International Civil Aviation Organization, the International Chamber of Commerce.
3. See WTO TFA Article 10.4 which defines SW as a platform for single-entry, non-duplicative submission of trade documentation, ideally supported by information technology.
4. The policy relevance of these indicators was tested with the support of, and in consultation with relevant international fora, including the Inter-American Network of International Trade Single Windows (*Red VUCE*), UNECE/CEFACT (Centre for Trade Facilitation and Electronic Business), and APEC's Sub-Committee on Customs Procedures (SCCP).
5. The Single Window indicators are not meant at this stage to assess the impact of these platforms on trade flows and trade costs, given the limited number of countries where they are operational and their widely varying levels of development.
6. This includes declarations, permits, certificates, visas and product inspections.
7. Without making any judgement as to the preferred form of financing for the Single Window, this element seeks to understand whether existing financing mechanisms are clear, sustainable over the long term and whether any fees charged correspond to the services provided.
8. Interactivity refers to the ability of users to interact directly with the Single Window; for example, by lodging forms online.
9. This feature refers to the data retained within the Single Window by participating agencies, whether this includes transaction data or just lodging and sign off.
10. Contingency mechanisms can include: communication contingencies (alternatives in case of Internet failure, failure of communication with participating agencies, etc.); update of master tables (countries, consignments, products, etc.); backup and recovery of data and applications; application contingencies (application crash, alternate channels).
11. This includes the incorporation of the following functionalities: Help Desk and user support services; Operating instructions and guidelines; Physical training for users; Wizard; E-learning; Other.
12. This can concern the following mechanisms: transmission of the information without encryption (in the clear); transmission of the information over a secure channel with exchange of digital certificates; encrypted and/or signed transmission.
13. The primary focus of this feature is the extent to which data requirements in the National Single Window are aligned with data requirements in other Single Windows.
14. ASEAN (2005), "Agreement to Establish and Implement the ASEAN Single Window".
15. In the absence of a Customs Union, and given the significant institutional, legal and operational complexities involved in integrating different national systems (including concerns about concentration of risk from channelling information through a single server), the ASW does not centralise the processing of information, but limits itself to electronic cross-border data exchange among NSWs.
16. Nevertheless, the electronic "stamping" of cross-border messages by the ASW is critical for establishing the sequence of exchanges in case of a regional dispute.
17. Brunei, Indonesia, Malaysia, the Philippines, Singapore, Thailand and Viet Nam.

18. Including ICT solutions, security protocols, interfaces, messaging, routing and synchronising functions.
19. This has included examining whether there is national enabling legislation in place; equivalence of electronic and paper copies; acceptance of electronic (including digital) signatures; electronic data retention and archiving; ability to use electronic data in judicial proceedings; and liability and dispute resolution issues.
20. Singapore has operated its Single Window for over two decades; Brunei Darussalam, Indonesia, Malaysia, Philippines, and Thailand are at relatively advanced stages of NSW completion. CLMV (Cambodia, Lao PDR., Myanmar, and Viet Nam) countries are implementing e-Customs platforms and launching NSW efforts with support from the donor community.
21. This would, for example, support the exchange of certificates of origin or advance cargo information with non-ASEAN trading partners. Related individual discussions with the People's Republic of China, Japan and Korea are currently underway.
22. Such as for electronic signatures, data protection, use of electronic data in judicial proceedings, data retention and archiving, liability and dispute settlement (Benjelloun et al., 2012).
23. Direct data input from traders against differing formalities and requirements also meant that such a portal could not operate without a unified automated processing system for all Member States and carefully co-ordinated and air-tight security procedures, meant to address failures and ensure the protection of confidential data.
24. New NSW progress indicators allow Members to report every six months.
25. This is the case in Indonesia, Thailand and Singapore.

Bibliography

APEC SCCP (2009), "Single Window Implementation Guide", Single Window Working Group, Phase 2 Final Report, July.

Benjelloun, R., D. Pantastico and M. Wong (2012), Cross-border E-Trade: The ASEAN Single Window, UN/ESCAP TID *Working Paper* 03/12.

Koh, J. and A. Feldman Mowerman (2013), "Towards a Truly Seamless Single Windows and Trade Facilitation Regime in ASEAN beyond 2015", *ERIA Discussion Paper Series* 2013-29.

Moise, E. and S. Sorescu (2017), "Single Window and Border Agency Co-operation: Expanding Selected OECD Trade Facilitation Indicators", TAD/TC/WP(2016)14/FINAL.

Nathan Associates Inc. (2013), "ASEAN Single Window Task Order", Final Report, USAID ADVANCE.

Nizeyimana, C. and L. de Wulf (2012), "Rwanda Electronic Single Window Supports Trade Facilitation", *World Customs Journal*, Vol. 9, No. 2.

OECD (2016), *Market Openness Review of Costa Rica*, TAD/TC/ACS(2015)3/FINAL.

Pitakdumrongkit, K. and M.T. Anna Robles (2014), "Assessing the Progress of AEC Projects: A New Approach", *RSIS Working Paper* No 280.

UN/CEFACT (2005), "Recommendation No. 33", *www.unece.org/fileadmin/DAM/cefact/recommendations/rec33/rec33_trd352e.pdf*.

USAID (2012), "Lao PDR National Single Window Roadmap Development: Technical Approach", USAID ASEAN Single Window Project.

USAID (2014), "ASEAN Single Window, Facilitating Trade for the ASEAN Economic Community", *www.sasec.asia/uploads/events/2014/SCS-II/asw-overview.pdf*.

Trade Facilitation and the Global Economy

PART 1

Chapter 5

Costs and challenges

This chapter highlights key costs and challenges in implementing trade facilitation reforms, from initial financial investments to the sustained policy commitment to adopt and maintain measures over the long term. It draws on reviews of experience in 24 developing and emerging economies to present evidence on the nature of the costs and how they compare with the benefits from implementing trade facilitation reforms.

The costs of TFA implementation are manageable compared to the expected benefits

The cost to developing countries of implementing trade facilitation measures was a central issue in the WTO negotiations on trade facilitation.[1] Unpacking the costs associated with trade facilitation reforms requires taking into the account not only the cost of introducing new measures, but also of sustaining reforms over the longer term. Upfront costs in diagnosing and designing what needs to be done need to be factored in, along with the costs and skills involved in changing laws and regulations. Reforms can involve investments in physical infrastructure, but these have to be accompanied by investments in training staff to operate new technology or perform new processes. A comprehensive and sequenced approach is important: for example, new equipment will not solve problems where policies still require cumbersome processes. Lastly, not all costs are financial: change management, and the associated challenges of changing organisational incentives and behaviours, are an important issue for trade facilitation reforms.

This chapter draws on country experience with implementing trade facilitation to identify and discuss the key cost components and challenges in implementing reforms. Based on work examining the experience of 24 developing and emerging economies, it highlights the extent to which trade facilitation processes can be undertaken in the framework of normal operating budgets and without additional resources, apart from donor support for the areas requiring more technically demanding and complex changes, and longer implementation and familiarisation periods. Overall, implementation and operating expenses are also seen to have been quite limited compared to expected benefits from the reforms.

Assessing the costs of implementing trade facilitation measures

A number of issues arise in assessing the costs of implementation, not least where costs may be financially small but require challenging organisational or behavioural change. Some measures may be relatively inexpensive to put in place but challenging both in terms of enforcement in practice and sustainability over the long run. Translating the introduction of formal measures into changes in the day-to-day operations of border agencies and other participants (such as firms and traders) can require addressing entrenched behaviours and values or the desire to preserve rents. Overcoming resistance to change can require not only technical and financial assistance to improve technical and human capacity, but also political momentum and time to adjust.

Another important issue in assessing the costs of implementation is the distinction between capital expenditure and recurring costs. *Capital expenditure* relates to the introduction of automated systems for advance lodging and processing of data, risk management or single windows; the purchase of equipment, vehicles or buildings; or initial training on certain tasks or operations. *Recurring expenses* primarily concern salaries, but also the operation and maintenance of equipment and regular training to maintain skills at the required level. Measures that entail a significant upfront investment are not necessarily costly to operate on an ongoing basis: Single Windows are a case in point. Yet the sustainability of reforms can also depend on building the capacity of local teams for strategic thinking and driving reforms, and to be able to diagnose and address new issues as they arise in the future.[2]

One challenge in assessing the costs of implementing trade facilitation reforms is that these annual operating expenses for reforms are difficult to separate from those related to the overall functioning of customs and other border administrations and are generally absorbed by these agencies' regular operating budgets. While it is important to ensure that budgets for maintenance of both equipment and skills are available in the long term to ensure the sustainability of reforms, experience also indicates that the efficiency gains from the reforms also enabled border authorities to do more with their existing resources. Private support can also be very valuable in providing know-how and complementing resources earmarked for reform. For example, Malaysia's Single Window was championed by the government, which ensured active and continuous involvement of various border agencies, but was established and run by the private sector.

Finally, it is not only the readiness of Customs but also of other agencies involved in the border process that need to be factored into assessments of the likely costs of reforms. In general, Customs are at the forefront of modernisation and facilitation, as the only government body that deals with all goods arriving in and departing from a country. Customs also tend to be the main beneficiaries of extensive financial and technical support from bilateral and institutional donors (Box 5.1) and specialised agencies, including the World Customs Organization (WCO). The upgrading and modernisation of the other agencies involved is gaining momentum but still has some way to go.

Identifying the main cost components of trade facilitation reforms

The introduction and implementation of trade facilitation measures entails costs and challenges in one or more of the following areas: diagnostics, new regulation, institutional changes, training, equipment and infrastructure, and awareness-raising and change management. While equipment and infrastructure are often the most expensive, training appears to be the most significant, as trade facilitation is primarily about changing border agencies' ways of doing business.

Diagnostic and re-engineering costs: Identifying priority areas for reform and devising appropriate action plans can be complicated, especially for developing countries that may have limited experience with diagnostic and reengineering endeavours. Prior to the conclusion of the TFA negotiations, technical assistance was provided by the WTO Secretariat, with the support of Annex D organisations[3] and experts from Members' national administrations, to help developing countries participate more effectively in the negotiations and to assess their trade facilitation needs and priorities.[4] Diagnostics and planning for trade facilitation reforms has also formed part of capacity building initiatives such as the Diagnostic Trade Integration Studies (DTIS) for Enhanced Integrated Framework countries, or the Diagnostic Needs Assessments and Implementation Support under the WCO Columbus Program. In some countries, these diagnostic projects may also mobilise domestic expertise from academia and the administration.

Regulatory costs: Trade facilitation measures may sometimes require new legislation, or the amendment of existing laws. Generally, these regulatory changes are undertaken in a

Box 5.1. **Trade facilitation has attracted significant donor support**

Many of the initial expenses for implementing trade facilitation reforms – such as purchasing equipment, training officials and putting in place new measures – have been financed by the increasing level of technical and financial assistance devoted to trade facilitation over the last decade.

Donor support directed to simplifying and modernising border rules and procedures reached USD 363 million in 2016, a fivefold increase over the 2002-05 base-line average. Donor support for trade facilitation was also relatively resilient during the global economic crisis; the decline experienced since 2013 may reflect difficulties related to ascribing assistance to the implementation of the WTO TFA while WTO Members' notifications of TFA Category B and C commitments were still at an early stage.

Figure 5.1. **Aid for trade facilitation has grown strongly since 2002**

Total aid for trade facilitation, commitments (USD million, 2015 constant prices), 2002-16

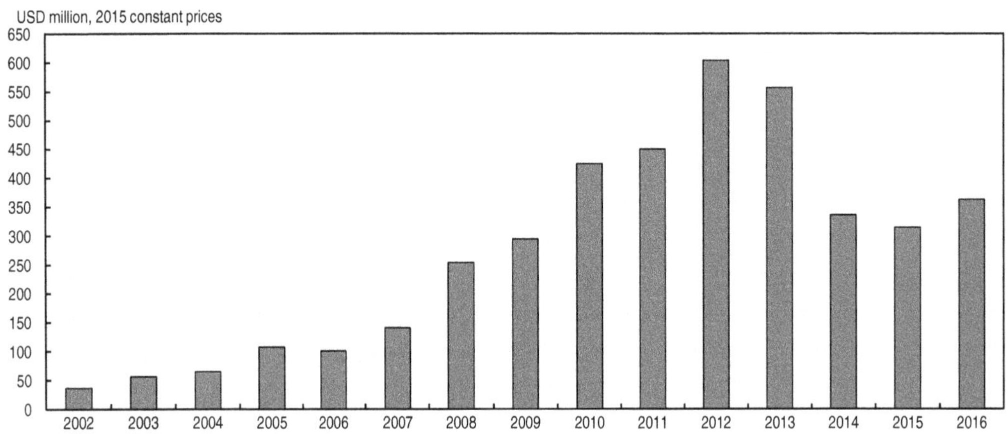

Source: OECD-DAC (2018), *Aid activities database* (CRS), *https://stats.oecd.org/qwids/.*

The clear majority of donor assistance for trade facilitation reforms has gone to least developed countries, although assistance for Lower Middle Income Countries and global programs have been steadily increasing.

Figure 5.2. **LDCs remain the largest beneficiaries of aid for trade facilitation**

Aid for trade facilitation by income group, commitments (USD million, 2015 constant prices), 2002-16

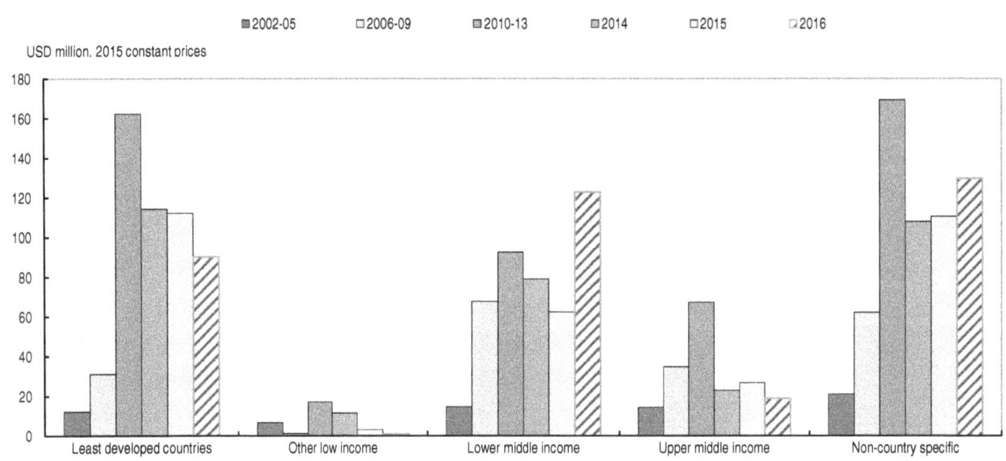

Source: OECD-DAC (2018), *Aid activities database* (CRS), *https://stats.oecd.org/qwids/.*

Box 5.1. **Trade Facilitation has attracted significant donor support** *(cont.)*

The largest beneficiaries of assistance for trade facilitation are countries in Africa, which received USD 161 million in 2016, a 17-fold increase since 2002-05.

Figure 5.3. **Aid for trade facilitation goes predominantly to countries in Africa and Asia**

Aid for trade facilitation by region, commitments (USD million, 2015 constant prices), 2002-16

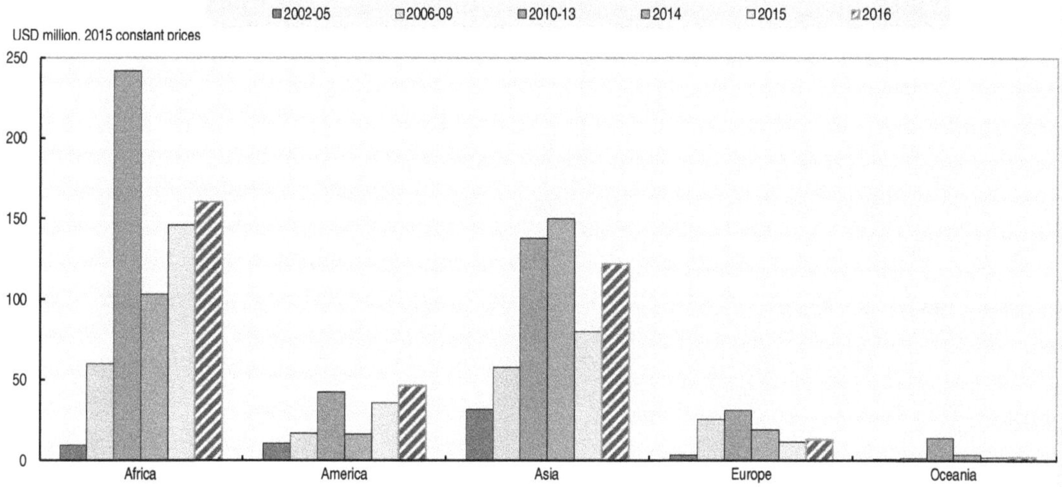

Note: Country groupings are those used by the OECD-DAC. Africa grouping: North Africa, Sub-Saharan Africa; America grouping: North and Central America, South America, Caribbean; Asia grouping: Middle East, Central Asia, South Asia, South and Central Asia, Far East Asia.
Source: OECD-DAC (2018), *Aid activities database* (CRS), *https://stats.oecd.org/qwids/*.

wider, customs modernisation context and are not narrowly confined to trade facilitation. They involve time and specialised staff in ministries, the centre of government and parliament. Preparatory work to assess the existing regulatory framework, ensure consistency and coherence with other domestic policies and identify potential unintended consequences on various users forms a significant part of this undertaking. Resources required for legislative and regulatory work differ depending on countries' legislative structures, procedures and frequency of changes in legislation. However, with the exception of major legislative changes, such as for electronic signatures, most changes pertinent to trade facilitation can be handled at the operational level and entail little additional cost. In countries with limited domestic expertise, support may be provided through international assistance. The TFA negotiation also generated a wealth of supporting material, produced by member governments and intergovernmental agencies, about the main regulatory and institutional aspects that need to be taken into account in reforming regulation.[5]

Institutional costs: Some trade facilitation measures require the establishment of new units, such as a post-clearance team, a risk management team or a central enquiry point, which may require additional human and financial resources. In terms of human resources, countries can either recruit new staff, which generally costs more, or redeploy existing staff, which may also entail costs related to training, physically relocating staff and forward planning. Relocation is not an uncommon management practice in customs, so redeployment linked to new trade facilitation measures may simply be part of the general practice of relocation. However, redeployment may be less viable where it would create significant service disruptions or where sophisticated, specialised functions are being introduced.

Although not actually expensive, the clarification of border agencies' respective fields of responsibility and co-ordination around border services and controls may be institutionally challenging. Customs administrations may be responsible for the application not just of their own procedures and requirements but also those of a range of other authorities, particularly in terms of ensuring compliance with any documentary requirements (licences, certificates, etc.). The ability to delegate controls, or the requirement to co-ordinate border agency activities in a way that minimises the burden to users, may require strong direction from the centre of government.

Training costs: Training often appears as the most critical cost component of trade facilitation reforms. Countries may choose between: i) recruiting new, expert staff; ii) training existing staff in a training centre; iii) on-the-job training; and iv) importing trained staff through personnel exchange with other ministries/agencies. Option i) is the most expensive since it implies a budgetary increase, but may not succeed if the salary scale is too low to attract suitably qualified staff. Moreover, there may only be a limited pool of potential staff with the necessary customs-specific skills and expertise. Regular training is common practice in many customs administrations around the world, though varying in frequency and duration, and training on specific trade facilitation measures (option ii) is often part of more general training.[6]

On-the-job training (option iii) results in no additional cost for the administration, but may give rise to temporary costs for traders, in the form of disruption to some service operations and this, along with financial considerations, may constrain the ability to train large numbers of officials in new techniques, such as risk assessment. Option iv) may be relevant for cases such as post-clearance audit, where appropriate expertise may be drawn from the inland tax administration. Although this is a costless option for the state and for the customs administration, the loss of qualified staff from the tax administration may make it difficult to implement without sustained political commitment, even when customs and tax are under the same agency or department.

Equipment/infrastructure costs: Equipment and infrastructure are not always a prerequisite for trade facilitation reforms, although some measures, such as advance lodgement and processing of data, risk assessment or special procedures, are more readily implemented with appropriate equipment and infrastructure. Border agencies usually demand information and communication technology (ICT) products and infrastructure and scanners to enhance their control functions, and only incidentally in relation to trade facilitation measures. For example, while telephones make communication far easier and office automation can greatly improve performance, neither can be counted as direct costs of trade facilitation. Yet insufficient equipment and infrastructure will inevitably make some facilitation measures more difficult to implement.

Equipment and infrastructure should be viewed as implementation tools to be carefully combined and sequenced with regulatory, institutional or human resource changes. For example, as long as a country has not introduced modern risk management for targeting high-risk consignments and continues to examine unnecessarily large numbers of low-risk consignments, scanners will not do much to help reduce clearance times or enhance control performance. Likewise, modern equipment and IT systems require a complementary investment in people, as any system can only be as efficient as the people who run it. Furthermore, purchasing implementation tools before elaborating the relevant policies (for instance introducing computer networks before modernising control and clearance procedures) runs the risk of reducing policy design options and making any subsequent changes lengthier and costlier.

Awareness-raising and change-management costs: The efficiency of a number of trade facilitation measures is also linked to capacity or willingness of the other economic actors with whom border agencies interact (such as firms and traders) to go along with new modes of operation. Awareness-raising activities can promote better understanding and the positive involvement of the private sector, and facilitate the introduction and enhance the sustainability of any new measures. Private stakeholders are frequently included in training and capacity building activities alongside customs and other government officials, possibly funded by the government or technical assistance programs. Lastly, the development of a communications strategy directed at both customs staff and other stakeholders, and the establishment of client service standards are important elements of change management.

What does country experience tell us?

No study can generate hard and fast figures about how much each country should be spending to promote trade facilitation. Countries circumstances differ: trade facilitation and customs reforms have different starting points and some expenses are simply a function of the size of the administration. The approach and level of ambition for pursuing and implementing some measures, such as Single Windows, also varies. And diverse country circumstances mean that the application in practice of the same trade facilitation measures will differ across countries.

Reviews of country experience (initially in 2005[7] and updated in 2012) explored costs and challenges in implementing trade facilitation measures in 24 developing countries.[8] The case studies show that trade facilitation measures have introduced new ways to fulfil the traditional mandates of border agencies, often making them more efficient and effective by rationalising resource use. The reported costs of implementing trade facilitation measures were not high, both as regards resources to introduce the measures, as well as operating expenditures, with the exception of costs related to information and communication technologies (ICT). The costs of introducing trade facilitation measures were primarily related to recruitment and training of specialised staff and for equipment, but the time necessary for satisfactory implementation of the measures constitutes an additional challenge. Reported operating costs were mainly related to salaries. Although aggregate figures of total trade facilitation costs in one country will not be directly transposable to other countries, budgeted or estimated capital expenditure to introduce trade facilitation measures in the reviewed countries ranged between EUR 3.5 and 19 million. Annual operating costs directly or indirectly linked to trade facilitation did not exceed EUR 2.5 million in any of the reviewed countries that reported such expenses. In both cases, the stated figures concern much more than trade facilitation as several reforms are part of a broader customs modernisation agenda that also covers productivity and improved revenue collection.

Some costly measures bring significant benefits

The costliest trade facilitation measures tend to be those related to the introduction and use of ICT. The single most expensive measure to introduce is generally Single Window mechanisms although, once in place, available evidence suggests that ongoing salary and maintenance expenditures are not necessarily very high.[9] Other trade facilitation measures that rely on ICT include risk management systems and the ability to lodge and process documentation prior to arrival of the consignment. Yet in assessing the cost it is important to remember that the introduction of ICT concerns far more than trade facilitation and some costs, for instance those related in risk management and control selectivity, would have been incurred even in the absence of a trade facilitation agenda. Furthermore, an accurate cost assessment needs to factor in linkages between different elements of trade facilitation that cannot be correctly implemented in isolation, such as separation of release from clearance and risk management.

Overall, authorities in the reviewed countries seemed to devote more resources to trade facilitation implementation in 2012 than was the case in the 2005 case studies. However, the amounts were not particularly large compared to the budget and total staff of their Customs agencies. The costs of introducing and implementing trade facilitation measures also need to be seen in the light of their effectiveness and against the significant gains in terms of trade cost reductions (Part II).

In addition, a cost-benefit evaluation of implementing trade facilitation measures should be set against a specific time frame, as some measures may involve important one-off costs but deliver long-term benefits. Institutional reforms take time to implement, and to translate into visible and measurable results. Customs modernisation in particular will result in cost savings, through the ability of the administration to handle a growing number of trade declarations without need for additional staff and through shorter clearance time but more effective screening of cargoes.

Transparency and predictability measures

The most resource-intensive transparency measures seem to concern Internet publication and online enquiry points. The principal challenge of these measures, past the inception stage, which mainly calls for IT equipment and expertise, is to maintain information that is accurate, reliable and updated immediately when changes come into effect. This implies an efficient institutional mechanism for feeding all relevant information: co-ordination by the host agency is useful but can be too resource intensive and ineffective without a timely and proactive supply of information from other relevant agencies. Country experience indicates a disparity between Customs and other border agencies in this regard. Advance ruling mechanisms have become more prevalent over time (73% of the countries covered by the OECD TFIs provide for some type of advance rulings, most often on classification) and do not appear overly expensive to launch.[10]

Procedural simplification and streamlining

Procedural harmonisation and streamlining includes harmonisation and simplification of documentary requirements; pre-arrival lodgement and processing of data; separation of release from clearance; risk management; post-clearance audits; and authorised economic operators.

Costs of automation are both overestimated and underestimated in terms of trade facilitation needs. They are overestimated because automation is generally part of a much larger customs modernisation effort, beyond trade facilitation; and underestimated because the full cost of measures supported by automation, such as risk management, across all concerned agencies are not necessarily captured.

While equipment purchasing and ICT are central for pre-arrival lodgement and processing of data or risk management, training and skills upgrading are critical for their effective implementation and sustainability. For example, one such project involved, in addition to infrastructure and equipment (which included backup generators and CCTV to monitor operations at border checkpoints), capacity building for Customs to effectively manage and maintain the system and its overall ICT infrastructure and network, including by progressively shifting responsibility for support and maintenance of ASYCUDA from UNCTAD staff to customs staff, gradual introduction of a risk management system and support for the design, development and integration of complementary ICT elements associated with the National Single Window.

Special procedures for Authorised Operators (AOs) rely extensively on the availability and efficient operation of risk assessment and audit techniques. They pose the additional challenge of the delicate balance between trust and impartiality in the relationship between the AO and the administration, particularly acute in countries with very small AO programs.

Co-ordination and co-operation between border agencies

As documented in Chapters 3 and 4, co-ordination and co-operation between border agencies and the establishment of Single Windows are currently the most challenging areas for progress in the implementation of trade facilitation reforms. The varying levels of expertise and capacity between border agencies and the reluctance to relinquish controls or abandon previous modes of operation are significant hurdles in the path of reforms. A further challenge is the difficulty of sustaining co-ordinating bodies during their early years of operation. Co-ordination and co-operation with neighbouring countries requires unwavering political will across the border and strong ties and good relations between the parties.

Single Windows are probably the most sophisticated instrument supporting the co-ordination of controls between border agencies, and the single most expensive trade facilitation measure – but also a very significant contributor to reducing trade costs. Beyond the purely financial constraints of purchasing the necessary equipment and software, the main challenges of introducing Single Windows relate to the complex interactions between the multiple entities involved, with each having their own work culture and wishing to retain their *modus operandi*. The task of mapping out each of the processes to be subsumed under the Single Window mechanism can also be complex and time consuming.

Notes

1. The TFA negotiating modalities contained in Annex D of the 2004 WTO General Council Decision stipulated that the negotiations "*shall also address the concerns of developing countries related to cost implications of proposed measures*".

2. For example, in Lao PDR the Second Trade Development Facility Project has included a subcomponent of USD 600 000 for building the capacity of senior and middle managers in all the involved agencies to lead and sustain trade facilitation reforms.
3. International organisations invited by virtue of Annex D of the 2004 WTO General Council Decision "*to undertake a collaborative effort ... to make technical assistance and capacity building more effective and operational and to ensure better coherence*" were since referred to as Annex D organisations. They include the IMF, OECD, UNCTAD, WCO and the World Bank.
4. Between September 2007 and December 2010, 94 needs assessments were undertaken, with another round of assessments launched after the conclusion of the negotiations to help countries prepare their special and differential treatment (SDT) notifications and determine their technical assistance needs (as of June 2017, 78 such assessments had been undertaken by the WTO Secretariat).
5. These include, for example, the WTO material for National Self-Assessments of Trade Facilitation Needs and Priorities, UNCTAD Technical Notes on Trade Facilitation, the WCO World Customs Centre of Learning, and the extensive list of country case studies on various topics of trade facilitation reform presented by WTO Members.
6. The development of a comprehensive human resource development capacity in Lao PDR was assessed at USD 850 000 in the ongoing World Bank Customs and Trade Facilitation Project, covering the establishment of a Customs training centre, endowed with the necessary equipment, the conduct of competency assessments, and the development of a comprehensive training curriculum and training materials, including the translation of WCO e-learning modules into Lao PDR.
7. "The Cost of Introducing and Implementing Trade Facilitation Measures" in *Overcoming Border Bottlenecks, The Costs and Benefits of Trade Facilitation*, OECD 2009.
8. Argentina, Barbados, Burkina Faso, Cambodia, Chile, Colombia, Costa Rica, the Dominican Republic, Jamaica, Kenya, Lao PDR, Latvia, Malaysia, Mauritius, Mongolia, Morocco, Mozambique, Philippines, Senegal, Sierra Leone, Tanzania, Thailand, Uganda and Zambia.
9. Expenditure to establish a Single Window mechanism ranged from EUR 17 million in Mongolia to EUR 3 million in Burkina Faso, with system upgrades costing between EUR 350 000 in Kenya and EUR 960 000 in Costa Rica. However, annual operating expenses ranged from around EUR 33 000 in Mongolia, to EUR 625 000 in Costa Rica. Between 80% and 90% of these amounts were devoted to salaries and the rest to computer equipment maintenance, supplies, insurance and marketing.
10. For example, the introduction of an advance rulings mechanism ranged between EUR 20 000 in Sierra Leone and Mongolia and EUR 25 000 in Kenya.

Bibliography

Moïsé, E. (2013), "The Costs and Challenges of Implementing Trade Facilitation Measures", *OECD Trade Policy Papers*, No. 157, OECD Publishing, Paris, *http://dx.doi.org/10.1787/5k46hzqxt8jh-en*.

OECD (2009), *Overcoming Border Bottlenecks: The Costs and Benefits of Trade Facilitation*, OECD Publishing, Paris, *http://dx.doi.org/10.1787/9789264056954-en*.

OECD-DAC (2018), *Aid activities database* (Creditor Reporting System, CRS), *https://stats.oecd.org/qwids/*.

PART 2

The economic case for trade facilitation

PART 2

Chapter 6

Trade facilitation, trade and global value chains

This chapter explores how specific border measures affect trade and the functioning of supply chains and what policy makers can do to optimise their operation. What are the trade facilitation policies and measures that have the strongest impact in reducing trade costs and enhancing trade flows? Which policies and measures matter most for boosting country participation in global value chains? The assessment focusses on the impact of trade facilitation measures on developing both the supply and the demand side of value chains.

While successive rounds of multilateral trade negotiations have contributed to a steady decline in conventional trade barriers, much remains to be done to lower the costs associated with the conduct of trade. Trade costs arise in getting to the border (such as transport or logistics costs); at or crossing the border, such as documentation and customs compliance requirements, lengthy administrative procedures and other delays; or behind the border, such as non-tariff regulatory measures, and general impediments on doing business (Figure 6.1). While the policies to address trade costs should be comprehensive and address costs at all three stages, the focus of this chapter is on costs arising at the border.

Figure 6.1. **Trade cost diagnostics**

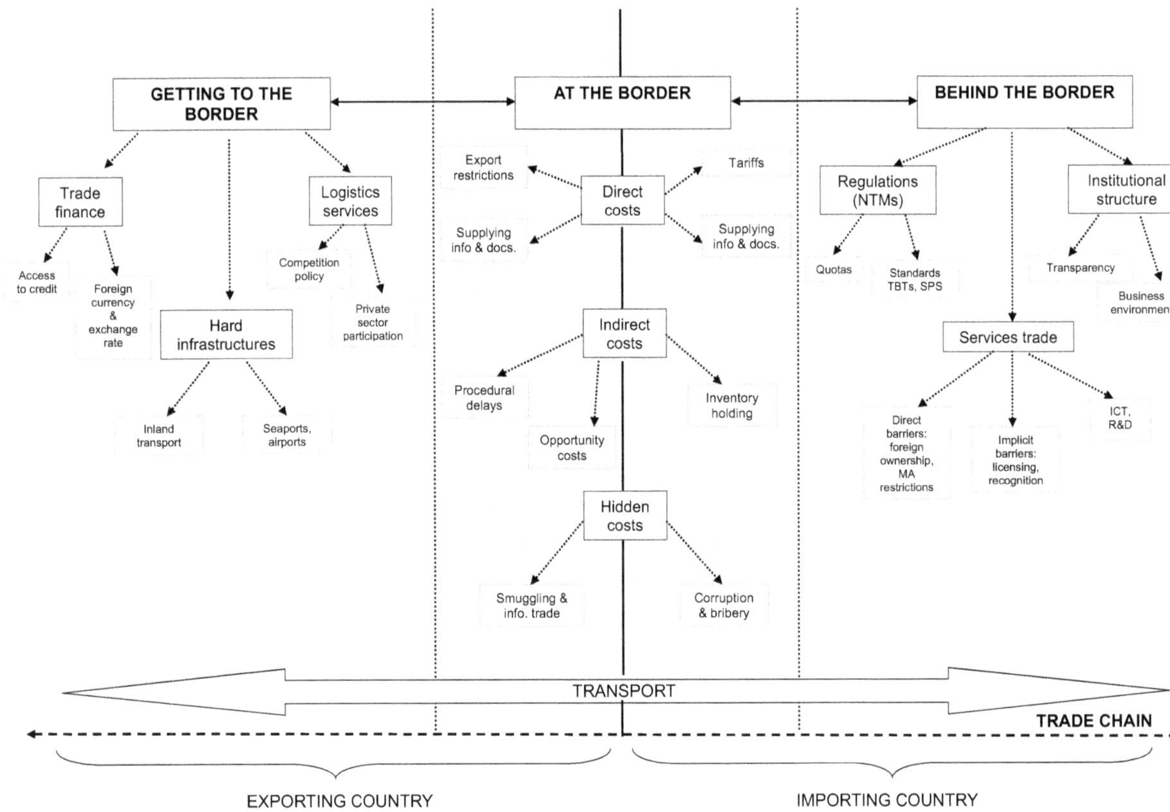

The internationalisation of production through global value chains (GVCs) has given rise to complex cross-border flows of goods, know-how, investment, services, and people. This has created a "magnification effect" for trade costs, as goods may be traded across borders multiple times, first as intermediates and then as final products, before reaching the consumer. Every time unfinished goods are shipped to another country for further processing, they encounter costs associated with border procedures. These costs accumulate and, by the time a finished good reaches its final consumer, these layers of additional costs may affect demand, as well as production and investment, at all stages of the value chain. Participation in a GVC means that trade facilitation actions on both the export and the import side matter for production and competitiveness. Firms involved in GVCs are affected not only by costs incurred at their own borders, but also by those between third countries at points upstream and downstream on the chain. The proliferation of GVCs means that national policies are increasingly interdependent (OECD, 2013).

Lengthy customs procedures or inefficient border infrastructure also add costs in the form of increased uncertainty, in turn constraining the ability of firms to engage in just-in-time production or to react quickly to demand shifts. This can have an impact on inventory management at each stage of production, increasing costs and tying up working capital which could be used more efficiently (OECD, 2013). The more products cross borders during their production, the more significant trade facilitation policies become. Trade in components is particularly time-sensitive: the cost of an extra day spent in transit is 60% higher for importers of intermediate goods than for importers of final goods (Hummels and Schaur, 2012).

Trade facilitation policies can be instrumental in minimising such costs and delays and improving the efficiency of GVCs, especially if undertaken by a large number of countries simultaneously. Such a collective effort could also help ensure that domestic firms in all countries benefit from further opportunities to participate in GVCs (OECD, 2013).

Against this background, this chapter draws on OECD Trade Facilitation Indicators (TFIs) data to explore the impact of implementation of the WTO Trade Facilitation Agreement (TFA) on trade costs, and on countries' participation in GVCs. Beyond the overall impacts of trade facilitation on reducing trade costs, it explores how specific border procedures impact trade costs, trade flows and the functioning of supply chains and the implications for policy.

The impact of the Trade Facilitation Agreement on trade costs

In order to determine how implementation of the TFA affects trade costs, two scenarios are explored: a) "full" implementation, where WTO Members implement all the provisions of the TFA, including those formulated on a "best endeavours" basis; and b) "limited" implementation, where WTO Members implement only the mandatory provisions of the TFA, leaving aside discretionary provisions, but where countries that already implement best practices would continue to do so. These two scenarios provide the upper and lower bounds of the potential reductions in trade costs likely to be achieved through implementation of the TFA (a brief description of the methodology for measuring trade costs is at Annex A). The effects of TFA implementation are considered for a wide range of countries, broken down by income and OECD membership (Figure 6.2) and also by regional grouping (Figure 6.3).

Full implementation of the TFA has the potential to reduce trade costs by around 12% to 18%, varying across country groupings, but with the largest gains accruing to countries in the lower income groupings. By contrast, limited implementation of only the mandatory provisions of the TFA leads to potential reductions in trade costs ranging from 10% to 14% across country groupings, between 2 and 4 percentage points less that than from full implementation. Opportunity costs from less than full implementation are particularly significant for low and lower middle income countries.

Broken down by geographic region, potential trade cost reductions for countries again range from between 14% to 18% (Figure 6.3), with the largest gains accruing to countries in Sub-Saharan Africa and Asia.

These estimates by income grouping or by region are conservative; benefits may be substantially larger, depending on the scope and pace of implementation of the TFA.

Figure 6.2. **Implementation of the TFA lowers trade costs for all countries, but especially for lower income countries**

Potential trade cost reductions by income group (%)

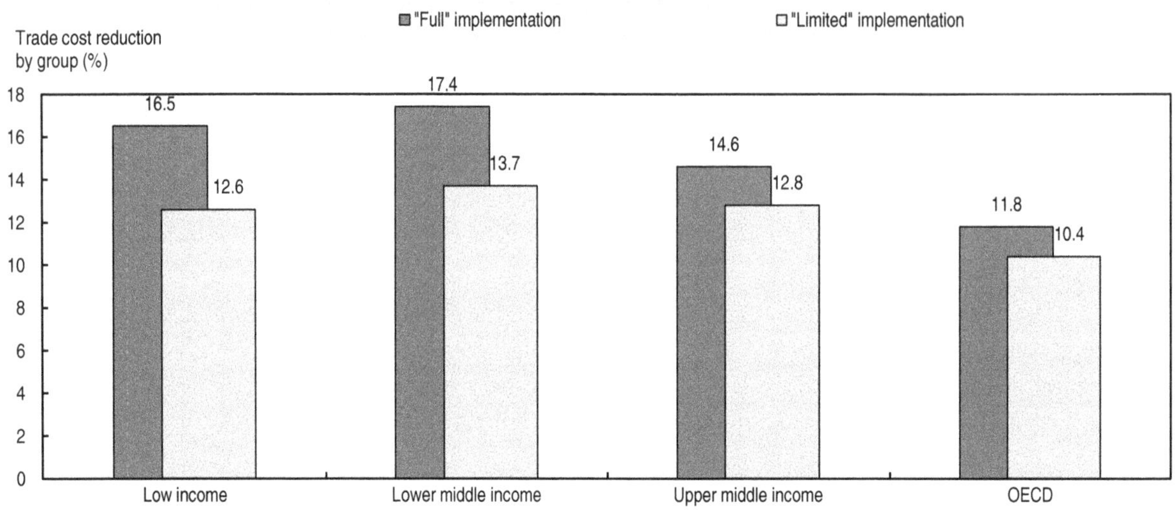

Note: In the "limited" scenario for OECD economies, only their non-OECD trading partners are considered to be implementing solely the mandatory provisions of the Agreement; OECD partners are considered to be undertaking full implementation. Trade costs are estimates from the World Bank – UN ESCAP International Trade Costs Database.

Source: OECD estimates.

Figure 6.3. **Sub-Saharan Africa and Asia stand to gain most from trade facilitation reforms**

Potential trade costs reductions by regions (%)

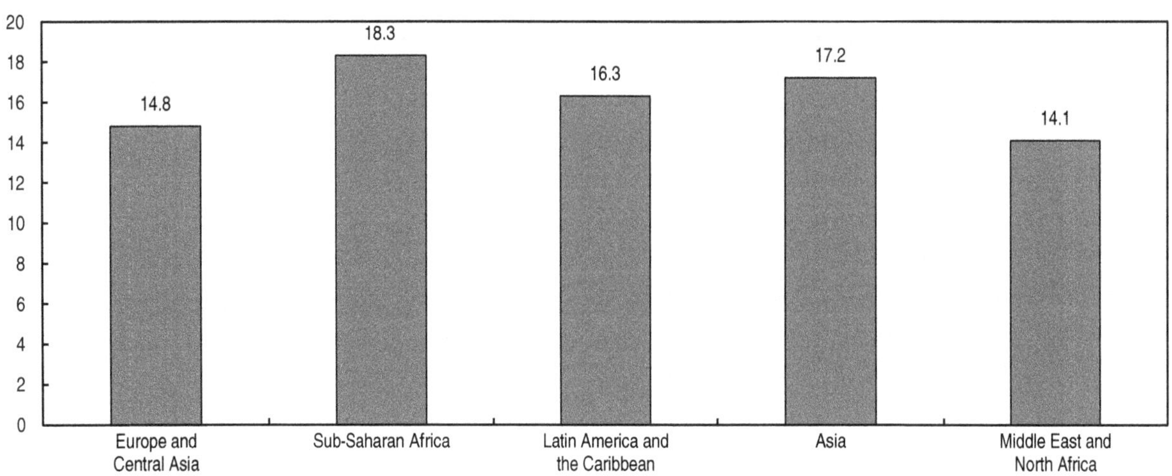

Source: OECD estimates.

Assessment of gains is strongly influenced by whether developing countries will require additional time and technical assistance to implement various measures, and by the timeframes for implementation.

Which trade facilitation measures matter most in reducing trade costs?

Beyond the overall impacts of trade facilitation on reducing trade costs, how do *specific* border procedures impact trade costs?

While their precise contribution varies, across all income groups, the policies that contribute most to reducing trade costs are the harmonisation and simplification of trade documents, the automation of border processes, the streamlining of trade procedures and formalities and the availability of information.[1] These same measures also have the strongest impact on reducing trade costs when countries are considered by geographical group (Figure 6.4).

Figure 6.4. **Some trade facilitation measures are particularly important for cutting trade costs**

Potential trade costs reductions for the "top" sets of measures (%)

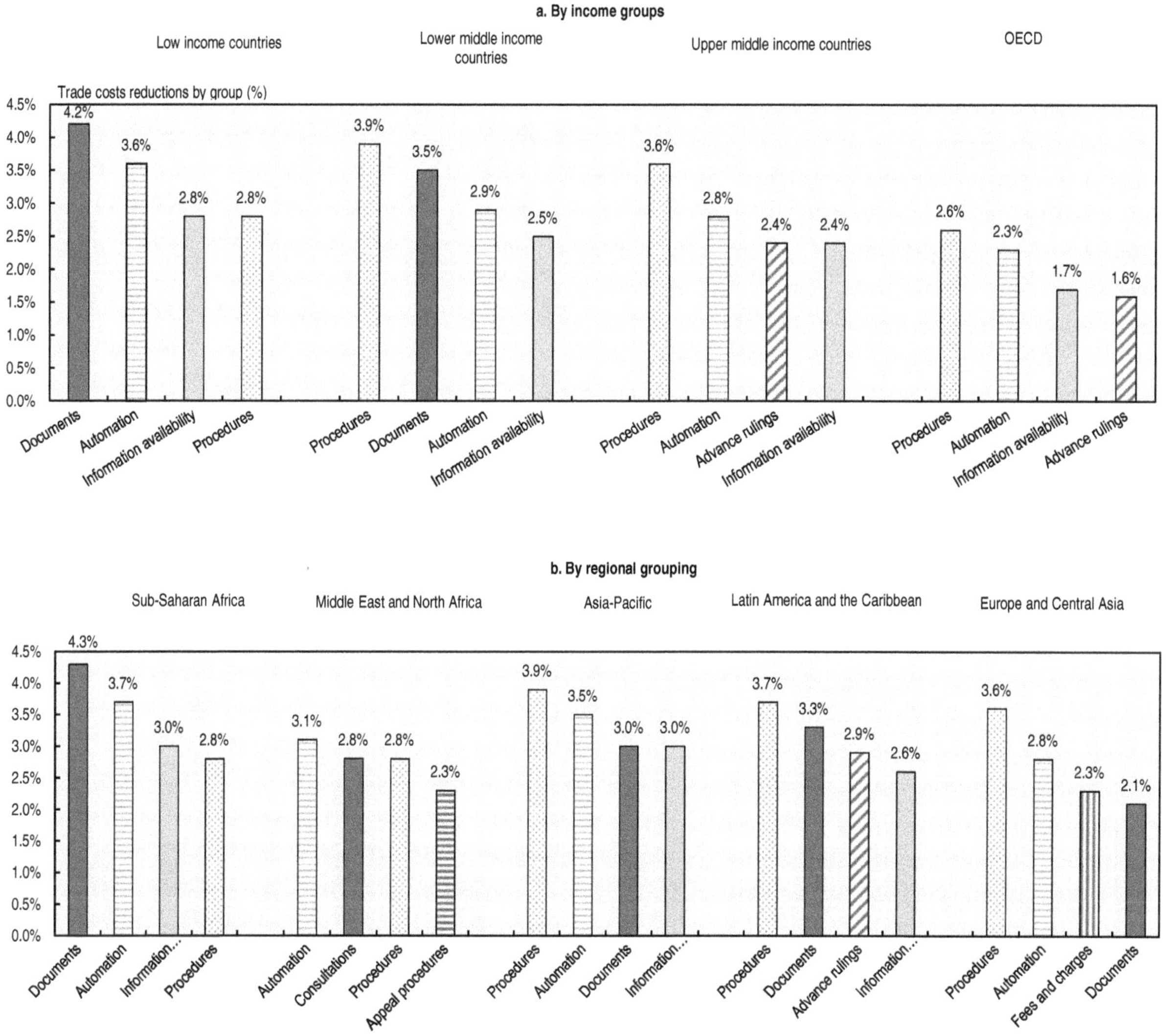

Source: OECD estimates, based on a scenario of full implementation of the TFA.

The combined effect of implementing all measures under the TFA is greater than the sum of the individual components.[2] This shows the additional benefits that can accrue when reforms are taken together and underscores the importance of undertaking trade facilitation in a comprehensive manner. It also underscores that potential cost reductions stand to benefit stakeholders as a whole, including both traders (importing and exporting firms), as well as public administrations.

The potential impact of trade facilitation on the operation of supply chains

The potential of trade facilitation measures to reduce trade costs can also affect participation in supply chains.[3] That is, they can shape the extent to which a given country's exports are used by firms in partner countries as inputs into their own exports (forward linkages, or selling into GVCs) and they can influence the extent to which foreign intermediate inputs are used in the exports of a given country (backward linkages, or buying from GVCs). (A brief description of the methodology for analysing impacts on GVCs participation is found in Annex A).

Trade facilitation can boost the demand side of value chains

The "demand" side of GVC activity (buying from GVCs, or backward linkages) is captured by imports of value-added. These backward linkages show the origin of foreign value-added components of final goods consumed in a given country, and the extent to which final users are connected to suppliers abroad. A country where inputs can be imported quickly and reliably is attractive to companies looking to build or integrate into GVCs: a relatively small increase in a country's trade facilitation performance (as measured by the TFIs) of 0.1 units can generate increases in imports of value-added ranging from 1.5 to 3.5% (Figure 6.5). The trade facilitation measures that appear to be most important in encouraging these "backward" linkages in GVCs are (in order of magnitude): availability of advance rulings; streamlining of border procedures and controls; proportionality and transparency of import and export fees and charges; and automation of border processes.

Figure 6.5. **Trade facilitation can boost participation in GVCs**

Improvements in TFIs and GVC participation

Potential increases in value-added trade from an increase in TFIs of 0.1 (%)

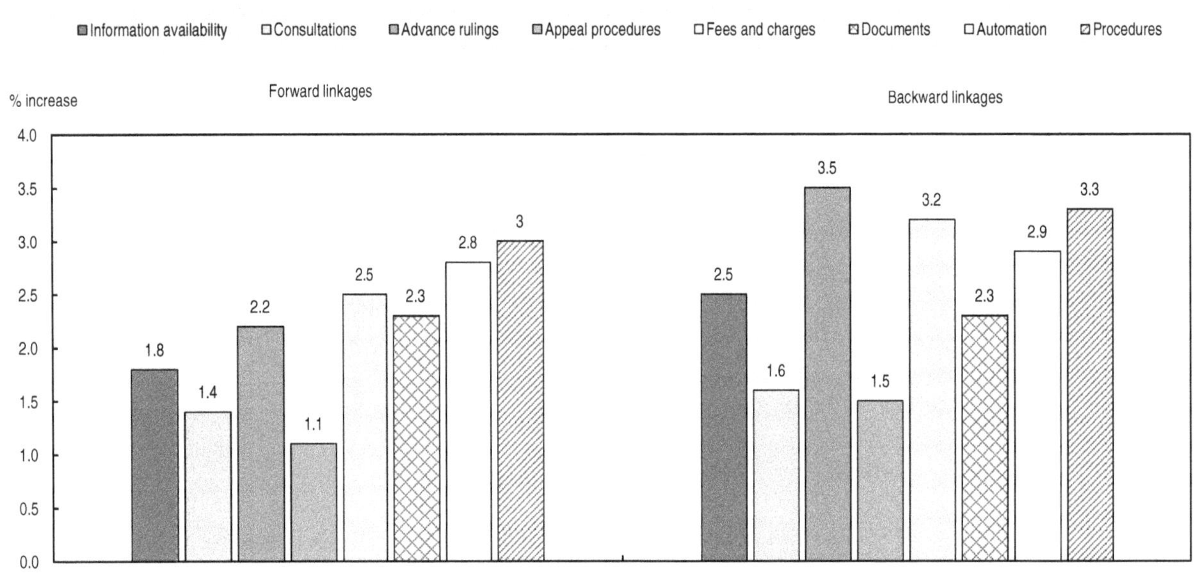

Source: Moïsé and Sorescu (2015).

Advance rulings bring higher certainty, predictability and reliability to the supply chain: the ability to know in advance how goods will be treated on a number of Customs issues, and that these determinations will be binding on all customs offices over a specified period of time, allows companies to minimise policy-related risks in their sourcing decisions. Similarly, it is the predictability afforded by the TFA's *disciplines on fees and charges* rather than the direct cost they represent for the trader that is most important in explaining the importance of these measures for GVC participation.

Streamlined border procedures and controls enable faster movement of imported value-added through measures such as submission of trade documents through Single Windows; processing of documents prior to arrival of goods; rationalisation of physical inspections; and efficient use of guarantees or post-clearance audits (PCAs) to allow faster release of goods. In particular, the trend towards Single Windows and grouping of documents required by various border agencies is generating impressive efficiency gains. Additional facilitation measures offered to trusted traders under Authorised Operators (AO) programmes, such as single customs declarations for all imports and exports in a given period, or goods clearance at the trader's premises, also help ensure the timely availability of imported inputs. Finally, *automation of procedures* also leads to greater speed and efficiency, by reducing the compliance costs associated with transmitting and processing trade information, and by enabling targeted controls based on risk management approaches.

Box 6.1. **Trade facilitation is particularly important in some sectors**

The impact of trade facilitation is most significant when imported inputs feed into a high or medium-high tech sector in GVCs. This is the case whether the input is relatively low or medium-tech, such as basic metals, or mining and quarrying, or medium-high or high tech, such as transport equipment, chemicals and electrical and optical equipment.

The trade facilitation measures that seem to matter most in terms of the backward linkages in these GVCs are the availability of trade-related information; opportunities for dialogue with the trade community; availability of advance rulings; simplification and harmonisation of trade documents; and streamlining of border procedures and controls.

Sufficient and easily accessible, up-to-date trade-related information, as well as simplified and internationally harmonised documentary requirements appear also to be particularly important in the case of foreign sourcing of inputs for the transport equipment, chemicals, and electrical and optical equipment sectors.

Trade facilitation can bolster the supply side of value chains

The "supply" side of the value chain activity (selling into GVCs, or forward linkages) is captured by exports of value-added. These forward linkages show how firms export value both through direct exports of final goods and indirectly, via exports of intermediates to other countries which then process them and sell or export them to final users. The most important trade facilitation measures in terms of how efficiently a country can export value-added into GVCs are: availability of trade-related information; opportunities for dialogue with the trade community; proportionality and transparency of import and export fees and charges; automation of the border process; and streamlining of border procedures and controls. In terms of forward linkages into GVCs, a 0.1 units improvement in trade facilitation policies (as measured by the TFIs) can generate increases in a country's value-added exports ranging between 1 and 2.5% (Figure 6.5).

Trade facilitation is central to countries' ability to benefit from GVCs

Both forward and backward linkages matter for GVC participation. Countries can increase their GVC participation both by increasing the imported content of their exports (increasing their backward linkages) and by creating more value-added through goods and services for use as inputs in the exports of third countries (increasing their forward linkages). Moreover, there can be a virtuous circle between importing and exporting in GVCs: evidence (OECD, 2013) suggests that the use of foreign value added is one of the most important factors in determining growth in domestic value added in exports across all types of activities (agriculture, manufacturing and services) for developed and emerging economies alike.

In a world of GVCs, where exports competitiveness requires import openness, border processes are crucial for lowering trade costs, participation in GVCs and overall competitiveness (OECD, 2013) – with significant benefits to be gained from the pursuit of even greater procedural efficiency. Policies promoting transparency and predictability and removing unnecessary transmission and processing costs are the most critical in supporting participation in GVCs. However, these findings also show that the decision to segment production across countries in a GVC is facilitated not only by the predictability and speed of the border process from advance rulings and streamlined procedures, and the harmonisation and simplification of trade documents, but also by the climate of trust that comes from a transparent, accountable regulatory environment, open to dialogue with economic operators.

Moreover, there appears to be a strong positive correlation between participation in GVCs and growth (measured in GDP per capita). By helping to promote participation in GVCs, trade facilitation reforms have significant potential to help generate higher growth. The question of the impact of trade facilitation on the economy as a whole building on the insights from GVCs is taken up further in the following chapter.

Notes

1. Other measures under the TFA are: dialogue with the trade community; the existence and operation of advance ruling mechanisms; the availability and performance of appeal procedures; disciplines on fees, charges and penalties; co-operation among domestic agencies responsible for border controls and trade procedures; and cross-border co-operation among countries' agencies responsible for border controls and trade procedures (Box 6.1)
2. This is the case even when all elements of the WTO TFA (outlined in the footnote above) are included in the calculation.
3. The impact of trade facilitation improvements on GVC participation can be tested using OECD-WTO Trade in Value Added (TiVA) indicators. TiVA indicators track both the direct and indirect flows of value added associated with international trade, thus revealing bilateral trade in value-added even when bilateral gross trade flows might be zero.

Bibliography

Hummels, D. and G. Schaur (2012), "Time as a Trade Barrier", *NBER Working Paper* No. 17758.

Johnson, R.C. and G. Noguera (2012), "Fragmentation and Trade in Value Added Over Four Decades", *NBER Working Paper* No. 18186, June.

Koopman, R., Z. Wang and S.J. Wei (2014), "How Much Chinese Exports Is Really Made in China – Assessing Foreign and Domestic Value-Added in Gross Exports", NBER *Working Paper* No. 14109.

Moïsé, E., T. Orliac and P. Minor (2011), "Trade Facilitation Indicators: The Impact on Trade Costs", *OECD Trade Policy Papers* No. 118, OECD Publishing, Paris, *http://dx.doi.org/10.1787/5kg6nk654hmr-en.*

Moïsé, E. and S. Sorescu (2015), "Contribution of Trade Facilitation Measures to the Operation of Supply Chains", *OECD Trade Policy Papers*, No. 181, OECD Publishing, Paris, *http://dx.doi.org/10.1787/5js0bslh9m25-en.*

Moïsé, E. and S. Sorescu (2013), "Trade Facilitation Indicators: The Potential Impacts on Developing Countries' Trade", *OECD Trade Policy Papers* No. 144, OECD Publishing, Paris, *http://dx.doi.org/10.1787/5k4bw6kg6ws2-en.*

OECD (2015), *Implementation of the WTO Trade Facilitation Agreement: The Potential Impact on Trade Costs*, OECD Policy Brief.

OECD (2013), "Implications of Global Value Chains for Trade Policy", in *Interconnected Economies: Benefiting from Global Value Chains*, OECD Publishing, Paris, *http://dx.doi.org/10.1787/9789264189560-en.*

Kowalski, P. et al. (2015), "Participation of Developing Countries in Global Value Chains: Implications for Trade and Trade-Related Policies", *OECD Trade Policy Papers*, No. 179, OECD Publishing, Paris, *http://dx.doi.org/10.1787/5js33lfw0xxn-en.*

OECD-WTO (2013), "Trade in Value-Added: Concepts, Methodologies and Challenges", joint OECD-WTO Note.

OECD, WTO and World Bank (2014), "Global Value Chains: Challenges, Opportunities, and Implications for Policy", Report prepared for submission to the G20 Trade Ministers Meeting, Sydney, July.

OECD, WTO and UNCTAD (2013), "Implications of Global Value Chains for Trade, Investment, Development and Jobs", Report prepared for the G-20 Leaders Summit Saint Petersburg, September.

UNCTAD (2013), "World Investment Report 2013: Global Value Chains: Investment and Trade for Development", *http://unctad.org/en/PublicationsLibrary/wir2013_en.pdf.*

PART 2

Chapter 7

Economy-wide impacts of trade facilitation

A full and swift implementation of the WTO Trade Facilitation Agreement (TFA) has the potential to generate important global economic benefits but quantifying these poses serious challenges. This chapter draws on analysis using the OECD METRO model to document the channels through which trade facilitation reforms can benefit the global economy and the distribution of those potential benefits across country groupings and sectors over the short and longer term. Impacts on labour income and employment and welfare over the longer term are also explored.

Beyond the reduction in worldwide trade costs, a full and swift implementation of the Trade Facilitation Agreement (TFA) has the potential to generate important global economic benefits. But how can these economy-wide benefits be measured? This chapter draws on analysis using the OECD's METRO model (Box 7.1) to document the channels through which trade facilitation reform can benefit the global economy, and to discuss the distribution of potential benefits across country groupings at different levels of development, across different sectors and on different use markets (i.e. intermediate, household, government and capital).

Capturing the economy-wide impacts of trade facilitation

Border procedures and formalities can have economy-wide impacts through different channels, including *price* and *efficiency* effects. *Price effects* increase the price of traded products over what they would otherwise be, with a generally dampening effect on the level of trade. They can be either direct, as in payments of customs fees, or indirect, as in costs resulting from inefficient and burdensome trading processes, as well as border clearance delays. *Efficiency effects* can arise from distortions in the allocation of resources in the economy. Both price and efficiency effects generate welfare losses for consumers and producers in both importing and exporting countries (OECD, 2009).

The nature and magnitude of the effects may differ depending on the type of products traded. For highly perishable products, delays at the border can generate product losses or increased costs for storage and refrigeration, imposing depreciation and inventory holding costs (including high opportunity costs). Multi-stage production may be especially sensitive to lags and variability in timely delivery. Most large manufacturers are heavily dependent on frequent and timely delivery of raw materials and intermediate goods for their production processes. When consumer preferences are taken into account, speed and flexibility also play a key role – especially where there is uncertainty in the quantity likely to be demanded, product quality, or desired product characteristics (this is particularly the case for products subject to changing consumer preferences, such as fashion clothing items or fashionable toys). Moreover, if the product has a limited shelf life, then prolonged waits at the border could be enough to take the product out of the market (OECD, 2009; Walmsley and Minor, 2016).

Trade facilitation generates efficiency gains from reduced shipping losses

Time savings associated with the elimination of customs-related delays can have an effect on international trade by reducing both "spoilage" and inventory holding costs (Hummels, 2001). Inventory costs include not only the capital costs of the goods while they are in transit, but also costs related to the need to hold larger inventories to accommodate variation in arrival time. These latter costs have become increasingly important due to the use of "just in time" production techniques (Hertel et al., 2001). Speedy delivery is critical for goods subject to rapid depreciation and for which demand is uncertain, but is less important for bulk commodities and simple manufactures (Hummels et al., 2007).

Losses and costs associated with border inefficiencies, spoilage or inventory holding can be modelled following the widely-used *iceberg* cost approach. The idea behind this approach is that the costs of transporting a good are being paid for by a portion of the transported good, rather than any other resources (Samuelson, 1954). Like an iceberg, the value of the product "melts" away, as it is "towed" to more distant destinations. Inefficient trade procedures increase the cost of trade and drive a wedge between the price received by the producer of the good and the price paid by the consumer – a pure deadweight loss. Following this "sand in the wheels" approach (Fugazza and Maur, 2008) for depicting efficiency losses, various empirical studies have tried to account for both direct and indirect transaction costs associated with trade facilitation deficiencies, to translate trade facilitation improvements into technological progress in trading activities, and to capture the magnitude and sources of indirect transaction costs.

In essence, the approach assumes that implementation of trade facilitation reforms lowers the iceberg costs of trade – meaning that for the same amount of imports sent, more will arrive at their destination than prior to the reforms. This approach is appropriate when time delays lead to real costs for importing firms, such as when agro-food products spoil due to long delays in customs or when the delay of an imported intermediate triggers delays in the entire production process. In many cases, however, such time delays are an inconvenience, rather than a real cost. In those cases, using the iceberg approach alone is likely to overstate the impact of a full implementation of the TFA on real costs and hence real GDP (Walmsley and Minor, 2016).

Trade facilitation generates gains associated with speed of delivery

Border procedures also need to be assessed in the context of dynamic production networks and fast-evolving consumer tastes. In the case of agro-food products, spoilage may not only affect the product quantity arriving in the market (as in the iceberg approach), but also influence consumer willingness to pay for that product. Assuming that both the quantity and quality of these products will lessen along the way, their importers will factor this into the price they are willing to pay for the goods, so as to account for any losses selling them on to customers.

Timeliness is also important when demand is uncertain, a characteristic of "lean retailing" in modern textile or apparel supply chains (Evans and Harrigan, 2005). Long lags between ordering and delivery require firms to commit to product specifications and quantities to be supplied before they can be certain as to the extent of demand (Hummels and Schaur, 2013). Consumer tastes are volatile, and retailers face the prospect of having to liquidate vast inventories of unpopular clothing at the end of a selling season or of running short of suddenly popular styles. "Lean retailing" – the combination of low inventories and frequent restocking – offers a partial solution to these problems. With low inventories, stores will not be stuck with large amounts of unsold goods even if demand collapses; the essence of lean retailing is to respond rapidly to demand fluctuations instead of holding large inventories. For producers, lean retailing demands great flexibility. If they want to sell to lean retailers, producers must be able to adjust output rapidly and ship products quickly. The benefit for flexible producers is that they can charge a premium over their less flexible competitors, who can compete only on selling cost and not on timeliness (Evans and Harrigan, 2005). But importers and exporters cannot be flexible without smooth border procedures.

In order to capture the importance of timeliness for the user or consumer, Walmsley and Minor (2016) developed a *willingness to pay* approach for trade facilitation. Consistent with previous literature,[1] the newly-developed alternative approach holds that consumers prefer goods delivered more quickly and are willing to pay more for them. This is true not only for final products, but also for intermediate goods throughout the supply chain. For firms, the ability to defer import decisions until better market knowledge is obtained, and then to receive those imports quickly once a decision has been made, has distinct advantages for retailers and importers (Walmsley and Minor, 2016). So, the *willingness to pay* approach explicitly treats the reduction in customs delays from the demand side as an increase in the consumer willingness to pay for faster delivery.

Quantifying the economy-wide impacts of trade facilitation and identifying the channels for these impacts and the implications for reform thus represents a major analytical challenge. The choice of the transmission mechanisms outlined above – willingness to pay or iceberg costs – can have important consequences for the estimated impacts in terms of GDP, trade, and welfare (Walmsley and Minor, 2016). A new approach to addressing this issue, by combining both the approaches above, is set out below.

A new approach to assessing the economy-wide impacts of trade facilitation reforms

A new approach to assessing the potential economy-wide impacts of full TFA implementation is to combine the two approaches described above in a single model, in this case, METRO, the OECD's static multi-regional computable general equilibrium (CGE) model (Box 7.1). Under this new approach, trade facilitation reforms are depicted partly as reducing losses ("iceberg costs") on the producer side, and partly as increasing "willingness to pay" on the consumer side. Both effects are likely to occur when trade facilitation measures are introduced: losses from shipping and clearance delays are likely to be reduced; and, in the context of GVCs and rapidly changing consumer preferences, firms and consumers are more willing to pay more for a product delivered faster and from which they therefore get greater use.

Improved product delivery times thus change the incentives for economic agents and ultimately impact worldwide production and consumption patterns, including changes in prices of inputs and outputs, overall production, and trade of goods and services. Employment and wages can also be affected, depending on the adjustment possibilities in the labour market and on how labour is employed across sectors.[2] These effects are explored further below.

In the short term, trade facilitation reforms bring efficiency-related gains

Over the short term, the ability of economies to adjust to changing market conditions is more limited; investment and government expenditures, for instance, are already committed. In addition, labour markets are more likely to be characterised by wage and other rigidities and unemployment. The analysis below of the efficiency effects of full implementation of the TFA in the short-term is based on these constraints.

Reducing inefficiencies and delivery delays increases GVC trade, especially for developing countries

Benefitting from GVCs depends not only on firms' ability to manage exporting costs, but also whether they have access to competitively-priced inputs, know-how and

Box 7.1. **The OECD METRO model**

In 2015, the OECD launched a new global computable general equilibrium (CGE) trade model, known as METRO (ModElling TRade at the OECD). CGE models are computer simulation models that use data to explore the economic impact of changes in policy, technology and other factors. They show how different sectors inside one economy are linked and how multiple economies are connected to each other, as well as how resources such as labour, capital and natural resources are best allocated across all economic activities.[1]

The METRO database currently covers 61 economies across 57 economic sectors. It is based on the GTAP (Global Trade Analysis Project) database, but allows users to analyse global value chains (GVCs) by drawing on the OECD-WTO Trade in Value Added (TiVA) database. METRO more fully integrates structural policy issues into trade policy analysis, and features an extensive library of trade-related policies, including current border tariff rates and export restrictions, as well as domestic taxes and support. Using METRO, it is now possible to track trade flows by their use (i.e. intermediate, household, government and investment) and to trace bilateral links between source and destination markets, greatly enhancing the ability to model movements of goods and services, especially along GVCs.

Incorporating the TFIs into the METRO model allows analysis to capture how changes in trade facilitation policies affect interconnected modes of production. This provides a means of tracing and quantifying the economy-wide effects of trade facilitation reforms.

1. The METRO model builds on the GLOBE model developed by Scott McDonald and Karen Thierfelder (2013).
Source: OECD (2015).

technologies (Lopez Gonzalez, 2016). Firms using a higher share of imported intermediates can enhance their productivity – via both the use of more varieties of (and potentially more competitively priced) intermediates, and the technology transfers "embodied" in foreign intermediates – and this allows them to access new export markets.[3]

By significantly reducing trade transaction costs and clearance times, worldwide implementation of the TFA has the potential to increase world trade by 0.6% compared to the base.[4] Trade increases in all sectors, including the agro-food sector, with manufacturing sectors showing the highest growth rates (Figure 7.1).

Trade in covered sector groups increases between 0.2 and 1%. Intermediates account for the largest share of this increase for the majority of selected sectors, in particular those sectors[5] characterised by strong GVCs linkages where firms are likely to see further cost savings from "just-in-time" access to a higher variety of competitively-priced intermediate inputs. Broken down by country, intermediates also account for the largest increase in exports from developing and emerging economies, underscoring the new opportunities offered to these countries by GVCs to engage in global markets without having to develop complete products.

Trade also increases for countries at all levels of development (Figure 7.2), with the countries in the low income country (LIC), lower middle income country (LMIC) and OECD groups increasing exports more than imports (for LICs, the increase in exports is twice as high as the increase in imports). While the largest share of the increase in imports is goods and services for final consumption, increasing imports of intermediates appears to be particularly important in enhancing LICs' competitiveness.

Figure 7.1. **In the short-term, full implementation of the TFA would increase trade in all sectors**

Trade effects by commodity (% changes by end use categories, short term)

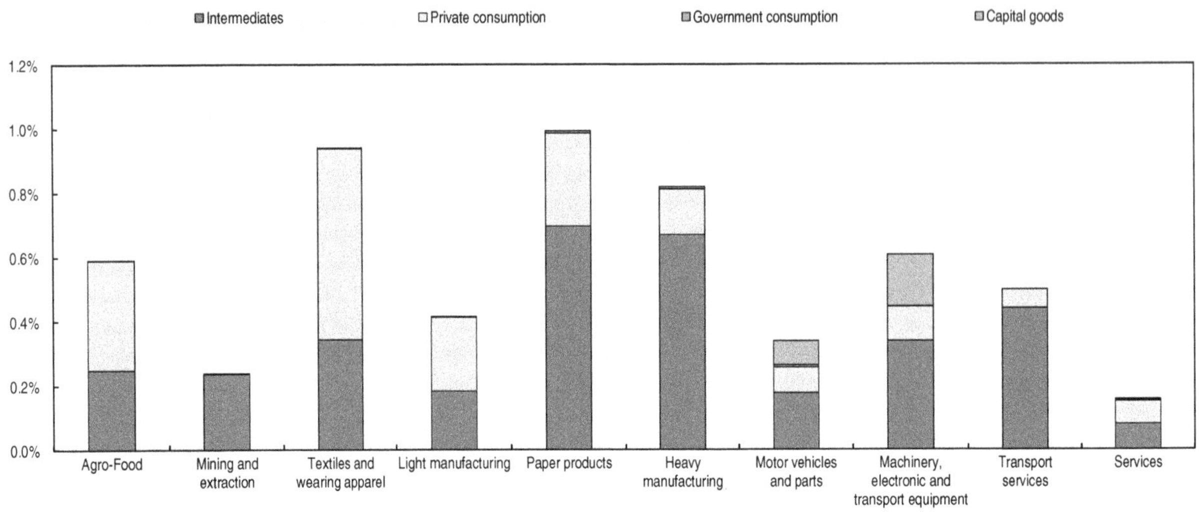

Source: OECD METRO model simulation results.

Figure 7.2. **Implementation of the TFA increases trade for countries at all levels of development, especially in intermediates**

Impacts on imports and exports by income group (% changes to base, short term)

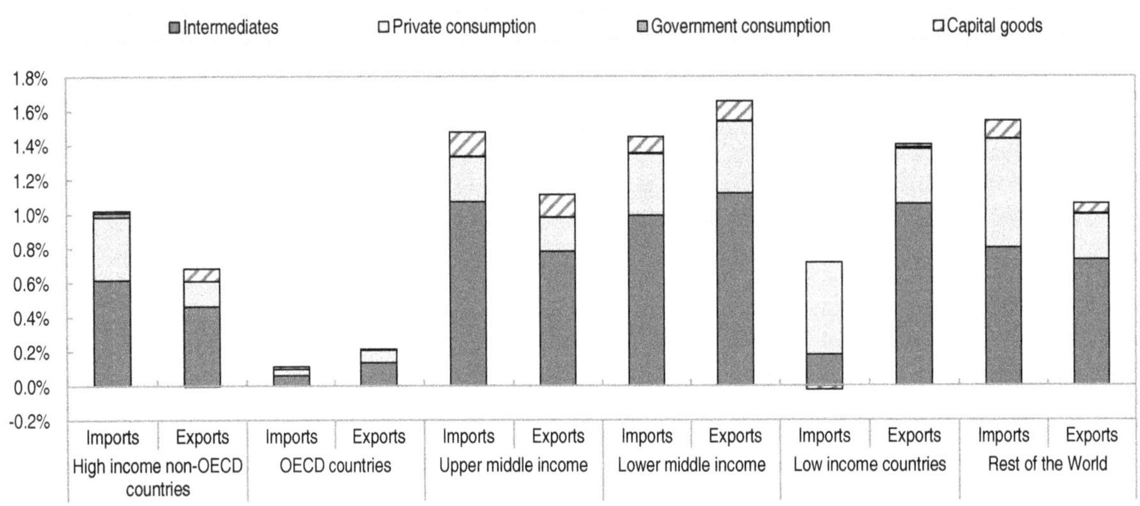

Source: METRO simulation results.

Falling input costs from trade facilitation reforms trigger production increases for all regions

Beyond trade, trade facilitation reforms generate positive effects on production by contributing to lowering overall input costs. This is the case across the large majority of sectors, with the exception of agro-food products (Figure 7.3) reflecting the agricultural sector's relatively small share of use of intermediates relative to primary production factors.[6] Lower costs for intermediate inputs are most pronounced in the machinery, transport and electronic equipment; heavy manufacturing; and transport service sectors. This indicates that importing also helps firms to remain competitive in the domestic economy, such that sectors not only benefit from lower costs for their own imported intermediates, but also from lower costs for domestically produced intermediates.

Figure 7.3. **Implementation of the TFA lowers the costs of inputs for almost all sectors**

Intermediate inputs costs, by sector and income group (% change to the base, short term)

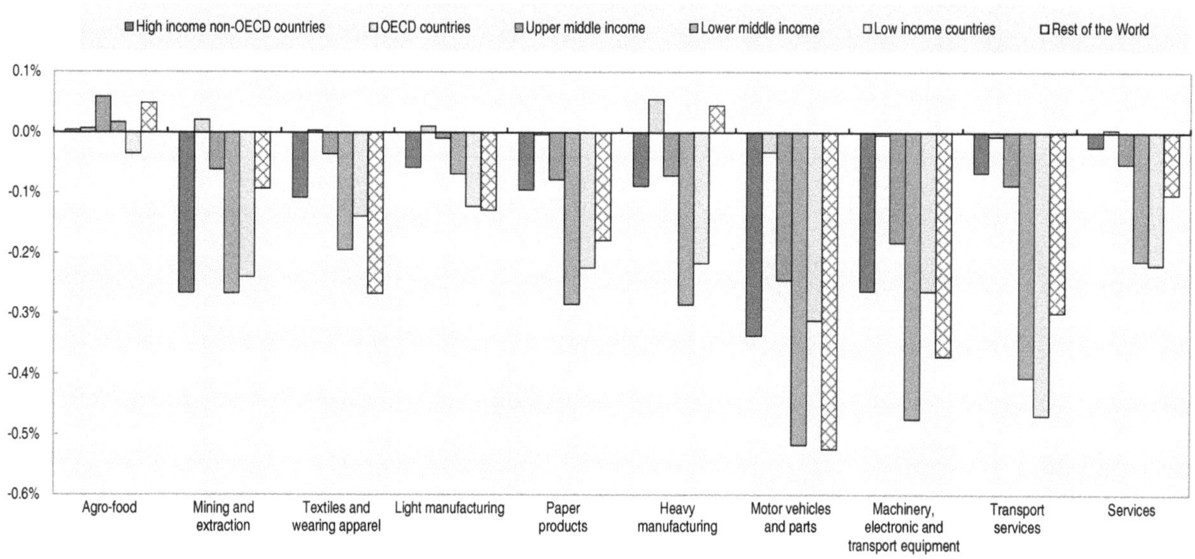

Source: OECD METRO model simulation results.

Production increases across all countries and almost all sectors

Declining inputs costs lower output prices and generate a positive impact on both domestic and export demand, and this in turn stimulates production. Full implementation of the TFA sees overall output levels increase by up to 0.5% across all income groups, with the strongest increases for LICs and LMICs, followed by high income countries (HICs) outside the OECD area and countries in the Rest of the World (RoW) (Figure 7.4). OECD countries experience smaller trade and production effects compared to other selected regions because of their already high level of trade facilitation performance and faster clearance times.

Output expands the most for the agro-food and heavy manufacturing sectors, across all the developing and emerging economy groups (including LICs, LMICs, upper middle income countries, and RoW).[7] A key share of this worldwide output increase comes from expansion of the services sectors, highlighting the importance of services both in connecting different production segments and as an increasingly important input to production processes. These "real" increases in output levels are complemented by the efficiency increase from improvements in trade facilitation (Figure 7.4) which reduce quality losses and shorten border processing time, increasing firms' and consumers' willingness to pay (WTP).

Regional gains vary, reflecting improved output in areas of comparative advantage for the selected regions. In Southeast and South Asia, the greatest expansion is in the heavy manufacturing, textile and wearing apparel, machinery, electronic and transport equipment, and services sectors. In South America and Sub-Saharan Africa, output increases in the agro-food sector, as well as heavy manufacturing and services. In other regions, such as North America and Europe, production increase is dominated by services.

Across all regions, the expansion of manufacturing is strongly linked to a growing role for services (Figure 7.5).

Figure 7.4. **By lowering input costs and raising efficiency, trade facilitation increases output across all regions**

Production effects by income region and sector (% change to base, short term)

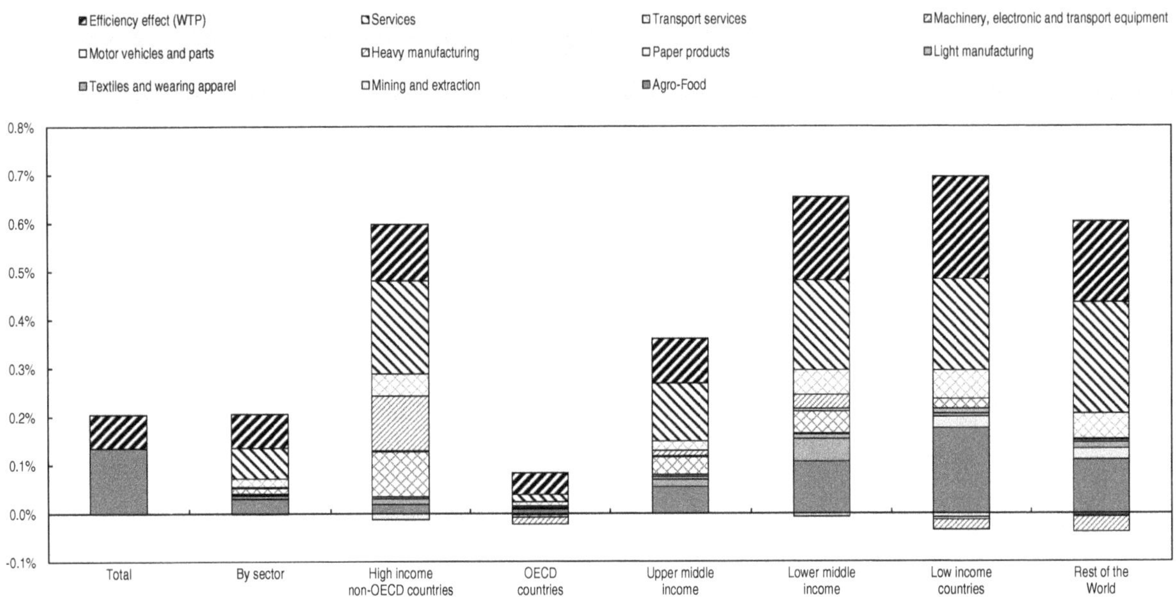

Note: The sectoral change represents the contribution to the overall production change of a country group. The efficiency effect (WTP) depicts the higher levels of utility resulting from faster delivery times. This applies for all production and welfare analysis charts.
Source: OECD METRO model simulation results.

Figure 7.5. **Manufacturing gains across all regions, but the role of services is increasing**

Production effects by geographical region and sector (% change to base, short term)

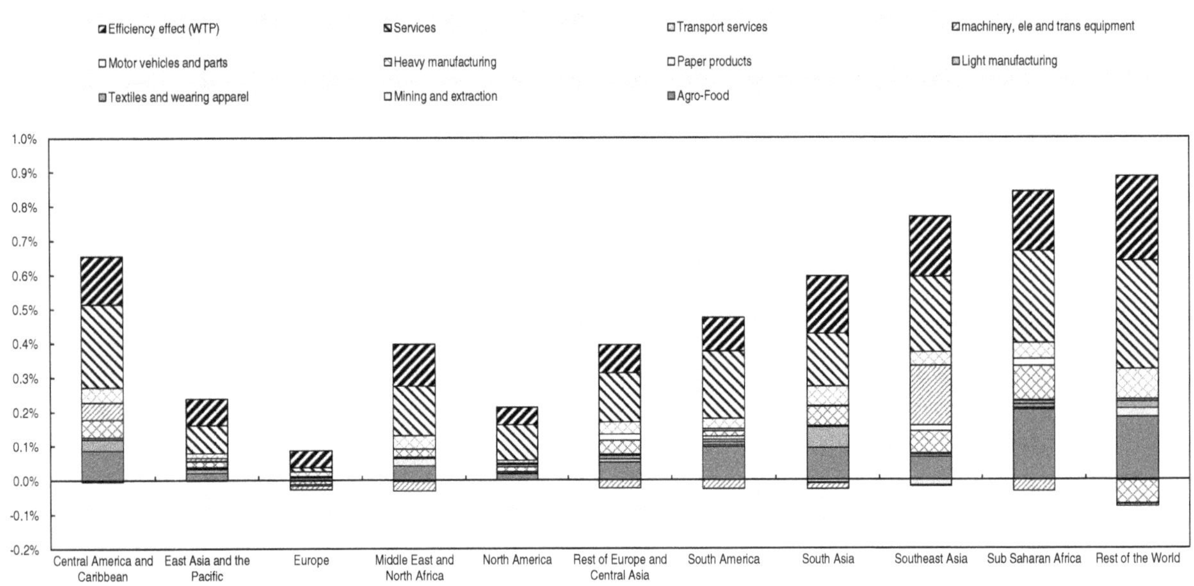

Source: OECD METRO model simulation results.

Over the long-term trade facilitation impacts resources allocation and wages

In the longer run, labour markets adjust to changing production needs through more flexible wage rates which sustain employment levels, so an assumption of full employment can be used. The longer-term scenario highlights the broader economic benefits that can stem from the efficiency spill-overs of trade facilitation reforms over a longer-term horizon, along with the associated impacts on the allocation of resources across sectors and on wages.

It leads to more efficient production and resource allocation

Over the longer term, improved worldwide trade facilitation performance would encourage specialisation and the reallocation of resources towards those activities that reflect a country's comparative advantage, again leading to increased production. Increased efficiency and lower costs, including from greater use of imported intermediates, would intensify the competition faced by domestic producers, leading to more efficient allocation and use of resources.[8] In a scenario where factors are free to adjust, increased competition would trigger production shifts both between and within regions. At the domestic level, certain sectors would grow by sourcing labour from other sectors. At the global level, intensifying competition in the world market may further increase price reductions triggered by trade facilitation.

In the longer run, the economic efficiency and competition gains spurred by trade facilitation would have positive effects on aggregate production across all regions, reaching up to 0.4% in Southeast Asia (Figure 7.6). As in the short-term, overall benefits from trade facilitation reforms would consist of both "real" production effects and increased willingness to pay derived from faster delivery times and reduced quality losses (reflecting increased utility for consumers and users). Production in Southeast Asia increases most in the machinery, transport and electronic equipment sectors, while South Asia shows potential to increase production in heavy manufacturing and textiles. There is also a key

Figure 7.6. **In the long term, production shifts take place within and among regions**

Production effects by geographical region and sector (% change to base, long term)

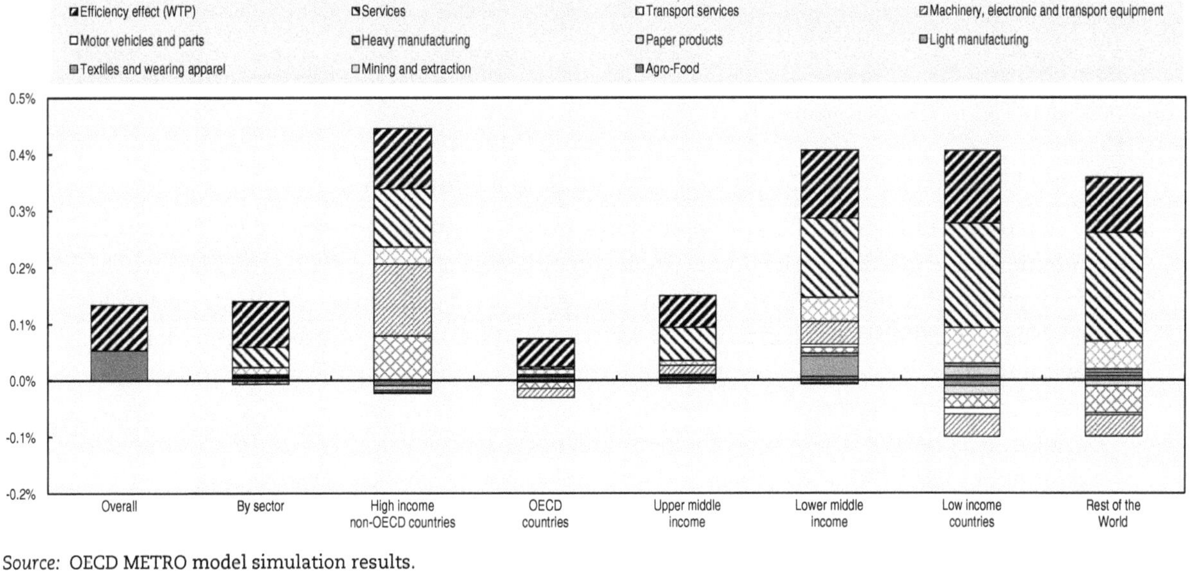

Source: OECD METRO model simulation results.

role for services (including transport services) for developing the production base in the Asian region. In Sub-Saharan Africa, notable increases would be experienced in the heavy manufacturing, motor vehicles and parts, and services sectors. Production in MENA is dominated by expansion in services, linked to the availability of cheaper imports of consumer goods, which encourages a shift in domestic production towards services.

And increased incomes

In the long run, trade facilitation reforms would also translate into rising incomes (Figure 7.7). All labour categories in developing and emerging economies, skilled and unskilled, would experience higher returns in the range of 0.3%, with the largest effects in LICs, LMICs, HICs outside the OECD area, and RoW. In OECD countries, income effects are more modest, given their already high level of trade facilitation performance and faster clearance times.

The rise in income also leads to increasing consumption in all regions, by up to 0.3% in LICs. This is compounded by lower losses at the border and faster delivery, both of which increase efficiency and thus total demand.

Figure 7.7. **In the developing world, trade facilitation raises labour income over the longer term**

Labour income evolution in the long run

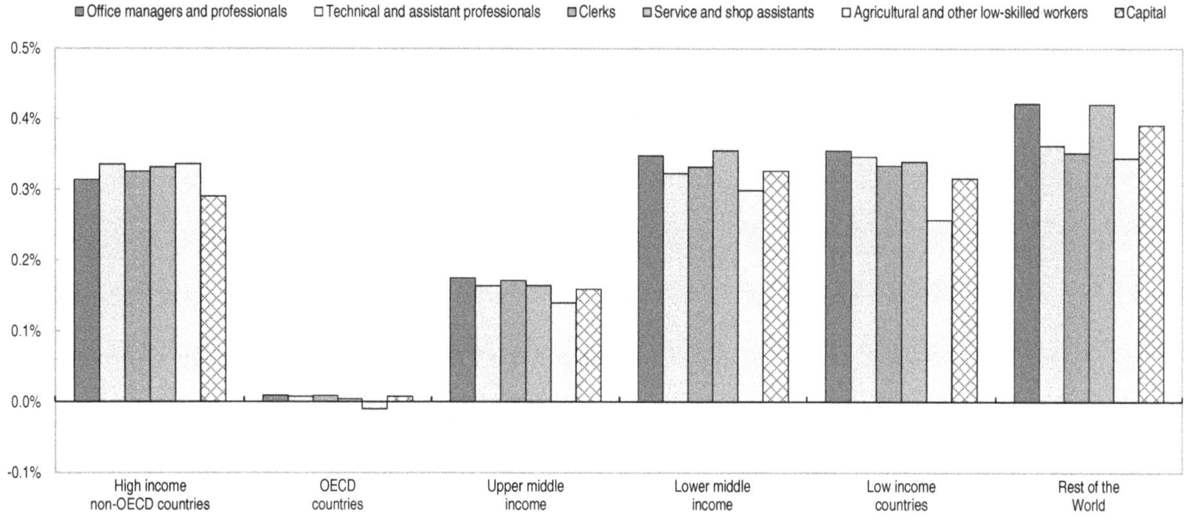

Source: OECD METRO model simulation results.

In the longer term, trade facilitation also leads to welfare gains

Increased efficiency of border procedures from full implementation of the TFA could potentially add between 0.04% and 0.41% to countries' GDP, depending on the level of development. But these figures do not include gains arising from the utility increase from faster delivery; these can be captured by welfare analysis, which provides a useful lens for assessing economic impacts beyond output from trade facilitation reforms over the longer term.[9] Using this analysis, full implementation of the TFA would see welfare increase by between 0.05 and 0.63% of total demand, depending on level of development and the assumptions used (Table 7.1 presents the slight variations between approaches).

Welfare increases across all selected income groups and major economic agents (including households, government and investment) (Figure 7.8), much of which stems not

Table 7.1. **Trade facilitation raises welfare over the longer term**

GDP and welfare effects by country income grouping

	High income non-OECD countries	OECD countries	Upper middle income	Lower middle income	Low income countries	Rest of the World
	Real GDP (expenditure)					
Iceberg – WTP[1]	0.18%	0.04%	0.13%	0.27%	0.41%	0.33%
Iceberg only[2]	0.35%	0.07%	0.22%	0.47%	0.77%	0.60%
WTP only[3]	0.01%	0.00%	0.04%	0.07%	0.03%	0.05%
	Welfare					
Iceberg – WTP[1]	0.16%	0.05%	0.28%	0.42%	0.50%	0.63%
Iceberg only[2]	0.15%	0.04%	0.26%	0.40%	0.51%	0.60%
WTP only[3]	0.17%	0.05%	0.31%	0.44%	0.49%	0.66%

1. Accounting for both decreasing losses on the supply side and increased utility from faster delivery times on the demand side.
2. Accounting only for decreasing losses.
3. Accounting only for increased utility from faster delivery times.

Source: OECD METRO model simulation results.

only from household consumption, but from the higher utility triggered by faster delivery times. LICs and RoW benefit the most, with welfare increases of 0.5 and 0.6% of total demand. Increasing household consumption in LICs is counterbalanced by a negative effect on household savings, suggesting a need for further inward FDI to compensate for the declining pool of domestic capital.

Figure 7.8. **Countries at all levels of development experience welfare gains**

Welfare decomposition by income groups (long term)

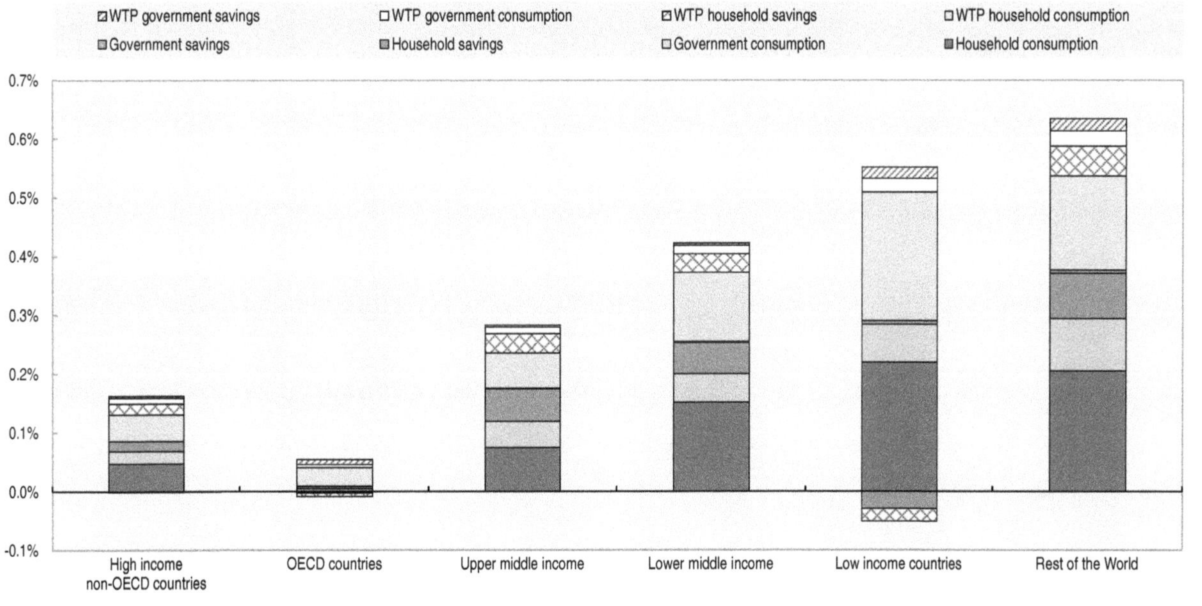

Source: OECD METRO model simulation results.

A closer look at welfare impacts indicates that, across all groups covered, increases in welfare over the longer term are driven by overall utility gains and technological changes, followed by allocative efficiency effects reflecting a more efficient allocation of resources in domestic economies (Figure 7.9).

Figure 7.9. **Longer term welfare gains are driven by technological changes and utility gains**

Further decomposition of welfare effects, by income groups

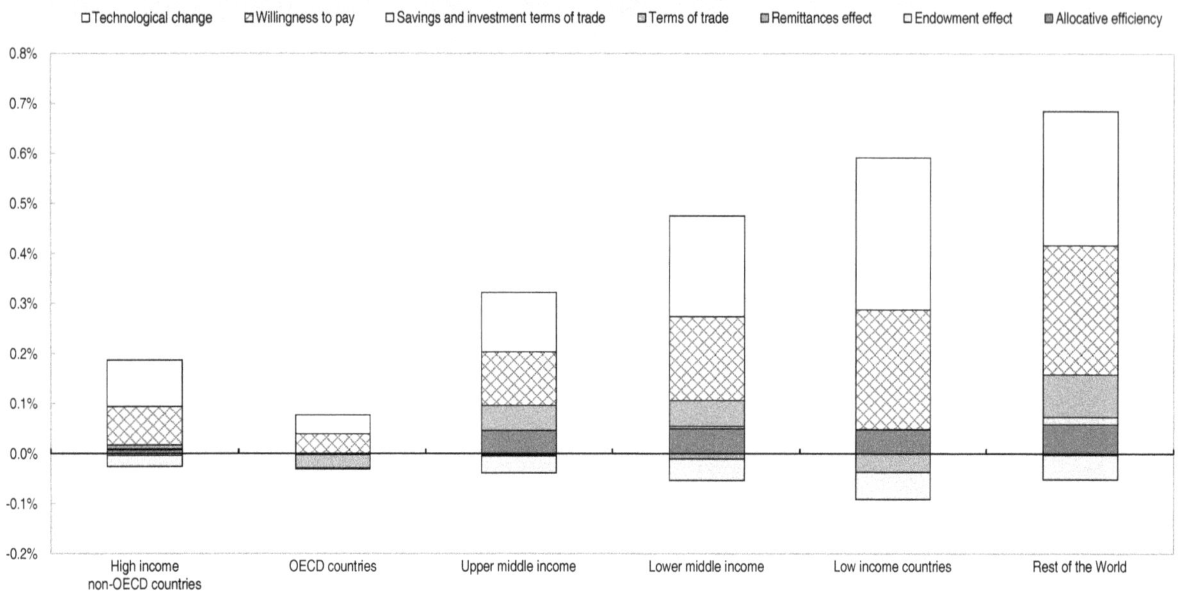

Source: OECD METRO model simulation results.

Figure 7.10. **Over the longer term, welfare increases in all regions**

Welfare decomposition by geographical regions

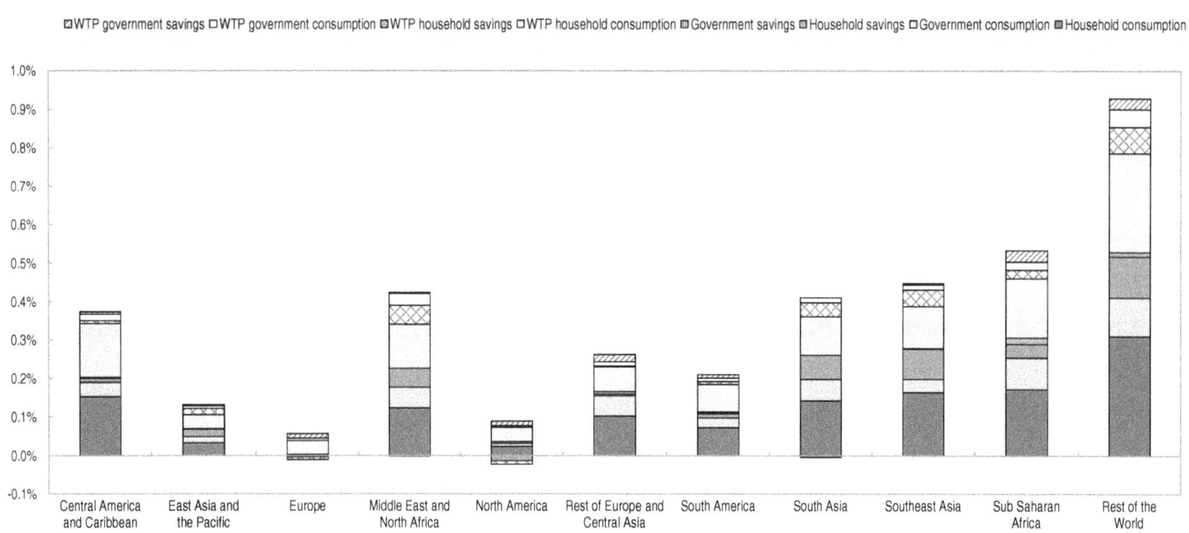

Source: OECD METRO model simulation results.

Over the longer term, trade facilitation reforms also lead to welfare increases in all selected geographical regions (Figure 7.10). Sub-Saharan Africa, Southeast Asia, South Asia, MENA, and Central America and the Caribbean experience welfare gains between 0.4 and 0.5% of their original regional demand. Effects are lower for South America and the Rest of Europe and Central Asia at 0.2%, and for Europe, North America, and East Asia and the Pacific at 0.1%. Households experience the largest welfare gains, followed by governments. The distribution of economy-wide benefits across regions and sectors heavily favours developing countries, particularly if they pursue ambitious WTO TFA implementation.

The longer run analysis highlights the broader economic benefits stemming from trade facilitation reforms, in terms of efficiency spill-overs and the associated impacts on the allocation of resources across sectors and on wages.

Overall, analysis based on the TFIs shows that implementation of the TFA can benefit all countries, as both exporters and importers of goods, by enabling better access to inputs for production and greater participation in the GVCs that characterise international trade today. Economies that currently face the biggest challenges in trade facilitation stand to reap the greatest benefits from implementation, with the nature and extent of those benefits depending on the extent and timeframes for implementation.

Notes

1. This refers to literature on importers' willingness to pay to reduce shipping times; see, for example, Hummels et al., 2007 and Hummels and Schaur, 2013.
2. Labour markets are currently characterised by rigid wages and unemployment, warranting the use of an unemployment assumption in the short term. This assumption would better depict economies with significant labour market rigidities and a larger pool of unemployed workers. In the long run, it is assumed that labour markets may be more likely to adjust to imbalances by adjusting wage rates while sustaining employment levels through a highly flexible and mobile labour force, and hence a fixed labour-supply assumption is used.
3. Imported intermediates from developed countries are found to provide a greater boost to productivity and exporting propensity (Bas and Strauss-Kahn, 2014).
4. The base refers to the 2011 data used in the METRO model to reflect the structure of the world economy.
5. Mining and extraction; paper and paper products; heavy manufacturing; motor vehicles and parts; and machinery, electronic and transport equipment.
6. Increasing demand for agricultural production increases demand for arable land and this in turn increases agricultural output prices. The food sector uses mainly agricultural goods as intermediate inputs for which prices for domestic supply have increased. This specific impact dominates the overall effect.
7. The rise in production is triggered by an increase in demand. Although the increasing production costs in agriculture dampen the positive demand effect in this sector, the overall impact on agro-food output is positive.
8. If streamlining of cumbersome border procedures were to increase competition, cheaper imports would put pressure on local firms to increase their efficiency and reduce production costs. Similarly, firms competing in the domestic market would also experience efficiency gains from accessing lower cost inputs.
9. The regional "Equivalent Variation" (EV) is used to enable utility increases to be captured. The EV measures the amount of money that a household and government would need in order to reach the same level of utility without the policy change. The measure depicted here is relative to total regional final demand (absorption) in the base situation.

Bibliography

Andriamananjara, S. et al. (2004), "The Effects of Non-Tariff Measures on Prices, Trade, and Welfare: CGE Implementation of Policy-Based Price Comparisons", *Working Paper* 15863, Office of Economics, United States International Trade Commission, Washington, DC.

Aguiar, A., B. Narayanan and R. McDougall (2016),"An Overview of the GTAP 9 Data Base", *Journal of Global Economic Analysis* 1, No. 1 (3 June): 181-208.

Armington, P.S. (1969), "A Theory of Demand for Products Distinguished by Place of Production", *IMF Staff Papers*, 16: 159-78.

Bas, M. and V. Strauss-Kahn (2015), "Input-trade Liberalisation, Export Prices and Quality Upgrading", *Journal of International Economics*, Vol. 95(2), pp. 250-262.

Beghin, J.C. et al. (2012), "Welfare Costs and Benefits of Non-Tariff Measures in Trade: A Conceptual Framework and Application", *World Trade Review*, Vol. 11(03), pp. 356-375.

Beghin, J.C. et al. (2013), "A Cost – Benefit Approach for the Assessment of Non-Tariff Measures in International Trade", in J.C. Beghin (ed.) Non-Tariff Measures with Market Imperfections: Trade and Welfare Implications (*Frontiers of Economics and Globalization*, Vol. 12), Emerald Group Publishing Limited, pp. 15-41.

Decreux, Y. and L. Fontagné (2015), "What Next for Multilateral Trade Talks? Quantifying the Role of Negotiation Modalities", World Trade Review, *Cambridge University Press*, Vol. 14(01), pp. 29-43, January.

Devarajan, S., J.D. Lewis and S. Robinson (1990), "Policy Lessons from Trade-Focused, Two-Sector Models", *Journal of Policy Modeling*, Vol. 12, pp. 625-657.

Evans, C.L. and J. Harrigan (2005), "Distance, Time, and Specialization: Lean Retailing in General Equilibrium", *American Economic Review*, Vol. 95(1), pp. 292-313.

Fontagné, L. and J. Fouré (2016), "Is Trade Facilitation a Free Lunch? A General Equilibrium Approach", Preliminary Draft, Presented at the 19th Annual Conference on Global Economic Analysis, Washington, DC, USA.

Fox, A., J. Francois and P. Londono-Kent (2003), "Measuring Border Costs and their Impact on Trade Flows: The United States-Mexican Trucking Case", Presented at the 6th Annual Conference on Global Economic Analysis, The Hague.

Francois, J., H. Van Meijl and F. van Tongeren (2005), "Trade liberalization in the Doha Development Round", *Economic Policy*, Vol. 20, pp. 350-391.

Fugazza, M. and J.C. Maur (2008), "Non-Tariff Barriers in Computable General Equilibrium Modelling", *Policy Issues in International Trade and Commodities Study Series*, No. 38, UNCTAD, Geneva.

Hertel, T., T. Walmsley and K. Itakura (2001), "Dynamic Effect of the "New Age" Free Trade Agreement between Japan and Singapore", *Journal of Economic Integration*, Vol. 16(4), pp. 446-84.

Hewitt, A. and I. Gillson (2003), "Income Distribution Impact of Trade Facilitation in Developing Countries", Background document prepared by the Overseas Development Institute for UNECE, Second International Forum on Trade Facilitation, 14-15 May 2003, Geneva.

Hilberry, R. and X. Zhang (2015), "Policy and Performance in Customs: Evaluating the Trade Facilitation Agreement", *Policy Research Working Paper* 7211, The World Bank, Washington, DC.

Hummels, D. (2007), "Transportation and International Trade in the Post War Era", *Journal of Economic Perspectives*, Vol. 21, pp. 131-154.

Hummels, D. (2001), "Time as a Trade Barrier", Purdue University, available at: *www.mgmt.purdue.edu/faculty/hummelsd/research/time3b.pdf*.

Hummels, D. and G. Schaur (2013), "Time as a Trade Barrier", *American Economic Review*, Vol. 103, pp. 1-27.

Hummels, D. et al. (2007), "Calculating Tariff Equivalents for Time in Trade", N.A. Inc. Arlington, VA, Report for the United States Agency for International Development (USAID).

Hummels, D. and A. Skiba (2004), "Shipping the Good Apples Out? An Empirical Confirmation of the Alchian-Allen Conjecture", *Journal of Political Economy*, University of Chicago Press, Vol. 112(6), pp. 1384-1402, December.

Huff, K. and T.W. Hertel (2001), "Decomposing Welfare Changes in GTAP", *GTAP Technical Paper* No. 5, Center for Global Trade Analysis, Purdue University, West Lafayette.

Lopez Gonzalez, J. (2016), "Using Foreign Factors to Enhance Domestic Export Performance: A Focus on Southeast Asia", *OECD Trade Policy Working Papers*, No. 191, OECD Publishing, Paris, *http://dx.doi.org/10.1787/5jlpq82v1jxw-en*.

McDonald, S. and K.E. Thierfelder (2013), *Globe v2: A SAM Based Global CGE Model using GTAP Data, Model documentation*, available at: *www.cgemod.org.uk/*.

de Melo, J. and S. Robinson (1989), "Product Differentiation and the Treatment of Foreign Trade in Computable General Equilibrium Models of Small Economies", *Journal of International Economics*, Vol. 27, pp 47-67.

Minor, P. and M. Tsigas (2008), "Impacts of Better Trade Facilitation in Developing Countries: Analysis with a New GTAP Database for the Value of Time in Trade", *GTAP Resource Paper* No. 2762.

Moïsé, E. and S. Sorescu (2013), "Trade Facilitation Indicators: The Potential Impact of Trade Facilitation on Developing Countries' Trade", *OECD Trade Policy Papers*, No. 144, OECD Publishing, Paris, *http://dx.doi.org/10.1787/5k4bw6kg6ws2-en*.

Moïsé, E., T. Orliac and P. Minor (2011), "Trade Facilitation Indicators: The Impact on Trade Costs", *OECD Trade Policy Papers*, No. 118, OECD Publishing, Paris, *http://dx.doi.org/10.1787/5kg6nk654hmr-en*.

OECD (2017a), "Economy-wide Effects of Trade Facilitation: a METRO Model Simulation", TAD/TC/WP(2016)15/FINAL.

OECD (2017b), "METRO Development: Modelling Non-Tariff Measures an Estimation of Trade Facilitation Impacts", TAD/TC/WP(2016)/20/FINAL.

OECD (2015), METRO v1 Model Documentation, TAD/TC/WP(2014)24/FINAL.

OECD (2009), *Overcoming Border Bottlenecks: The Costs and Benefits of Trade Facilitation*, OECD Publishing, Paris, *http://dx.doi.org/10.1787/9789264056954-en*.

Robinson, S. et al. (1993), "Agricultural Policies and Migration in a US-Mexico Free Trade Area: A Computable General Equilibrium Analysis", *Journal of Policy Modeling*, Vol. 15, pp 673-701.

Robinson, S., M. Kilkenny and K. Hanson (1990), *USDA/ERS Computable General Equilibrium Model of the United States*, Economic Research Services, USDA, Staff Report AGES 9049.

Samuelson, P.A. (1954), "The Transfer Problem and Transport Costs, II: Analysis of Effects of Trade Impediments", *The Economic Journal*, 64(254): 264-289.

van Tongeren, F. et al. (2010), "Case Studies of Costs and Benefits of Non-Tariff Measures: Cheese, Shrimp and Flowers", *OECD Food, Agriculture and Fisheries Working Papers*, No. 28, OECD Publishing, Paris, *http://dx.doi.org/10.1787/5kmbt57jjhwl-en*.

van Tongeren, F., J.C. Beghin and S. Marette (2009), "A Cost-Benefit Framework for the Assessment of Non-Tariff Measures in Agro-food Trade", *OECD Food, Agriculture and Fisheries Papers*, No. 21, OECD Publishing, Paris, *http://dx.doi.org/10.1787/220613725148*.

Walkenhorst, P. and T. Yasui (2005), "Benefits of Trade Facilitation: A Quantitative Assessment," in P. Dee and M. Ferrantino (eds.), *Quantitative Measures for Assessing the Effect of Non-Tariff Measures and Trade Facilitation*, Singapore: World Scientific Ltd. for APEC, pp. 161-192.

Walmsley, T. and P. Minor (2016), "Willingness to Pay in CGE Models: Estimating the Benefits of Improved Customs Efficiencies within the WTO Trade Facilitation Agreement", *ImpactEcon Working Paper* Rev2.

Zaki, C. (2014), "An Empirical Assessment of the Trade Facilitation Initiative: Econometric Evidence and Global Economic Effects", *World Trade Review*, Vol. 13, pp. 103-130.

ANNEX A

The trade facilitation indicators: Methodology

The OECD Trade Facilitation Indicators (TFIs) are composed of a set of variables, expressed in the form of factual questions and used to collect data on country policies in the area of trade facilitation. These variables measure the actual extent to which countries have introduced and implemented trade facilitation measures in absolute terms, but also their performance relative to others, using a series of quantitative measures on key areas of the border process. The aim is to ensure factual information that is geographically comparable and consistent over time irrespective of the various public and private entities providing the data. The variables and the possible scores that can be attributed to them are expressed in unambiguous terms, borrowing heavily from the TFA text which is widely understood among the trade policy and the business community.

Several iterations and extensive fine-tuning were necessary at the indicators' conceptualisation and drafting stage in order to ensure that terms were understood in the same way across countries, agencies and economic actors. The indicators and their composing variables were developed between 2010 and 2013 and further fine-tuned between 2014 and 2016 to better reflect implementation challenges and worldwide best practices, provide depth to the analysis of various components of TFA, and clarify variables to ensure consistent interpretation from answering entities.

The TFIs mirror the substantive provisions covered by Section I of the TFA, spanning TFA Article I Publication and Availability of Information (covering publication; information available through the Internet; enquiry points; and notifications) through to Article 12 (Customs Co-operation). An additional OECD indicator going beyond the scope of the TFA has been added to capture elements of good governance and impartiality of border administrations.

Each TFI indicator is composed of several specific, precise and fact-based variables related to existing trade-related policies and regulations and their implementation in practice. The approach taken to scoring in the TFIs is to transform qualitative regulatory information into a multiple binary scheme where the top score (2) corresponds to the best performance: variables representing measures within each of the 11 aggregate TFIs are coded with 0, 1, or 2. These seek to reflect not only the regulatory framework in the concerned countries but also delve – to the extent possible – into the state of implementation of various trade facilitation measures.

Where variables depend on numerical answers, these are broken down on thresholds to which 0/1/2 scores are applied. A scoring system that assigns discrete numerical values according to some metric of performance requires determining thresholds for what is best, worst or in between. In most cases, there are "natural" thresholds, as for example for a variable such as the "Establishment of a national Customs website". Thus, a country without a customs website will be assigned a score of 0; a country with a customs website will be assigned 1; and a country with a customs website which makes available a minimum set of information related to import or export procedures in one of the official WTO languages will be assigned a 2. In the cases where no natural thresholds can be identified, in order to reconcile the complexity of trade facilitation policies and implementation with the multiple binary scoring scheme, non-binary measures are broken down to multiple thresholds: if the variable is numerical in nature (e.g. number of advance rulings, percentage of post-clearance audits, percentage of physical inspections, etc.), the score can be determined by its percentile rank (e.g. below the 30th percentile of the country sample, between the 30th and 70th percentiles, above the 70th percentile of the country sample).

The TFIs are derived by aggregating variables across each of the 11 composite areas (Table 1.1 in Chapter 1). There are no hierarchies between variables. Within one aggregate indicator, variables are given equal weights. The TFIs represent a compromise between the comprehensive handling of the issues under review and the risk of including in the set certain variables for which the country coverage is incomplete. The expansive approach taken to the TFI variables was driven by the need to offer wide-ranging analysis across income levels, geographical regions and stages of development and to allow comparisons that will help countries move their reform agenda forward.

Using the TFIs for analysis

The TFIs are used to estimate economic impacts of trade facilitation reforms, and in particular of the implementation of the TFA, in a number of ways in this publication. Details of the methodology used in the main areas for analysis are below.

Implementation of the TFA

Calculation of the potential impact of the TFA is based on two scenarios: a) a "full" implementation scenario where countries implement all the options contained in the Agreement, including those formulated on a "best endeavours" basis; and b) a "limited" implementation scenario where countries implement only the mandatory provisions contained in the agreement, but taking into account that some of the best endeavours measures have already been implemented by some of these countries. These two scenarios provide upper and lower bounds of potential trade cost reductions likely to be obtained by implementing the TFA.

Trade costs

Trade costs include all costs incurred in getting a good to the final user, other than the cost of production itself. Given the difficulties involved in directly measuring trade costs, indirect methods can be used to infer the magnitude of trade costs from the volume of trade flows or price differences across borders. Trade costs estimates are thus drawn from the UN ESCAP-World Bank Trade Cost database. The calculated trade costs between two trading partners are a geometric average of trade costs in both directions.

Global Value Chains (GVCs)

Analysis linking the TFIs to the operation of supply chains has focused on three different measures of integration into GVCs, as mapped by selected OECD-WTO Trade in

Value Added (TiVA) indicators: the amount of foreign value-added embodied in final domestic demand or in gross exports of a reference country, and the amount of domestic value-added embodied in foreign final demand. These measures give a metric of engagement in the form of buying from and selling to GVCs, so as to enable the exploration within a gravity model framework of the impact of trade facilitation measures on the demand and the supply sides of value chain activity.

The TiVA indicators – available both at country and industry level – track both the direct and indirect flows of value added associated with international trade, thus revealing bilateral trade in value-added even when bilateral gross trade flows might be zero. At the industry level (agriculture-primary products, low-tech industries, medium-low tech industries, and high and medium-high tech industries), the average foreign value-added is a proxy for the extent to which industry value chains are segmented or "fine-sliced" into distinct tasks and activities that generate trade, compounding the double-counting effect. The model tests the response of the selected TiVA indicators to improvements in trade facilitation policies as expressed through the TFIs.

In addition to the TFIs, the set of explanatory variables includes the economic masses of the originating country and the destination country (proxies for the market size), the distance between the originating country and the destination country, and a series of other gravity variables (tariffs, the existence of a free trade agreement between the originating and destination countries, common border, common language), the distance to the closest manufacturing hub.

Time to trade and economy-wide effects

Trade facilitation improvements in the policy areas covered by the TFIs are shown to lead to reductions in both the import and export clearance times (available from the World Bank *Doing Business* indicators for *Trading Across Borders*), measured in hours, for each individual country. By linking the clearance time improvements with the value associated to one hour "saved" in transit, the trade facilitation policy changes are incorporated within the OECD METRO trade model using a novel methodological approach, which accounts for both supply and demand side gains triggered by trade facilitation improvements.

On the supply side, efficient border procedures are linked to decreasing losses resulting from fewer delays of goods at the border ("iceberg" effects). Delays in delivery increase the costs for firms of managing stocks and undermine their ability to respond rapidly to changes in consumer preferences. On the demand side, trade facilitation improvements are associated with an increase in the consumer's "willingness to pay" for faster delivery, as consumers derive more utility from goods delivered earlier rather than later. Faster delivery of intermediate goods through the supply chain also improves final delivery times and increases consumers' willingness to pay for the final product.

Trade facilitation policy changes are introduced in the METRO model as *ad valorem* equivalents (AVEs), expressing the value associated with a reduction in clearance delays triggered by improvements in border procedures. There are currently no data available on the relative importance of supply and demand effects (iceberg and willingness to pay) for the various product categories considered. The analysis therefore assumes equal importance and applies a mixed approach where the AVE estimate is introduced 50% as iceberg cost and 50% as willingness to pay.

ANNEX B

Trade facilitation indicators: Country lists

Table A.2.1. **Country groupings**

(a) By income criteria

Grouping	List of economies
OECD countries	Australia, Austria, Belgium, Canada, Chile, Czech Republic, Denmark, Estonia, Finland, France, Germany, Greece, Hungary, Ireland, Israel,[a] Italy, Japan, Korea, Latvia, Luxembourg, Mexico, Netherlands, New Zealand, Norway, Poland, Portugal, Slovak Republic, Slovenia, Spain, Sweden, Switzerland, Turkey, United Kingdom, United States
High income non-OECD economies	Antigua and Barbuda, Bahamas, Barbados, Bahrain, Brunei Darussalam, Cyprus,[b, c] Croatia, Hong Kong, China, Kuwait, Lithuania, Malta, Oman, Qatar, Saudi Arabia, Singapore, Chinese Taipei, Trinidad and Tobago, United Arab Emirates, Uruguay
Upper middle income countries	Albania, Algeria, Angola, Argentina, Azerbaijan, Belarus, Bosnia and Herzegovina, Botswana, Brazil, Bulgaria, People's Republic of China, Colombia, Costa Rica, Cuba, Dominica, Dominican Republic, Ecuador, Gabon, Georgia, Jamaica, Jordan, Kazakhstan, Lebanon, Macedonia FYR, Malaysia, Maldives, Mauritius, Montenegro, Namibia, Panama, Paraguay, Peru, Romania, Russian Federation, Serbia, South Africa, Suriname, Thailand, Venezuela
Lower middle income countries	Armenia, Bangladesh, Belize, Bhutan, Bolivia, Cambodia, Cameroon, Republic of Congo, Côte d'Ivoire, Djibouti, Egypt, El Salvador, Fiji, Ghana, Guatemala, Honduras, India, Indonesia, Kenya, Kyrgyz Republic, Lao PDR, Lesotho, Moldova, Mongolia, Morocco, Nicaragua, Nigeria, Pakistan, Papua New Guinea, Philippines, Sri Lanka, Sudan, Swaziland, Tunisia, Ukraine, Uzbekistan, Viet Nam, Yemen, Zambia
Low income countries	Benin, Burkina Faso, Burundi, Central African Republic, Chad, Comoros, Democratic Republic of Congo, Ethiopia, Gambia, Liberia, Madagascar, Malawi, Mali, Mozambique, Myanmar, Nepal, Niger, Rwanda, Senegal, Sierra Leone, Tajikistan, Togo, Tanzania, Uganda, Zimbabwe

a) The statistical data for Israel are supplied by and under the responsibility of the relevant Israeli authorities. The use of such data by the OECD is without prejudice to the status of the Golan Heights, East Jerusalem and Israeli settlements in the West Bank under the terms of international law.

b) Note by Turkey: The information in this document with reference to "Cyprus" relates to the southern part of the Island. There is no single authority representing both Turkish and Greek Cypriot people on the Island. Turkey recognises the Turkish Republic of Northern Cyprus (TRNC). Until a lasting and equitable solution is found within the context of United Nations, Turkey shall preserve its position concerning the "Cyprus" issue.

c) Note by all the European Union Member States of the OECD and the European Union: The Republic of Cyprus is recognised by all members of the United Nations with the exception of Turkey. The information in this document relates to the area under the effective control of the Government of the Republic of Cyprus.

Note: Based on World Bank's classification. The classification as of March 2017 is used.

(b) By geographic criteria

Grouping	List of economies
South America	Argentina, Bolivia, Brazil, Chile, Colombia, Ecuador, Peru, Paraguay, Suriname, Uruguay, Venezuela
Central America and Caribbean	Antigua and Barbuda, Bahamas, Barbados, Belize, Costa Rica, Cuba, Dominica, Dominican Republic, Guatemala, Honduras, Jamaica, Nicaragua, Panama, El Salvador, Trinidad and Tobago
North America	Canada, Mexico, United States
East Asia and the Pacific	Australia, People's Republic of China, Fiji, Hong Kong, China, Japan, Korea, Mongolia, New Zealand, Papua New Guinea, Chinese Taipei
Southeast Asia	Brunei Darussalam, Indonesia, Cambodia, Lao PDR, Malaysia, Myanmar, Philippines, Singapore, Thailand, Viet Nam
South Asia	Bangladesh, Bhutan, India, Sri Lanka, Nepal, Pakistan
Europe	Albania, Austria, Belgium, Bulgaria, Belarus, Bosnia and Herzegovina, Cyprus,[a, b] Czech Republic, Denmark, Estonia, Finland, France, Germany, Greece, Croatia, Hungary, Ireland, Italy, Latvia, Lithuania, Luxembourg, Malta, Macedonia FYR, Moldova, Montenegro, Netherlands, Norway, Poland, Portugal, Romania, Serbia, Slovak Republic, Slovenia, Spain, Sweden, Switzerland, United Kingdom, Ukraine
Rest of Europe and Central Asia	Armenia, Azerbaijan, Georgia, Kazakhstan, Kyrgyz Republic, Russian Federation, Tajikistan, Turkey, Uzbekistan
Middle East and North Africa	Algeria, Bahrain, Egypt, Israel,[c] Jordan, Kuwait, Lebanon, Oman, Qatar, Morocco, Saudi Arabia, Tunisia, United Arab Emirates
Sub-Saharan Africa	Angola, Benin, Botswana, Burkina Faso, Burundi, Cameroon, Central African Republic, Chad, Democratic Republic of Congo, Republic of Congo, Comoros, Côte d'Ivoire, Djibouti, Ethiopia, Gabon, Gambia, Ghana, Kenya, Lesotho, Liberia, Madagascar, Malawi, Mali, Mauritius, Mozambique, Namibia, Niger, Nigeria, Rwanda, Senegal, Sierra Leone, South Africa, Sudan, Swaziland, Tanzania, Togo, Uganda, Zambia, Zimbabwe

a) Note by Turkey: The information in this document with reference to "Cyprus" relates to the southern part of the Island. There is no single authority representing both Turkish and Greek Cypriot people on the Island. Turkey recognises the Turkish Republic of Northern Cyprus (TRNC). Until a lasting and equitable solution is found within the context of United Nations, Turkey shall preserve its position concerning the "Cyprus" issue.

b) Note by all the European Union Member States of the OECD and the European Union: The Republic of Cyprus is recognised by all members of the United Nations with the exception of Turkey. The information in this document relates to the area under the effective control of the Government of the Republic of Cyprus.

c) The statistical data for Israel are supplied by and under the responsibility of the relevant Israeli authorities. The use of such data by the OECD is without prejudice to the status of the Golan Heights, East Jerusalem and Israeli settlements in the West Bank under the terms of international law.

ANNEX C

Trade facilitation indicators questionnaire

Q ID	QUESTIONS
	A. INFORMATION AVAILABILITY
Q1.	**Is there a clearly identified Customs' website on the Internet?*** (0) There is no clearly identified Customs' website on the Internet. (1) Yes, there is an official website. (2) The website makes available a minimal set of information related to import or export procedures** in one of the official WTO languages.*** * A national Customs website can be part of a wider website like the Ministry of Trade and Finance website. ** An official Customs website should at least cover the description of import, export and transit procedures, and electronic links to the forms and documents required. (**Art.2.1**) *** *Whenever practicable, the description ... shall also be made available in one of the official languages of the WTO* (**Art.2.2**). The official WTO languages are English (EN), Spanish (ES) and French (FR).
Q2.	**Is there the possibility to provide online feedback to Customs?** (0) There is no possibility to provide feedback.* (1) There is a possibility by telephone or human contact only. (2) There are online means (email, forms) to provide feedback. * This refers to the possibility for users to provide feedback on the organization of the website: user-friendliness of the website, availability of information, explanation on new systems.
Q3.	**Is the applicable rate of duties published?*** (0) It is not possible to find the applicable rate of duties on the Customs website. (1) There is information (or an electronic link) on the applicable rate of duties. (2) Information is kept up to date. * **Art.1.1.b**.
Q4.	**Are there Enquiry Points to answer reasonable enquiries?*** (0) There are no Enquiry points to answer reasonable enquiries.** (2) There are one or more enquiry points to answer reasonable enquiries. * **Art.1.3**. ** Enquiries of traders may refer to issues such as: importation, exportation and transit procedures, applicable rate of duties, rules for classification or valuation, fees and taxes, laws, regulations and rulings on origin, restrictions or prohibitions, penalty provisions, appeal procedures, agreements with third countries and tariff quotas related provisions.
Q5.	**Adjustment of enquiry points' operating hours to commercial needs** (0) Enquiry points' operating hours are not adapted to commercial needs (telephone centres operating less than the normal working hours / no possibility to submit enquiries online). (2) Enquiry points offer a full time hotline (7/24).Enquiries may be submitted 7/24 and an answer will be provided within 24 hours on working days. **Art.1.3** *The enquiry points shall answer enquiries and provide the forms and documents within a reasonable time period set by each Member, which may vary depending on the nature or complexity of the request.*
Q6.	**Timeliness of enquiry points** (0) The administration's service charter does not indicate a standard time of response for the various means of enquiry (telephone, email or written correspondence), taking into account the nature or complexity of the enquiry. (2) The administration's service charter indicates a standard time of response for the various means of enquiry (telephone, email or written correspondence), taking into account the nature or complexity of the enquiry.

Q ID	QUESTIONS
Q7.	**Is information on import and export procedures published?*** (0) Import and export procedures are not described and the required forms and documents are not made available in a way as to allow undertaking the basic steps of the procedures. (1) Import and export procedures are described and the required forms and documents are made available in a way as to allow undertaking the basic steps of the procedures. (2) There are summary guides and/or specific highlights on these topics. * **Art.1.1.a.** This question does not specify a standardized minimum level of information, because this varies across the regulations of each country which are more or less burdensome and the friendliness of each customs website.
Q8.	**Is the required documentation easily accessible for downloading?** (0) No documents and forms required for the procedures of border agencies are available online. (1) Some but not all documents and forms required for those procedures are available online. (2) All required forms and documents required for the procedures of border agencies are available online.
Q9a.	**Is information about procedures published in advance of entry into force?*** (0) There is no interval between the publication of new or amended trade related laws and regulations, and their entry into force. (1) There is only an interval for selected new or amended trade related laws and regulations. (2) There is an interval between the publication of new or amended trade related laws and regulations, and their entry into force.** * *Each Member shall … ensure that new or amended laws and regulations … are published, or information on them made otherwise publicly available, as early as possible before their entry into force, in order to enable traders and other interested parties to become acquainted with them* (**Art.2.1.2**). ** Without prejudice to minor changes or to exceptions for measures that have a relieving effect, measures whose effectiveness would be undermined by the pre-publication, and measures applied in urgent circumstances.
Q9b.	If the answer to **Q8.a** is (2), please specify the average time*** between publication end entry into force: *** The average time is the interval generally applied in the country, whether on the basis of applicable rules, such as an Information Act, or on the basis of practice.
Q10.	**Are agreements with third countries relating to the above issues published?*** (0) There is no information on the official Customs website about international agreements relating to importation, exportation or transit. (1) Such agreements are available on the official Customs website.** (2) Agreements are available together with topic-specific annotations.*** * **Art.1.1.i.** ** At least an electronic link exists. *** The most relevant parts of the agreements (related to export, import or transit matters) are explained and highlighted.
Q11.	**Is there information on appeal procedures available through the Internet?*** (0) No information on appeal procedures is provided online. (1) Information on appeal procedures is displayed online. (2) Information is displayed and guidance on how to undertake these procedures is included or information is always given on an individual basis. * *Each Member shall make available … through the Internet a description of its … procedures, including appeal procedures, that informs governments, traders and other interested parties of the practical steps needed …* (**Art.1.2.a**).
Q12.	**Are decisions and examples of Customs classification published?** (0) Decisions and examples of Customs classification are not published. (1) Decisions and examples of Customs classification are publicly available. (2) Decisions and examples of Customs classification are displayed on the Customs website.
Q13.	**Is information on advance rulings* published?** (0) Information is not published or it is only available in the relevant legislation (Customs Code). (1) There is a specific page on the Customs website dealing with Advance Ruling procedures. (2) There is a specific page and an online request procedures is available (e.g. forms sent by email). * *An advance ruling is a written decision provided by a Member to an applicant prior to the importation of a good covered by the application that sets forth the treatment that the Member shall provide to the good at the time of importation with regard to the good's tariff classification, and the origin of the good. (**Art.3.9**)* In addition it could cover valuation methods and their application, duty drawback, or quotas. Following this definition, Binding Tariff Information (BTI) is regarded as an *advance ruling mechanism.Information* in the sense of this variable includes *at a minimum a) the requirements for the application for an advance ruling, including the information to be provided and the format; b) the time period by which it will issue an advance ruling; and c) the length of time for which the advance ruling is valid. (**Art.3.6**)*
Q14.	**Are penalty provisions for breaches of import and export formalities published?*** (0) There is no information on penalty procedures and the amount of penalties.** (1) There is no information available on the Customs website, but it is available in the relevant legislation (Customs Code). (2) Information is displayed on a dedicated page in the Customs website. * **Art.1.1.g.** ** Including in the relevant legislation.

Q ID	QUESTIONS
Q15.	**Is applicable legislation published on Internet?** (0) There is no information on the Customs website (no electronic links). (1) Traders can find the relevant legislation on the Customs website.* (2) There are quick references among the different pages of the website or user friendly guidance on key issues. * Through electronic links or a specific webpage.
Q16.	**Are judicial decisions on Customs matters published?** (0) No judicial decisions on Customs matters are published. (2) Judicial decisions on Customs matters are published on the Customs website (or electronic link).
Q17.	**Is there a dedicated interactive page for professional users/companies?*** (0) There is no dedicated interactive page for professional users/companies. (2) There is a dedicated page for companies or a "pro" version of the website. * A dedicated interactive page for professional users/companies provides specific information and tools for electronic interfaces and downloadable forms. It is more than a simple (or quick) distinction between companies and private individuals.
Q18.	**Are there user manuals available online?** (0) There are no manuals online to help users when a new system is implemented. (2) User manuals are available online.
	B. INVOLVEMENT OF THE TRADE COMMUNITY (CONSULTATIONS)
Q19.	**Are there public consultations between traders and other interested parties and government?** (0) There are no public consultations between traders and other interested parties and governments. (1) There are specific public consultations when introducing or amending trade related laws, regulations and administrative rulings of general application. (2) There are one or more structures for regular public consultations. * *Each Member shall, to the extent practicable and in a manner consistent with its domestic law and legal system, provide opportunities and an appropriate time period to traders and other interested parties to comment on the proposed introduction or amendment of laws and regulations of general application related to the movement, release and clearance of goods, including goods in transit.(Art.2.1.1)*
Q20.	**Are there general notice-and-comment framework procedures in place, applicable to trade and border issues?*** (0) There are no notice-and-comment procedures in place. (1) There are notice-and-comment procedures but they do not apply to trade and border issues and regulation. (2) Notice-and-comment procedures apply to trade and border issues and regulation. *** The score to this variable is (0) if variable Q10 scores (0).**
Q21.	**Are there established guidelines and procedures in place, governing the public consultation process?*** (0) There are no established guidelines and procedures in place, consultation take place at random. (2) There are established guidelines and procedures to ensure a systematic handling of consultation structures and opportunities. *** The score to this variable is (0) if variable Q10 scores (0).**
Q22.	**Who are the targeted stakeholders?*** (0) There are less than 2 stakeholder groups** involved. (1) There are at least 3 stakeholder groups involved. (2) There are 4 or more stakeholder groups involved. * This variable refers to the scope of the public consultations launched by the authorities on Customs and border related matters. ** The stakeholder groups are: Small and Medium Enterprises (SMEs), Large traders, Transporters, Customs brokers, Citizens.
Q23.	**What is the average number of public consultations?*** Please provide the number of public consultations (during the three previous years) : * Average number of public consultations, including both regular and specific consultations, open to all parties, taking place per year.
Q24.	**Are drafts published prior to entry into force?*** (0) Drafts** are not published before the entry into force of a rule. (1) Drafts are available before entry into force of a rule and stakeholder comments are possible. (2) The trading community is involved at the stage of drafting new trade related legislation. **Each Member shall, to the extent practicable and in a manner consistent with its domestic law and legal system, ensure that new or amended laws and regulations of general application related to the movement, release and clearance of goods, including goods in transit are published or information on them made otherwise publicly available, as early as possible before their entry into force, in order to enable traders and other interested parties to become acquainted with them.(**Art.2.1.2**)* **Drafts (or summaries) of trade related laws, regulations or administrative rulings of general application.
Q25.	**Are public comments taken into account?** (0) Public comments are not taken into account. (1) Public comments are taken into account. (2) The administration explains how public comments have been dealt with online or in the legislation's final draft.

Q ID	QUESTIONS
	C. ADVANCE RULINGS
Q26.	**Does the country issue binding advance rulings?** (0) Binding advance rulings are not issued. (2) Binding advance rulings are issued. * *An advance ruling is a written decision provided by a Member to an applicant prior to the importation of a good covered by the application that sets forth the treatment that the Member shall provide to the good at the time of importation with regard to the good's tariff classification, and the origin of the good. (***Art.3.9***)* In addition it could cover valuation methods and their application, duty drawback, or quotas. Following this definition, Binding Tariff Information (BTI) is regarded as an *advance ruling mechanism.* *An advance ruling issued by a Member shall be binding on that Member in respect of the applicant that sought it.***(Art.3.5)**
Q27.	**What is the annual number of advance ruling requests on tariff classification?** Please provide the average number of advance ruling requests per year on tariff classification:
Q28.	**What is the annual number of advance ruling requests on origin?** Please provide the average number of advance ruling requests per year on origin:
Q29.	**What is the total annual number of advance ruling requests?** Please provide the average total number of advance ruling requests per year:
Q30.	**What is the length of time for which the advance ruling is valid (duration)?*** Please provide the length of time for which the advance ruling is valid: * *The advance ruling shall be valid for a reasonable period of time after its issuance unless the law, facts or circumstances supporting the original advance ruling have changed. (***Art.3.3***)* The validity of the ruling may vary according to the policy area. The variable focuses on tariff classification.
Q31a.	**Is the maximum time by which the advance ruling will be issued published?*** (0) The maximum time by which the ruling will be issued is not published on the Customs website or in the related legislation. (2) The maximum time by which the ruling will be issued is published on the Customs website or in the related legislation.
Q31b.	**If your answer to Q31a is (2), please provide the maximum issuance time as published:** * *Each Member shall publish, at a minimum, the time period by which it will issue and advance ruling* (**Art.3.6.b**).
Q32.	**What is the percentage of advance rulings issued within the maximum issuance time provided for in Q31?** Please provide the percentage of advance rulings issued within the maximum issuance time:
Q33.	**Is information on advance rulings of significant general interest published?*** (0) Information on advance rulings of significant interest to other interested parties (governments, traders…) is not published. (2) Information on advance rulings of significant interest to other interested parties is made publicly available. * *Each Member shall endeavour to make publicly available any information on advance rulings which it considers to be of significant interest to other interested parties, taking into account the need to protect commercially confidential information* (**Art.3.8**).
Q34.	**Is it possible to request a review of an advance ruling or its revocation / modification?** (0) It is not possible to request a review of an advance ruling or its revocation / modification. (2) It is possible to request a review of an advance ruling or its revocation / modification. * *Each Member shall provide, upon written request of an applicant, a review of the advance ruling or the decision to revoke, modify or invalidate the advance ruling.* (**Art.3.7**)
Q35.	**Is the refusal to issue or the revocation of advance rulings motivated?*** (0) The refusal to issue or the revocation of advance rulings are not motivated. (2) The refusal to issue or the revocation of advance rulings are motivated. * *Where the Member revokes, modifies or invalidates the advance ruling, it shall provide written notice to the applicant setting out the relevant facts and the basis for its decision.* (**Art.3.4**)
	D. APPEAL PROCEDURES
Q36.	**Is information on procedural rules for appeal* publicly available?** (0) There is no appeal mechanism for Customs matters or the related laws are not publicly available. (2) There is an appeal mechanism and it is explained in the customs Code. ***Art.1.1.h**This variable is different from Q11 within the Information Availability area, which focuses on information available online.
Q37.	**Are independent or higher level administrative and/or judicial appeal procedures available for customs decisions?*** (0) There is no possibility of independent or higher level administrative, or judicial appeal of customs decisions. (1) There is the possibility of an independent or higher level administrative appeal of customs decisions and established policies/ procedures for the processing of appeals. (2) There is in addition a possibility of a judicial appeal following, or independent of, the administrative appeal of customs decisions. * *Each Member shall provide that any person to whom customs issues an administrative decision has the right, within its territory to administrative appeal to or review by an administrative authority higher than or independent of the official or office that issued the decision; and/or judicial appeal or review of the decision.* (**Art.4.1.1**)

Q ID	QUESTIONS
Q38.	**Timeliness of the appeal mechanism – time available for lodging and appeal?** (0) Time limits fixed for contesting a decision of border agencies do not provide sufficient time to study the contested decision and prepare the appeal. (2) Time limits fixed for contesting a decision of border agencies provide adequate time to study the contested decision and prepare the appeal. * *Each Member shall ensure that, in a case where the decision on appeal or review … is not given … (a) within set periods as specified in its laws and regulations … the petitioner has the right to either further appeal to or further review by the administrative authority or the judicial authority or any other recourse to the judicial authority.* (**Art.4.4**)
Q39.	**Timeliness of the appeal mechanism – avoidance of undue delays?** (0) There are no set periods specified in the laws and regulations for providing a decision on appeal or review. (1) There are set periods specified in the laws and regulations for providing a decision on appeal or review. (2) There are set periods specified and the petitioner can further appeal of the decision is not given within that set period or without undue delay; or the administrative silence is recognized as a decision in favour of the petitioner. * *Each Member shall ensure that, in a case where the decision on appeal or review … is not given either (a) within set periods as specified in its laws and regulations; or (b) without undue delay, the petitioner has the right to either further appeal to or further review by the administrative authority or the judicial authority or any other recourse to the judicial authority. Nothing in this paragraph shall prevent a Member from recognizing administrative silence on appeal or review as a decision in favour of the petitioner in accordance with its laws and regulations* (**Art.4.4**)
Q40.	**Is information available on the motives of the administration's decisions?*** (0) There is no information on the motives. (2) Information about the motives of the administration's decision is provided. * *Each Member shall ensure that the person … is provided with the reasons for the administrative decision so as to enable such a person to have recourse to appeal or review procedures where necessary* (**Art.4.1.5**).
Q41a.	**What is the average percent of appeals introduced by Customs or other border agencies that is resolved in favour of traders?** Please provide the percentage of appeals introduced by Customs or other border agencies that is resolved in favour of traders (over the last 3 years):
Q41b.	**What is the average per cent of appeals introduced by traders that is resolved in favour of Customs or other border agencies?** Please provide the percentage appeals introduced by traders that is resolved in favour of Customs or other border agencies (over the last three years):
Q41c.	**What is the average number of administrative appeals per year?** Please provide the average yearly number of administrative appeals (over the last 3 years):
Q41d.	**What is the average number of judicial appeals per year?** Please provide the average yearly number of judicial appeals (over the last 3 years) if available:
Q42a.	**Is there a time limit for deciding judicial appeals?** (0) There is no time limit for deciding judicial appeals. (2) There is a time limit for deciding judicial appeals.
Q42b.	**If the answer to Q40.a. is (2), please specify the time limit:**
	E. FEES AND CHARGES
Q43.	**Is information on fees and charges imposed by governmental agencies on, or in connection with, importation, exportation or transit,* published?** (0) Information on fees and charges is not published**. (1) Information is available in paper publications (Gazette, Bulletin, Customs Code). (2) Information is displayed on relevant agencies' website (on a dedicated page). * This variable refers to *all fees and charges other than import and export duties and other than taxes within the purview of Article III of GATT 1994 imposed by Members on or in connection with importation or exportation of goods.*(**Art.6.1.1**). ** *This information shall include the fees and charges that will be applied, the reason for such fees and charges, the responsible authority and when and how payment is to be made.*(**Art.6.1.2**)
Q44.	**How are fees and charges calculated*?** (0) Fees and charges are calculated on an ad-valorem basis.* (1) Some fees and charges are calculated on an ad-valorem basis.* (2) Fees and charges are not calculated on an ad-valorem basis or are limited in amount to the approximate cost of the services rendered on or in connection with the specific import or export operation. * However, the score is (2) if the fees and charges are less than the approximate cost of the service rendered. *Fees and charges for customs processing shall be limited in amount to the approximate cost of the services rendered on or in connection with the specific import or export operation in question*(**Art.6.2.1.i**)
Q45.	**What is the total amount of fees collected (value in USD)?** Please provide the total amount of fees and charges collected by customs and other governmental agencies in one civil year for importation/exportation : Please provide the total amount of fees and charges collected by customs and other governmental agencies in one civil year for transit:

Q ID	QUESTIONS
Q46.	**Is the information on fees and charges all-inclusive?** (0) No information about fees and charges is available, on paper or online. (1) Available information does not account for all applicable fees and charges or does not include all information required in Art. 6.1.2.* (2) All applicable fees or charges have been accounted for when providing information and it includes the fees and charges that will be applied, the reason for such fees and charges, the responsible authority and when and how payment is to be made. * *Information on fees and charges (...) shall include the fees and charges that will be applied, the reason for such fees and charges, the responsible authority and when and how payment is to be made* (**Art.6.1.2**).
Q47.	**What is the total number of fees collected (number-diversity)?**
Q47a.	Please specify the number of (different categories of) fees and charges collected by all entities involved in the border process:
Q47b.	Please specify the collecting entities and the type of fees (Veterinary inspections, inspections outside normal working hours, etc.):
Q48.	**Fees for answering enquiries and providing required forms and documents** (0) There are fees requested for answering enquiries and/or providing required forms and documents. (1) If any, these are limited to the approximate cost of services rendered. (2) There are no fees requested for answering enquiries and/or providing required forms and documents. **Art.1.3.3** *Members are encouraged not to require the payment of a fee for answering enquiries and providing required forms and documents. If any, Members shall limit the amount of their fees and charges to the approximate cost of services rendered.*
Q49.	**Are fees and charges periodically reviewed to ensure they are still appropriate and relevant?** (0) There is no periodic review of fees and charges. (1) Fees and charges are reviewed periodically. (2) Fees and charges are reviewed periodically and adapted to changed circumstances. **Art.6.1.4** *Each Member shall periodically review its fees and charges with a view to reducing their number and diversity, where practicable.*
Q50.	**Is there an adequate time period granted between the publication of new or amended fees and charges and their entry into force?** (0) Fees and charges may be applied even without being published or prior to their publication. (1) New or amended fees and charges enter into force immediately upon their publication (2) There is a time period accorded between the publication of new or amended fees and charges and their entry into force. **Art.6.1.3** *An adequate time period shall be accorded between the publication of new or amended fees and charges and their entry into force, except in urgent circumstances. Such fees and charges shall not be applied until information on them has been published.*
Q51.	**Are there fees for Customs services during normal working hours?** (0) There are fees for Customs services during normal working hours. (2) There are no fees for Customs services during normal working hours.
Q52.	**Implementation of penalty disciplines for the breach of customs laws, regulations or procedural requirements-transparency** (0) The rules, regulations or procedures regarding penalty disciplines for the breach of customs laws, regulations, or procedural requirements are not publicly available. (1) The rules, regulations or procedures regarding penalty disciplines for the breach of customs laws, regulations, or procedural requirements are publicly available. (2). The rules, regulations or procedures regarding penalty disciplines for the breach of customs laws, regulations, or procedural requirements are publicly available and they clearly specify the persons that can be held responsible for such breach. **Art.1.1.g** *Each Member shall promptly publish ...penalty provisions against breaches of import, export or transit formalities* **Art.6.3.2** Each Member shall ensure that penalties for a breach of a customs law, regulation, or procedural requirement are imposed only on the person(s) responsible for the breach under its laws.
Q53.	**Implementation of penalty disciplines for the breach of customs laws, regulations or procedural requirements-proportionality** (0) Penalties imposed for the breach of customs laws, regulations, or procedural requirements are assessed and applied regardless of the circumstances and the severity of the breach. (2) Penalties imposed for the breach of customs laws, regulations, or procedural requirements depend on the facts and circumstances of the case and are commensurate with the degree and severity of the breach. **Art.6.3.3.** *The penalty imposed shall depend on the facts and circumstances of the case and shall be commensurate with the degree and severity of the breach.*
Q54.	**Procedural guarantees on penalties*** (0) The administration does not provide any explanation in writing on the basis for assessing and applying the penalty. (2) The administration provides an explanation in writing to the person upon whom the penalty is imposed, specifying the nature of the breach and the applicable regulation. **Art.6.3.5** *Each Member shall ensure that when a penalty is imposed for a breach of customs laws, regulations, or procedural requirements, an explanation in writing is provided to the person(s) upon whom the penalty is imposed specifying the nature of the breach and the applicable law, regulation or procedure under which the amount or range of penalty for the breach has been prescribed.*
Q55	**Conflicts of interest in the assessment and collection of penalties and duties** (0) Remuneration of customs officials is based on a fixed portion or percentage of any penalties or duties that they assess or collect. (2) Remuneration of customs officials is independent of any penalties or duties that they assess or collect **Art.6.3.4** *Each Member shall ensure that it maintains measures to avoid: i) conflicts of interest in the assessment and collection of penalties and duties; and ii).creatingan incentive for the assessment or collection of a penalty that is inconsistent with paragraph 3.3.*

Q ID	QUESTIONS
Q56	**Is voluntary disclosure of the breach of customs regulation by the person responsible a mitigating factor when establishing penalties?** (0) Voluntarily disclosure of the breach of a customs regulation, by the person responsible, prior to the discovery of the breach by the customs administration, is not considered a mitigating factor when establishing penalties. (2) Voluntarily disclosure of the breach of a customs regulation, by the person responsible, prior to the discovery of the breach by the customs administration, is considered a mitigating factor when establishing penalties. **Art.6.3.6** *When a person voluntarily discloses to a Member's customs administration the circumstances of a breach of a customs law, regulation, or procedural requirement prior to the discovery of the breach by the customs administration, the Member is encouraged to, where appropriate, consider this fact as a potential mitigating factor when establishing a penalty for that person.*
	F. FORMALITIES-DOCUMENTS
Q57.	**Are copies of documents* accepted?** (0) Customs and other border agencies do not accept copies of documents. (1) Copies are accepted with exceptions (related to the type of good, the circumstances or the agency). (2) Copies are accepted without exceptions, although the original may need to be presented upon request. **Each Member shall, where appropriate, endeavour to accept paper or electronic copies of supporting documents required for import, export and transit formalities.* (**Art.10.2.1**)
Q58.	**What is the percent of supporting documents required for import, export and transit formalities for which copies are accepted?*** Please provide the percentage of supporting documents required for import, export and transit formalities for which border authorities accept copies: ** Each Member shall, where appropriate, endeavour to accept paper or electronic copies of supporting documents required for import, export or transit formalities.* (**Art.10.2.1**) The percentage should be calculated on the basis of the total number of supporting documents required by the country for import, export or transit.
Q59.	**Are copies accepted where another government agency already holds the original?** (0) Customs and other border agencies do not accept copies of documents. (2) Copies are accepted where another government agency holds the original of the document. ** Where a government agency of a Member already holds the original of such a document, any other agency of that Member shall accept a paper or electronic copy, where applicable, from the agency holding the original in lieu of the original document.* (**Art.10.2.2**)
Q60.	**How widely are international standards* used?** **Please indicate which of the following Conventions have been ratified:** Convention (2005) on Facilitation of International Maritime Traffic Convention (2006) on International Civil Aviation Convention (1990) on the Temporary Admission of Goods (Istanbul Convention) International Convention (1986) on the Harmonized Commodity Description and Coding System (HS Convention) General Annex of the International Convention (1999) on the Simplification and Harmonisation of Customs procedures (Revised Kyoto Convention) * As a proxy of acceptance of international standards we consider the ratifications to the following conventions: Convention (2005) on Facilitation of International Maritime Traffic, Convention (2006) on International Civil Aviation, Convention (1990) on the Temporary Admission of Goods (Istanbul Convention), International Convention (1986) on the Harmonized Commodity Description and Coding System (HS Convention), General Annex of the International Convention (1999) on the Simplification and Harmonisation of Customs procedures (Revised Kyoto Convention).
Q61.	**What is the number of documents for import?** Please provide the number of documents necessary for importation:
Q62.	**What is the number of documents for export?** Please provide the number of documents necessary for exportation:
Q63.	**Are relevant border agencies required to carry out a periodic review of their documentation requirements?** (0) Relevant border agencies do not carry out a periodic review of their documentation requirements. (1) Relevant border agencies carry out periodic reviews of their documentation requirements and ensure that requirements that are no longer required are discontinued. (2) Relevant border agencies carry out periodic reviews of their documentation requirements and proceed to simplify requirements that are unduly consuming or costly for traders. **Art.10.1.1** *(…) each Member shall review (…) documentation requirements, and, based on the results of the review, ensure, as appropriate, that (they…) b. are adopted and/or applied in a manner that aims at reducing the time and cost of compliance for traders and operators; c. are the least trade restrictive measure chosen, where two or more alternative measures are reasonably available for fulfilling the policy objective or objectives in question; and d. are not maintained, including parts thereof, if no longer required*
	G. FORMALITIES-AUTOMATION
Q64.	**What is the percent of import declarations cleared electronically?** Please provide the percentage of import declarations cleared electronically:
Q65.	**What is the percent of export declarations cleared electronically?** Please provide the percentage of export declarations cleared electronically:

Q ID	QUESTIONS
Q66.	**What is the percent of import and export procedures that allow for electronic processing?*** Please provide the percentage of all import and export procedures, including processing of documents and payment of duties, taxes, fees and charges that allow for electronic processing: * *Members shall, as appropriate, provide for advance lodging of documents in electronic format for pre-arrival processing of such documents* (**Art.7.1.2**) *Each Member shall, to the extent practicable, adopt or maintain procedures allowing the option of electronic payment for duties, taxes, fees and charges collected by customs incurred upon importation and exportation.* (**Art.7.2**)
Q67.	**How much are border agencies spending on automation annually* (in USD)?** Please provide the total automation spending (in USD): * This variable refers to the amount spent for automating formalities connected with importation, exportation or transit, whether in charge of the Customs agencies or other agencies dealing with goods import, export or transit, such as sanitary and phytosanitary control agencies, port authorities, etc. during the current year.
Q68.	**Is pre-arrival processing* supported by the possibility to lodge documents in advance in electronic format?** (0) Documents cannot be lodged in advance in electronic format.. (1) Advance lodging of documents in electronic format is in the process of implementation, not yet fully operational. (2) There is a fully operational mechanism, allowing for the advance lodging of documents in electronic format. * Pre-arrival processing refers to the *procedures allowing for the submission of import documentation (...) in advance, in order to begin processing prior to the arrival of goods* (**Art.7.4.3**)
Q69.	**Do import and export procedures allow for the electronic payment of duties, taxes, fees and charges (including inspections fees, licenses, permits, other fees) collected upon importation and exportation?** (0) Import and export procedures do not allow for the electronic payment of duties, taxes, fees and charges collected upon importation and exportation. (1) Some of the duties, taxes, fees and charges collected upon importation and exportation can be paid electronically. (2) All duties, taxes, fees and charges collected upon importation and exportation can be paid electronically. **Art.7.2** *Each Member shall, to the extent practicable, adopt or maintain procedures allowing the option of electronic payment for duties, taxes, fees and charges collected by customs incurred upon importation and exportation*
Q70.	**Is the electronic payment system integrated with the automated declaration/cargo processing systems?** (0) The electronic payment system is not integrated with the automated declaration/cargo processing systems. (1) The electronic payment system is in the process of being integrated with the automated declaration/cargo processing systems. (2) The electronic payment system is integrated with the automated declaration/cargo processing systems.
Q71.	**Is Risk Management* applied and operating in an automated environment?** (0) There are no risk management mechanisms in place. (1) Risk management mechanisms, whether fully operational or in the process of implementation, are not supported by information technology. (2) There is a fully operational mechanism, supported by information technology. * Risk Management means the systematic application of management procedures and practices providing Customs and other relevant border agencies with the necessary information to address movements or consignments on the basis of risks they represent. "Risk" is defined as the potential for non-compliance with Customs and/or other relevant laws. *Each Member shall concentrate customs control and, to the extent possible other relevant border controls, on high risk consignments and expedite the release of low risk consignments.* (**Art.7.4.3**)
Q72.	**Is the single window supported by information technology?** (0) There is no single window, or the single window operates totally in a non-automated environment. (1) The automation of the single window is work in progress. (2) The single window is fully supported by information technology. **Art.10.4.4** *Members shall, to the extent possible and practical, use information technology to support the single window.*
Q73.	**Are IT Systems capable of accepting and exchanging data electronically?*** (0) IT systems are not ready for EDI accepting and exchanging data electronically. (1) In the process of implementation, not yet fully operational. (2) IT systems are ready for EDI accepting and exchanging data electronically.
Q74.	**Does the automated processing system include functions allowing for the release of goods subject to conditions (i.e. guarantee)?** (0) The release of goods is not separated from the final determination and payment of Customs duties, taxes, fees and charges, or such .separation cannot take place in the context of automated declaration processing. (2) The automated declaration processing includes functions allowing for the release of goods subject to conditions, such as the deposit of appropriate guarantee.
Q75.	**Are digital certificates and signatures in place?** (0) No use of electronic signatures. (2) Use of electronic signatures.

Q ID	QUESTIONS
Q76.	**Is automated processing for Customs declarations available full-time (24/7)?** (0) There is no full-time automated processing. (2) There is full-time automated processing.
	H. FORMALITIES-PROCEDURES
Q77.	**Is there a Single Window?*** (0) There is no Single Window. (1) A Single Window is planned or in the process of implementation.** (2) There is a Single Window. * A Single Window is defined as a facility that allows parties involved in trade and transport to lodge standardized documentation and/or data with a single entry point to fulfill all import, export and transit-related regulatory requirements (**UN/CEFACT Recommendation No.33**). *Members shall endeavour to establish or maintain a single window, enabling traders to submit documentation and/or data requirements for importation, exportation or transit of goods through a single entry point to the participating authorities or agencies* (**Art.10.4.1**) ** It can be a facility already in place acting as a Single Window (i.e not covering all the aspects of a Single Windows facility) or a facility in the process of implementation but not yet fully operational.
Q78.	**Are Average Release Times published?*** (0) The average time for the release and clearance of goods is not published in a consistent manner on a periodic basis. (2) The average time for the release and clearance of goods is published in a consistent manner on a periodic basis, for major customs offices. *Members are encouraged to measure and publish their average release time of goods periodically and in a consistent manner ...* (**Art.7.6.1**)
Q78b.	**What is the average Clearance Time?*** Please provide the average clearance time (hours):
Q79.	**Are there procedures allowing for the pre-arrival processing of goods?*** (0) Procedures allowing for the submission of import documentation and other required information so as to begin processing prior to the arrival of goods are not in place. (1) Procedures allowing for the submission of import documentation and other required information so as to begin processing prior to the arrival of goods are in the process of implementation. (2) Procedures allowing for the submission of import documentation and other required information so as to begin processing prior to the arrival of goods are in place. **If the answer is (2), please provide the percentage of pre-arrival processing:** * *Each Member shall adopt or maintain procedures allowing for the submission of import documentation and other required information, including manifests in order to begin processing prior to the arrival of goods with a view to expediting the release of goods upon arrival.* (**Art.7.1.1**)
Q80.	**What is the percent of goods undergoing physical inspections?** Please provide the percentage of physical inspections:
Q81.	**Are perishable* goods treated differently than non-perishable goods with regards to physical inspections**regarding timeliness?** (0) Physical inspection procedures do not allow to accelerate the control for perishable goods. (1) Border agencies give appropriate priority to perishable goods when scheduling required examinations. (2) Border agencies give appropriate priority to perishable goods when scheduling required examinations and have the possibility to clear such goods outside business hours.
Q81b.	**Please provide the percentage of physical inspections for perishable goods:** * *Perishable goods are goods that rapidly decay due to their natural characteristics, in particular in the absence of appropriate storage conditions.* *Each Member shall give appropriate priority to perishable goods when scheduling any examinations that may be required.* (**Art. 7.9.2**)
Q82.	**Are perishable goods treated differently than non-perishable goods with regards to physical inspectionsstorageconditions ?** (0) There are no proper storage facilities for perishable products and the Customs border agencies do not have the authority to clear perishable goods at storage facilities arranged by the importer. (2) Storage facilities have been arranged by the authorities to ensure perishable products benefit from appropriate storage conditions or Customs border agencies have the authority to clear perishable goods at storage facilities arranged by the importer.
Q83.	**Is the release of goods separated from final determination and payment of Customs duties?*** (0) There is no such possibility. (1) Yes, but it is restricted to the Authorized Economic Operator status. (2) Yes, provided that all other regulatory requirements have been met, without conditions other than the submission of guarantee or a deposit for any amount not yet determined. **Each Member shall adopt or maintain procedures allowing the release of goods prior to the final determination of customs duties, taxes, fees and charges, if such a determination is not done prior to, or upon arrival, or as rapidly as possible after arrival and provided that all other regulatory requirements have been met. As a condition for such release, a Member may require ... payment of any amount not yet determined in the form of a ... deposit ... or a guarantee in the form of a surety, a deposit or other appropriate instrument provided for in its laws and regulations.* (**Art.7.3**)

Q ID	QUESTIONS
Q84.	**What is the percent of goods released prior to final determination and payment of Customs duties, taxes, fees and charges?**
Q84a.	Percentage of releases prior to final determination and payment of Customs duties, taxes, fees and charges:
Q84b.	Percentage of releases for perishable goods prior to final determination and payment of Customs duties, taxes, fees and charges:
Q85.	**Are perishable goods treated differently than non-perishable goods concerning the separation of release from clearance?*** (0) There is no preferential treatment of perishable goods. (2) Perishable goods enjoy preferential treatment concerning the separation of release from clearance. ** With a view to preventing avoidable loss or deterioration of perishable goods, and provided all regulatory requirements have been met, each Member shall:* *a. provide for the release of perishable goods under normal circumstances within the shortest possible time; and* *b. provide for the release of perishable goods, in exceptional circumstances where it would be appropriate to do so, outside the business hours of customs and other relevant authorities.***(Art. 7.9.1)**
Q86.	**Are customs controls supported by a risk management system allowing risks to be assessed through appropriate selectivity criteria?** (0) There is no risk management system for customs controls. (1) A risk management system to support customs controls is in the process of implementation. (2) A risk management system is fully operational and allows customs controls to concentrate on high-risk consignments, expediting the release of low-risk consignments. **Art 7.4.1**. *Each Member shall, to the extent possible, adopt or maintain a risk management system for customs control.* **Art.7.4.3**. *Each Member shall concentrate customs control and, to the extent possible other relevant border controls, on high risk consignments and expedite the release of low risk consignments.* **Art.7.4.4.** *Each Member shall base risk management on assessment of risk through appropriate selectivity criteria. Such selectivity criteria may include, inter alia, HS code, nature and description of the goods, country of origin, country from which the goods were shipped, value of the goods, compliance record of traders, and type of means of transport.*
Q87.	**Are other border controls supported by a risk management system?** (0) There is no risk management system for border controls other than customs. (1) Risk management systems to support border controls other than customs are in the process of implementation. (2) Border controls other than customs are supported by a risk management system, allowing those controls to concentrate on high-risk consignments and expedite the release of low-risk consignments. *** Please indicate the border agencies having in place, or in the process of implementing a risk management system:** ______________________________
Q88.	**Does Customs use risk channels (green, yellow, red – or equivalent) for customs clearance? If yes, please indicate the percentage of shipments that are allocated to the red, green and yellow channel in the total number of shipments of cargo cleared in a year?** Red channel: Yellow channel: Green channel:
Q89.	**Is compliance with customs and other related laws and regulations supported by post-clearance audits (PCAs)?*** (0) PCAs are not conducted: (1) PCAs are conducted (2) PCAs are conducted and the results are used in applying risk management. If the answer is (1) or (2), please indicate the percentage of Post-Clearance Audits (PCAs) carried out: ** With a view to expediting the release of goods, each Member shall adopt or maintain post-clearance audit to ensure compliance with customs and other related laws and regulations.*(**Art.7.5.1**)
Q90.	**Establishment of standard policies and procedures to guide PCAs** (0) There are no standard policies and procedures to guide the conduct of PCAs. (1) Standard policies and procedures are established to guide the conduct of PCAs. (2) Standard policies and procedures ensure the conduct of PCAs in a transparent and risk-based manner.
Q91.	**Is the use of pre-shipment inspections required on Customs matters?*** (0) The country requires pre-shipment inspection on tariff classification and customs valuation. (1) No pre-shipment inspection is required on tariff classification and customs valuation. (2) No pre-shipment inspection is required on any Customs matter. **Members shall not require the use of pre-shipment inspections in relation to tariff classification and customs valuation. Without prejudice to the rights of Members to use other types of pre-shipment inspection … Members are encouraged not to introduce or apply new requirements regarding their use* (**Art.10.5.1** and **Art.10.5.2**)

Q ID	QUESTIONS
Q92.	**Is it possible to provide additional trade facilitation measures to operators meeting specified criteria (authorized operators or AOs)?*** (0) There is no possibility to provide additional facilitation to Authorized Operators. (1) Additional trade facilitation measures are provided to Authorised Operators meeting criteria related to compliance or the risk of non-compliance.** (2) The applied Authorised Operator scheme is developed on the basis of relevant international standards. * This can be offered either under a separate scheme or as part of *customs procedures generally available to all operators.* ** Such as an *appropriate record of compliance with customs and other related laws and regulations; a system of managing records to allow for necessary internal controls; financial solvency; supply chain security* (**Art.7.7.2**) **Art.7.7.1** *Each Member shall provide additional trade facilitation measures related to import, export or transit formalities and procedures, (...) to operators who meet specified criteria, hereinafter called authorized operators. Alternatively, a Member may offer such facilitation measures through customs procedures generally available to all operators and not be required to establish a separate scheme.*
Q93.	**Transparency of the criteria for qualifying as an Authorized Operator (AO) and the procedures for submission and review of applications for AO status** (0) The criteria for qualifying as an Authorized Operator (AO) and the procedures for submission and review of applications for AO status are not defined or published. (1) The criteria for qualifying as an Authorized Operator (AO) and the procedures for submission and review of applications for AO status are made available in paper publications. (2) The criteria for qualifying as an Authorized Operator (AO) and the procedures for submission and review of applications for AO status are published on a dedicated webpage and an online request procedure is available. **Art.7.7.2** *The specified criteria shall be related to compliance, or the risk of non-compliance, with requirements specified in a Member's laws, regulations or procedures.*
Q94.	**What is the percentage of Authorized Operators (AOs)* against the total number of traders?** Please provide the percentage of AOs against the total number of traders: Please provide the percentage of SMEs in the total number of AOs **Art 7.7.2**. *Criteria to qualify as an authorized operator ... shall not ... to the extent possible, restrict the participation of small and medium-sized enterprises.*
Q95.	**What is the annual percentage of trade volume handled by Authorized Operators?** Please provide the annual percentage of trade volume handled by AOs:
Q96.	**How long does it take on average to obtain Authorized Operator certification?*** Please specify the time necessary on average to obtain AO certification: * This question is not applicable if the country provides additional trade facilitation measures as part of *customs procedures generally available to all operators*, and not by establishing a separate scheme, as provided in **Art.7.7.1**
Q97.	**What are the benefits provided for Authorized Operators?** **Please specify which of these benefits are linked to the AO status:** Deferred payment of duties, taxes, fees and charges Use of comprehensive guarantees or reduced guarantees Low rate of physical inspections Low documentary and data requirements A single Customs declaration for all imports and exports in a given period Rapid release time Clearance of goods at the premises of the AO
Q98.	**Adjustment of working hours of Customs personnel to commercial needs** (0) The working hours of Customs personnel are not adapted to commercial needs. (1) The working hours of Customs personnel are partially adapted to commercial needs. (2) The private sector considers that working hours of Customs personnel are entirely adapted to commercial needs.
Q99.	**Requirement for clearance by a third-party customs broker** (0) The use of a third-party customs broker is mandatory. (1) The use of a third party customs broker is mandatory for certain types of consignees. (2) The use of a third-party customs broker is not mandatory **Art.10.6.1** *(...) from the entry into force of this agreement Members shall not introduce the mandatory use of customs brokers*
Q100.	**Expedited release procedures** (0) There are no procedures allowing for the rapid release of expedited shipments. (1) Goods may benefit from expedited release to persons meeting specific qualifying criteria,* but this is limited to certain types of goods only.** (2) Goods of any type, weight or value may benefit from expedited release to persons meeting specific qualifying criteria.* * Including an adequate infrastructure and payment of customs expenses related to processing of expedited shipments; advance submission of the information necessary for the release; a high degree of security, logistics and tracking control over the shipment; a good compliance record.

Q ID	QUESTIONS
	**** Please specify :** **Type of goods** **Yes/no** **Goods entering through air cargo facilities only** **Low value goods only** **Other ____________________**
Q101.	**Procedures for the re-export of rejected goods** (0) The importer does not have the right to return to the exporter goods that have been rejected for import due to failure to comply with prescribed sanitary and phytosanitary regulations or technical regulations. (1) The importer has the right to return rejected goods that are not subject to specific prohibitions. (2) The importer has this right to return rejected goods and a reasonable period of time is granted to complete the re-export. **Art. 10.8.1** *Where goods presented for import are rejected by the competent authority of a Member on account of their failure to meet prescribed sanitary or phytosanitary regulations or technical regulations, the Member shall, subject to and consistent with its laws and regulations, allow the importer to re-consign or to return the rejected goods to the exporter or another person designated by the exporter*
Q102.	**Temporary Admission of Goods and Inward and Outward Processing** (0) Goods moved into or out of the customs territory for a specific purpose, including for inward or outward processing are not relieved from the payment of import duties and taxes. (2) Goods moved into or out of the customs territory for a specific purpose, including for inward or outward processing are relieved totally or partially from the payment of import duties and taxes. **Art. 10.9.9** *Each Member shall allow … goods to be brought into a customs territory conditionally relieved, totally or partially, from payment of import duties and taxes if such goods are brought … for a specific purpose, are intended for re-exportation within a specific period, and have not undergone any change except normal depreciation and wastage due to the use made of them.* *Goods allowed for outward processing may be reimported with total or partial exemption from import duties and taxes in accordance with the Member's laws and regulations in force*
	I. BORDER AGENCY CO-OPERATION INTERNAL* *within the same country
Q103.	**General co-operation and co-ordination of the activities of domestic agencies involved in the management of cross border trade, with a view to improving border control efficiency and facilitating trade*** (0) There is no co-operation and co-ordination between the various domestic agencies involved in the management of cross border trade. (1) Co-operation, co-ordination, exchange of information and mutual assistance involves substantially all domestic agencies involved in the management of cross border trade. (2) There is an explicit co-ordination strategy led at a high political level. * *A Member shall ensure that its authorities and agencies responsible for border controls and procedures dealing with the importation, exportation and transit of goods co-operate with one another and co-ordinate their activities in order to facilitate trade.* **(Art. 8.1)**
Q104.	**Institutionalised mechanism to support inter-agency co-ordination** (0) There is no inter-agency co-ordination body. (2) An inter-agency co-ordination body is established to facilitate domestic co-ordination. **The above score of (2) is multiplied with the percentage of listed features* to which the body meets the terms of.** **This is a continuous variable,i.e. the final score of the variable ranges from 0 to 2.** **TFA Art 23.2** ***Please specify whether the co-ordination platform** **Yes/no** Has established terms of reference and procedures for conducting its activities Has a permanent technical Secretariat Its decisions and recommendations are made publicly available on a dedicated webpage Has a Steering Committee which monitors the implementation of decisions Has clear provisions for its financing Includes at least 60% of relevant agencies (a number of ____ agencies of a total of ____ relevant agencies in the country)
Q105.	**Domestic inter-agency co-ordination mechanisms meet regularly to develop strategy and oversee implementation of border agency co-operation*** (0) There are no meetings between the different public agencies involved in the procedures required to import or export goods or such meetings are only ad hoc. (1) Regular meetings are held to improve co-operation. (2) Regular meetings are held and the proceedings are publicly available. * If the score of the previous question Q104 is zero, this variable is also scored zero.

Q ID	QUESTIONS
Q106.	**Domestic co-ordination / harmonisation of data requirements and documentary controls among agencies involved in the management of cross border trade** (0) Data requirements of various border agencies are not co-ordinated / harmonised. (1) Data requirements are co-ordinated / harmonised through common data definitions and types of information requested and mechanisms established to ensure timely exchange of information among the relevant border agencies. (2) Data requirements are co-ordinated/harmonised and a single data entry is possible for traders.* **TFA Art 8.1** * for instance through a single window platform
Q107.	**Interconnected or shared computer systems and real time availability of pertinent data among domestic agencies involved in the management of cross border trade** (0) There are no interconnected or shared computer systems and no exchange of data among domestic agencies involved in the management of cross border trade. (1) Exchange or transmission of data is provided between the different systems on a regular basis (daily, weekly, monthly). (2) There are interconnected or shared computer systems and data is commonly available in real time.* **TFA Art 8.1**
Q108.	**Domestic co-ordination of inspections among agencies involved in the management of cross border trade** (0) There is no domestic co-ordination of physical inspections and controls between the various agencies involved in the management of cross border trade. (1) There is informal and ad hoc co-ordination to address contingencies. (2) A single location and co-ordinated timing is established for the physical inspection of consignments by the various concerned agencies. **TFA Art 8.1**
Q109.	**Shared results of inspections and controls among agencies involved in the management of cross border trade with a view to improving border control efficiency and facilitating trade** (0) No, inspection results are not shared among the agencies involved in the management of cross border trade. (2) Inspection results are shared among the agencies involved in the management of cross border trade. **TFA Art 8.1**
Q110.	**Control delegation at the national level** The score is (0) if government agencies do not delegate controls to another agency involved in the management of cross border trade. Otherwise, the score is the percentage* of government agencies delegating controls to another agency involved in the management of cross border trade multiplied by the top score (2). As an example, 60% of agencies delegating controls leads to a score of 1.2, while 40% delegating leads to a score of 0.8. This is a continuous variable, i.e. the score of the variable ranges from 0 to 2. ***Please specify the number of agencies ________ of the total ______ relevant agencies which are currently delegating controls.**
Q111.	**Co-ordinated / shared risk management mechanisms** (0) Domestic agencies involved in the management of cross border trade maintain separate risk management mechanisms. (1) Domestic agencies involved in the management of cross border trade maintain separate risk management mechanisms but share intelligence with a view to improving risk management efficiency. (2) There are interagency synergies in terms of risk analysis and shared data and risk profiling of goods.
Q112.	**Authorised Operators programs** (0) Each agency certifies its own Authorised Operators. (1) Ad hoc collaboration exists among certain agencies on the certification of Authorised Operators. (2) Explicit strategies have been implemented among the agencies to harmonise the requirements, co-ordinate the certification, manage the follow-up and co-ordinate the inspection of Authorised Operators.
Q113.	**Co-ordinated / shared infrastructure and equipment use** (0) Domestic agencies involved in the management of cross border trade do not share infrastructure and equipment. (2) Domestic agencies involved in the management of cross border trade share infrastructure and equipment.
	J. BORDER AGENCY CO-OPERATION EXTERNAL* *with other countries
Q114.	**Cross-border co-operation and co-ordination of the activities of agencies involved in the management of cross border trade, with a view to improving border control efficiency and facilitating trade*** (0) There is no cross-border co-operation and co-ordination with border agencies in neighbouring countries. (1) National legislation allows for cross-border co-operation, co-ordination, exchange of information and mutual assistance with border authorities in neighbouring countries. (2) There is an explicit co-ordination strategy led at a high political level, or the concerned countries belong to a Customs Union. **TFA Art. 8.1**

Q ID	QUESTIONS
Q115.	**Alignment of working days and hours with neighbouring countries at land borders where applicable** (0) Working days and hours are not aligned with neighbouring countries. (2) Working days and hours are aligned with neighbouring countries. **TFA Art. 8.2 (i)**
Q116.	**Alignment of procedures and formalities with neighbouring countries at borders where applicable** (0) Procedures and formalities are not aligned with neighbouring countries. (1) Local arrangements exist in order to facilitate goods' traffic (2) Procedures and formalities are aligned with neighbouring countries. **TFA Art. 8.3 (ii)**
Q117.	**Cross-border co-ordination / harmonisation of data requirements and documentary controls** (0) Data requirements are not co-ordinated / harmonised with neighbouring countries. (1) Work is under way with neighbouring countries in order to identify strategies for co-ordination/harmonisation of data requirements. (2) Data requirements are co-ordinated / harmonised with neighbouring countries through common data definitions and types of information requested and mechanisms established to ensure timely exchange of information,* or the concerned countries belong to a Customs Union. * for instance by means of interoperability of National Single Windows
Q118.	**Cross-border co-ordination / harmonisation of the different computer systems** (0) Computer language and systems are not co-ordinated / harmonised with neighbouring countries. (1) Work is under way with neighbouring countries in order to identify strategies for co-ordination/harmonisation of computer language and systems. (2) Computer language and systems are co-ordinated / harmonised with neighbouring countries.
Q119.	**Risk management co-operation** (0) There is no risk management co-operation with border agencies in neighbouring countries. (1) Border agencies in neighbouring countries share intelligence with a view to improving risk management efficiency and facilitating licit trade. (2) There are interagency synergies in terms of shared risk profiling of traders or goods, or of risk analysis and exchange of the results thereof.
Q120.	**Systematic sharing of control results among neighbouring countries at border crossings with a view to improving the risk analysis as well as the efficiency of border controls and to facilitating licit trade** (0) The control results are not shared with border agencies in neighbouring countries. (1) National legislation allows for exchanging information about control results. (2) The control results are shared with border agencies in neighbouring countries.
Q121.	**Development and sharing of common facilities with neighbouring countries at border crossings, where applicable** (0) Common facilities are not developed and shared with neighbouring countries. (1) There are no common facilities, but some infrastructure and equipment is shared between neighbouring countries at land borders. (2) Common facilities are developed and shared with neighbouring countries. **TFA Art. 8.3 (iii)**
Q122.	**Joint controls with neighbouring countries at border crossings, where applicable** (0) There are no joint controls performed in co-operation with neighbouring countries. (1) Joint controls are performed with neighbouring countries. (2) One stop border posts are shared with neighbouring countries. **TFA Art. 8.3 (iv, v)**
Q123.	**Mutual Recognition Agreements/Arrangements on Authorized Operators* (AOs), where applicable** **The score is (0) if the Customs administration has not signed any MRAs on AOs. The score is also (0) if the country does not have AO programs in place.** **If MRAs on AOs have been signed with partner countries, an assigned score of (2) is multiplied with the percentage of listed features** the MRAs cover.** **This is a continuous variable,i.e. the score of the variable ranges from 0 to 2.** **TFA Art. 7.5** *"Mutual Recognition (MR) is a broad concept embodied within the WCO SAFE Framework whereby an action or decision taken or an authorization that has been properly granted by one Customs administration, is recognized and accepted by another Customs administration (...)The objective of Mutual Recognition of AEOs is that one Customs administration recognizes the validation findings and AEO authorizations by the other Customs administration issued under the other programme and agrees to provide substantial, comparable and – where possible ? reciprocal benefits/facilitation to the mutually recognized AEOs." (WCO, *Guidelines for Developing a Mutual Recognition Arrangement/Agreement*)

Q ID	QUESTIONS
	****Please specify whether MRAs cover:**
	Yes/no
	Agreed benefits that can be delivered to the AOs covered by the MRA
	The practical arrangements enabling the participating Customs administrations to provide the agreed benefits
	Use of compatible technologies for the AO data exSchange with the partner country
	Storing of AO data is reconciled with data protection and data security concerns
	Reference to the procedures to be followed if one MRA partner finds irregularities involving the AOs of the other partner country
	Include consultations with the private sector
Q124.	**Exchange of staff and training programmes at the international level**
	(0) There are no programmes to exchange staff with partner countries.
	(1) There are occasional exchanges of know-how with neighbouring or third countries.
	(2) There are regular exchange programmes, as well as training seminars on best practices, with both neighbouring and third countries.
	TFA Art. 12.1.2
	K. GOVERNANCE AND IMPARTIALITY
Q125.	**Are the structures and functions in the border agencies clearly established and transparent?**
	(0) Structures and functions of the various administrations involved in the border process are not publicly described.
	(2) Structures and functions of the various administrations involved in the border process are clearly established and publicly available.
Q126.	**Is there an ethics policy applied to border agencies?**
	(0) There is no ethics policy applied to the various agencies involved in the border process
	(1) There is an ethics policy applied to the various agencies involved in the border process
	(2) Violations of ethics regulations are prosecuted. The ethics policy observes all of the principles of the Revised Arusha Declaration.
Q127.	**Have the various border agencies established a Code of conduct?**
	(0) There is no Code of conduct in the various agencies involved in the border process.
	(1) A Code of Conduct is developed.
	(2) The Code of Conduct is published and there is a communications strategy to make it available to all employees.
Q128.	**Are there effective sanctions against misconduct of border agency staff?**
	(0) Sanctions against misconduct are not published.
	(2) The code of conduct includes disciplinary provisions specifying what constitutes misconduct and the sanctions which apply.
Q129.	**Is there efficient internal communication about policies and procedures of agencies involved in the border process?**
	(0) There are no arrangements in place to ensure that staff receives relevant information in good time about new legislation and regulation, and changes to existing legislation and regulation.
	(2) Arrangements are in place to ensure that staff receives relevant information in good time about new legislation and regulation, and changes to existing legislation and regulation.
Q130.	**Is there an internal systems audit function in the various agencies involved in the border process?**
	(0) There is no internal audit mechanism.
	(2) An audit function for internal systems is established, adequately empowered and operational.
Q131.	**Are non-compliance penalties for border agency staff transparent and proportional?**
	(0) There is no publicly available information on non-compliance penalties.
	(2) Systems of non-compliance penalties are transparent and balanced.
Q132.	**Are there clear provisions for the financing of the Customs administration?**
	(0) There is no public information as to the financing of the Customs administration.
	(2) Financing is determined and set out in legal provisions and related information is publicly available.
Q133.	**Do Customs publish an annual report?**
	(0) Customs do not publish annual activity reports.
	(1) Annual reports are available, but they contain insufficient information on customs activities.*
	(2) Annual reports are available and contain sufficient information on Customs activities.
	* Information is viewed here as insufficient if it does not include information on budget and duties collected, complaints or efficiency indicators.

ORGANISATION FOR ECONOMIC CO-OPERATION AND DEVELOPMENT

The OECD is a unique forum where governments work together to address the economic, social and environmental challenges of globalisation. The OECD is also at the forefront of efforts to understand and to help governments respond to new developments and concerns, such as corporate governance, the information economy and the challenges of an ageing population. The Organisation provides a setting where governments can compare policy experiences, seek answers to common problems, identify good practice and work to co-ordinate domestic and international policies.

The OECD member countries are: Australia, Austria, Belgium, Canada, Chile, the Czech Republic, Denmark, Estonia, Finland, France, Germany, Greece, Hungary, Iceland, Ireland, Israel, Italy, Japan, Korea, Latvia, Luxembourg, Mexico, the Netherlands, New Zealand, Norway, Poland, Portugal, the Slovak Republic, Slovenia, Spain, Sweden, Switzerland, Turkey, the United Kingdom and the United States. The European Union takes part in the work of the OECD.

OECD Publishing disseminates widely the results of the Organisation's statistics gathering and research on economic, social and environmental issues, as well as the conventions, guidelines and standards agreed by its members.

OECD PUBLISHING, 2, rue André-Pascal, 75775 PARIS CEDEX 16
(51 2017 07 1 P) ISBN 978-92-64-27756-4 – 2018

www.ingramcontent.com/pod-product-compliance
Ingram Content Group UK Ltd.
Pitfield, Milton Keynes, MK11 3LW, UK
UKHW051505290926
15471UKWH00008B/1420